M000033365

TUMBLING DICE

BECAUSE JOURNALISTS ARE HUMAN TOO

BY LESLEY-ANN JONES,
SUNDAY TIMES BESTSELLING AUTHOR OF
'BOHEMIAN RHAPSODY: THE DEFINITIVE BIOGRAPHY OF
FREDDIE MERCURY'

FOREWORD BY PHILIP NORMAN,
INTERNATIONALLY ACCLAIMED BIOGRAPHER OF THE BEATLES,
THE ROLLING STONES, ELTON JOHN & ERIC CLAPTON

ON THE RUN WITH MICHAEL JACKSON

TERRORISING BOWIE

BREAKING THE LAW WITH A ROLLING STONE

SPARRING WITH SINATRA

REHAB WITH STEVIE NICKS

DOUBLE-CROSSED BY GARY GLITTER

HANGING WITH RAQUEL WELCH

GETTING PREGNANT WITH JOAN COLLINS

FISHING WITH MARCO PIERRE WHITE

FLYING WITH HUGH GRANT

FIGHTING WITH RICHARD GERE

FINDING PRINCESS DIANA'S SECRET LOVER

MOTHERING WITH MADONNA

ALSO BY LESLEY-ANN JONES

Bohemian Rhapsody: The Definitive Biography of Freddie Mercury

Hero: David Bowie

Ride a White Swan: The Lives and Death of Marc Bolan

Naomi: The Rise and Rise of the Girl from Nowhere

Imagine, a novel

With Gray Jolliffe: Excuses, Excuses

With Robin Eggar & Phil 'The Collector' Swern: the Sony Rock Review

WHAT PEOPLE ARE SAYING ABOUT TUMBLING DICE

Brilliant, unputdownable, a tour de force. The best book about celebrities that I have ever read. I wish I'd written it.

> Simon Napier-Bell, rock manager, the Yardbirds,
> Marc Bolan, Wham!, Sinead O'Connor, George Michael.

LAJ has always shone her light brilliantly, if sometimes too accurately, on others. She now turns it articulately and entertainingly onto herself – a scoop!

> Sir Tim Rice, author & Academy Award-winning lyricist,
> 'Jesus Christ Superstar', 'Evita', 'Chess', 'The Lion King'

Hilarious, revealing, shocking and hugely enjoyable account of the wild, weird world of celebrity and even wilder, weirder world of tabloid journalism.

> Piers Morgan, TV presenter, journalist and former Editor,
> News of the World, Daily Mirror, mailonline, Mail on Sunday

Lesley-Ann was both the glamour and the guts of rock journalism. No one got closer to the story, nor nearer to the core of a crazy time. She was there and she was all there.

> Robert Elms, broadcaster, BBC Radio London

This is a book I'd have expected to hate. I despise celebrity journalism, have minimal interest in celebrities, page past the celeb sections of newspapers, and have never even looked at *Hello!* magazine. But, boy oh boy, *Tumbling Dice* is sensational! The stories are amazing and the storyteller, Lesley-Ann Jones, brings such intelligence, self-knowledge and honesty to a life recollected, that by the second page of the introduction, I was hooked.

Matthew Parris, The Times columnist, broadcaster and former politician

It was almost impossible to be at a gig, party reception or other rock-related shindig from the late '70s, '80s and beyond without seeing Lesley-Ann. She was everywhere, and seemed to know everyone, from rock stars to hotel doormen. I remember once, at the infamous Sunset Marquis hotel in Hollywood, wondering if LAJ was in town, only to have her suddenly appear from behind a large potted palm at breakfast. LAJ lived, loved and breathed rock'n'roll, and brought the extraordinary stories she uncovered, and was often a part of, to Fleet Street with the skill and confidence of a true insider. Smart, tireless, indefatigable but always with a maverick's smile on her face, Lesley-Ann Jones might be the closest to a rock'n'roll legend that newspapers have ever produced.

Martin Townsend, former Editor, Sunday Express

Searing, raw, vivid, compelling! This is as real and as outrageous as memoirs get. Jones's account of celebrity journalism, Fleet Street during its heyday and some of the biggest scandals of the age is 100% accurate, and all too true. I know: I was there. I worked with her. The way in which the author sets these explosive revelations against her own sometimes devastating private life is shocking and heart-breaking. Do yourself a favour and read this book: all human life is here.

Stuart White, former US Editor, News of the World, and best-selling author of 'Death Game' and 'Kiss of the Angel'.

Lesley-Ann Jones has long been regarded as the doyenne of showbiz writing and reporting. For three decades she has moved in the social circles of the megastars of the modern music era, from Bowie and Boy George to Mercury and Fleetwood Mac. LAJ spent days and nights, weeks and months with these people, witnessing cultural history in the making. She maintained such a stunning presence, you could easily believe she was a rock-chick herself. No other journalist has ever been more immersed in the industry's explosive kaleidoscope. No one got closer. No one saw more.

Mike Parry, broadcaster and former Fleet Street executive

CONTENTS

FOREWORD BY PHILIP NORMAN

We members of the strange literary minority known as rock biographers tend not to socialise with each other like authors of detective stories or science-fiction. For me, the chief deterrent is the lamentable standard of most rock biographising; if ever I were to meet Peter Guralnick or Paul Morley, whatever charm they may possess would be neutralised by the thought of their dreary presences in print. Consequently, almost the only fellow professional I ever see – or want to – is Lesley-Ann Jones.

I first became aware of 'LAJ', as she signs herself, with the insightful first biography of Freddie Mercury she published in 1997. I've since got to know her at the reunions of old rock stars and the music writers who once chronicled them – nicknamed the Scribblers, Pluckers, Thumpers and Squawkers lunch – which take place twice-yearly at a riverside pub in Barnes. Entertaining though these gatherings are, the attendees are predominantly male and grey-haired. LAJ adds a welcome touch of glamour and an even more welcome one of naughtiness.

I've always rather envied those for whom newspapers were a family tradition rather than (as in my own case) a refuge for an otherwise un-employable misfit. LAJ comes from fine old Fleet Street stock: her father, Ken Jones, was a highly esteemed sportswriter for the Daily and Sunday Mirror and The Independent; as she fondly writes, 'one of an intrepid band of men who crashed around the country and across the world on a relentless mission to bring the stench of the prize fight, the elegance of the test match, the frenzy of football to the breakfast table.' But here the traditional nepotism did not apply: it was only after a colourful start in radio and the music industry that she found her own way to the Street of Shame and took up Britain's last legal bloodsport, otherwise known as celebrity journalism.

She was 'blooded' in the late 1980s, an era when British celebrity sleaze and tabloid amorality reached an unsurpassed high water-mark, notching up an impressive series of exclusives with contemporary splash-hogs such as Boy George, Madonna and Whitney Houston. While as adept at getting her foot in the door as any of her rivals, she had an ability to make friends with her quarry – through natural empathy, intelligence, humour and that winning air of naughtiness – which often led to personal entanglement in the stories she covered. Tumbling Dice reprises hilarious examples such the Bill Wyman-Mandy Smith marriage, the unmasking of Gary Glitter as the first national treasure-turned serial paedophile, and Hugh Grant's 'moment of madness' (that quintessential '8os phrase!) with an LA prostitute named Divine, which showed the floppiness of his hair didn't extend to other regions.

It's worth noting that the cruelty of mad-dog tabloids to celebrities was nothing compared with their brutality towards their own staff. LAJ came in for more than her share, thanks to her refusal to write lies to fit a pre-determined headline. In those 'hot-metal' days, now so rose-tinted, bullying was still thought to be something that went on only among schoolkids and sexual harassment deemed a male prerogative, both in the newsroom and on assignments. 'You know we're going to fuck, don't you?' was the opening gambit of one celebrity chef she interviewed – an objective he sought to advance by being horrible to her young daughter, whom she'd brought with her. The reader will admire the professionalism with which she resists an urge to give him a swift kick in the goujons.

Aside from what Fleet Street threw at her, she has come through skin cancer, peritonitis, meningitis, life-or-death surgery, having the Last Rites read over her, a miscarriage and swine 'flu; she's been held at gun-point in Tobago, kidnapped in LA and taken away to be locked in a po-lice-cell from outside her own home in London; since a 'shattering' di-vorce, she has managed to raise a son and two daughters on freelance journalism, the only commodity apart from cocaine whose price is con-tinually falling.

In this rollicking but not unserious memoir she characterises herself as a cut-price Gloria Gaynor, whose 'I Will Survive' is the anthem of inde-fatigable womanhood. I prefer to think of her, rather, as a value-added Etta James.

Philip Norman

INTRODUCTION

I was a nerdy kid on a mission impossible: to get a job on a newspaper and write about music and musicians. Against the odds, I did it. I could never have imagined, however, how far the caper would go. Lucky for me that I landed on Fleet Street at the height of the twentieth century's obsession with celebrity culture. Having progressed from college to work experience at London's Capital Radio, and having worked with Debbie Harry and Blondie, Spandau Ballet, Ultravox, Pat Benatar, Leo Sayer and the rest at Chrysalis Records, I was suddenly risking everything as a reporter and interviewer of the stars. I hooked a few good scoops, including Boy George's admission of heroin addiction, Madonna's heartbreak following the collapse of her marriage to Sean Penn, and the earliest indication that all was not well in the mind of Whitney Houston. More significantly, I was personally involved in three of the most explosive celebrity scandals of the age: Bill Wyman's affair with schoolgirl Mandy Smith, Gary Glitter's exposure as a paedophile after he had groomed my younger sister, and Hugh Grant's arrest in Los Angeles following his dalliance with prostitute Divine Brown. These were stories and experiences that changed my life. Not in a good way. To this day, I have nightmares about them. But it's not all bad. Not only did I survive the hardest street on earth, but I am also living proof that, if writers and reporters do eventually become the story, it is because we were actually there.

Looking back, I realise that 'the cult of celebrity' never existed. It was a mirage. We who pursued stars around the globe on an endless quest for splash-headline interviews and world exclusives wanted them to walk on water, and to be different from the rest of us. But they weren't. While getting close enough to talk to them, drink with them, dine with them and travel with them might have been a dream come true for our millions of readers, what we found, to our disappointment, was that celebrities were more human than we were. There were exceptions, of course. But they tended on the whole to be weak, vulnerable and dependent. They were insecure and fallible. The truth was often an irrelevance to them. And they were scared. Every one of them was terrified of something: surprisingly often, of mortality. The realisation that their hard-earned wealth would never protect them from the inevitable and could not save them from the abyss was the last unmentionable. I often felt let down and disappointed by artists I'd long looked up to. But because there was a job to be done, and because that job was following them about and recording their perambulations and performances against a newspaper deadline, I just got on with it.

I often had to pinch myself. I was a coalminer's granddaughter with stars in my eyes. The few celebrities with whom I'd come into contact as a child hailed almost exclusively from the sporting world. I would sometimes go to Fleet Street with my father Ken Jones during school holidays in the Seventies, for a treat, because that was where he worked. Specifically, in the hinterland of the Street itself, in a vast red- and blue-panelled building diagonally opposite the Victorian Prudential Assurance Building, which peered down with disdain upon Holborn Circus, and which was home in those days to the Mirror Group newspapers. Dad was a sportswriter, one of an intrepid band of men who crashed about the country and across the world on a relentless mission to bring the stench of the prize fight, the elegance of the test match, the frenzy of football to the breakfast table. The words he typed in triplicate were read weekly in millions of homes. He had a Bond-like picture byline and a portable typewriter in a rubber zip-up case slapped with stickers from far-flung lands. He spoke compellingly about sport on 'Grandstand', a popular television sports magazine show which went out live on Saturday afternoons. He was fond of teasing us that he toiled on 'the hardest street on earth.' How did he wind up there? Just as the fat lady got to Carnegie Hall. Although the nationals have since relocated and the industry is now in decline, the thoroughfare between Ludgate Circus and the old Temple Bar whose name remains synonymous with and evocative of the print media is still a living place of work, if only for bankers, lawyers, publicans, retailers and restaurateurs. Yet it is haunted to this day by the ghosts of Fleet Street's golden age; by those who designed, edited, wrote, drew, photographed, typeset, printed and sold advertising space for newspapers.

'Did your dad get you in?' was a question I was often asked, after I landed my first job there. Not exactly. Not that it hurt that I had a connection, nor indeed that my father was well-known. At least, thanks to the fact that my field of interest was showbusiness, not sport, I would never suffer the indignity of comparison that Dad had been subjected to during his first career. Ken had been a professional footballer, and part of an extraordinary clan known as 'the Jones Boys'. Five brothers including my grandfather Emlyn 'Mickey' Jones had followed their father 'Big Daddy' down the pit, as miners. All five discovered out of nowhere that they could play football, though their father had never kicked a ball. They signed to Merthyr Town FC, and were eventually sold to First Division English clubs. My grandfather played for Everton. My great uncle Bryn became the world's most expensive player when he left Wolverhampton Wanderers for Arsenal in 1939. The appointment prompted an angry demonstration in Downing Street, mounted by protesters opposing the 'vast' sum squandered on a mere footballer at a time when Europe stood on the brink of war. A generation later, three of their sons became professionals, including my father. When our 'Uncle Cliff' was sold by Swansea to Tottenham Hotspurs for the world-record transfer fee, family history repeated itself.

While my small, modest grandfather had been a star player and the darling of the fans, turning out for Southend United between 1929 and 1936 in more than five hundred games, Dad was by his own admission a 'marginal pro'. He was all too often dismissed, to his disgruntlement, as 'not as good as your father.'

It was when I discovered David Bowie that things began to fall into place. My schoolfriends and I started doorstepping our local hero in Beckenham, Kent, and were eventually invited in for tea with him. Having realised that I wanted to grow up to live and work among artists like him, but being not remotely musical or artistic, it occurred to me that I could emulate my father, go on the road with rock bands, and write about them.

I got more than I bargained for on Fleet Street. I was forced to compromise myself at every turn. I was at first relieved when the Daily Mail poached me from the Sun, perceiving an escape route from the vulgar 'Shock and Amaze on Every Page!' ethos flaunted ruthlessly by the paper's then editor Kelvin MacKenzie, who hired me after seeing me on television. But what I was subjected to at the Mail was infinitely worse. I was dismayed to find myself on a hotbed of bloodthirsty goons obsessed with conspiracy and exaggeration, some of whom peddled downright lies as 'news' and 'fact'. Even the Editor David English invented interviews.

At the Daily Mail, the writing of fiction was rife. I was set to work on endless stories that were essentially untrue, and merely the product of an editor's wild imagination. 'Never let the truth get in the way of a good story' was the unspoken rule. I fought fierce battles with my immediate editors to get unadulterated copy and genuine interviews into the paper, to protect my music business friends from being turned over and to preserve my contacts book. I succeeded as often as I failed, occasionally thanks, I admit, to committing a cardinal sin of journalism by granting copy approval, without which some celebrity interviewees would never have talked. This almost always backfired, however, because I would subsequently find that the words had been ruined and the artist's wrath incurred by a disastrously crass headline or compromising photographs.

When I found that I was expecting my first child after having separated from the father, it became obvious that I could no longer do the job I had been assigned to. Management could not sack me for being pregnant, so they mounted a campaign to get me to resign. This culminated in my being despatched to stand on the doorstep of outgoing BBC Director General Alasdair Milne, where I was made to remain throughout the night, trying to secure an interview with him.

It was 1987. Mobile phones were not yet in general use. The assignment meant tramping through snowdrifts every hour on the hour to a phone box at the corner of Holland Park, to call in to the news desk with updates. It happened during the most severe spell of winter weather the country had seen since January 1740. A newspaper could be sued spectacularly for such abuse of a pregnant reporter today. In those days, if you didn't like it, you knew where the door was.

My eventual escape, post-birth, was to YOU magazine, the colour supplement of the Mail's sister and rival paper, the Mail on Sunday. YOU's new editor Nick Gordon had read my pieces on the Mail and offered me a rolling contract travelling the world seeking stories about 'ordinary people doing extraordinary things' and 'extraordinary people doing ordinary things'. It was still mostly, naturally, about celebrities. On YOU, my interviews were not doctored, nor edited sensationally against my will. The headlines were clever, and they served the copy. I stayed there for six years. Then Management fired the editor. Dee Nolan, his successor, offloaded Nick's favourite writers, and redesigned the magazine as an homage to lipstick and tights.

Piers Morgan, then at the helm of the News of the World, and at twenty-nine the youngest-ever Fleet Street editor, invited me out of the blue to work for him. I had a great run at Wapping, penning the weekly 'Lesley-Ann Jones Big Interview'. Once again, Fate intervened.

In June 1995, Hugh Grant was caught in a compromising position on Sunset Boulevard. The 'Four Weddings and a Funeral' superstar was in Los Angeles to promote his latest film, the tepid rom-com 'Nine Months'. I was there too: I had been sent to interview him for my column in the News of the World. The screening was held on the 20th Century Fox lot. During the drinks reception afterwards, Grant was conspicuously absent. It was revealed only later that he had 'taken a walk on the wild side'. When he was arrested in a street off the Strip that night, he was being entertained in his car by a prostitute called Divine Brown. Charged with 'lewd conduct in a public place', Grant tumbled temporarily from grace. Thanks to what he later described as a 'moment of insanity', he now faced a jail sentence. While hundreds of hacks in London flew into overdrive to bag the exclusive with Grant's long-term girlfriend, actress and model Elizabeth Hurley, the race was on for the scoop of the decade, an interview with Divine. The News of the World's West Coast editor Stuart White nabbed it, paying $100,000 for the privilege. He then capitalised on his jealously-guarded British Airways contacts and landed me a seat in First Class on the next flight back to Heathrow, sitting next to Hugh Grant...

Hugh whined for the next twenty years that his career had been destroyed by the media. It really would have been finished, had Divine been allowed to speak the truth.

I was researching my first biography of Freddie Mercury when I met my first (as it turned out, only) husband, a management consultant and recreational pilot. He proposed over lunch in a Stellenbosch vineyard half an hour outside Cape Town on New Year's Day 1996. We were married in London a few weeks later, on 17th February. A traditional sort, he wanted me to stay at home and have babies while he went out to work. Against my better judgement, I acquiesced. A hack's job is never nine-to-five. I knew that the notion of working women 'having it all' was a redundant myth. We can have it all, I think, but not all at once. I decided to content myself with giving my second and third children the time and commitment I'd been unable to lavish on my first. I would focus 'in my spare time' on writing books.

But the fabled Fleet Street stories never faded. And the tales behind them are more sensational than anything that appeared in print.

I was an unsuspecting foil for Rolling Stone Bill Wyman's relationship with thirteen-year-old Mandy Smith. I was a fly in the ointment of

Richard Gere's ego, when they despatched me to quiz him about the so-called showbiz urban myth of the decade, that he was partial to a particularly sordid sexual practice. When I relocated from New York to Los Angeles, I found myself the unwitting new best friend of Raquel Welch. I witnessed Live Aid from the wings at Wembley Stadium, and the collapse of Janet Jackson's pop extravaganza at New York's Madison Square Garden, when the singer's terrified pet panther went berserk. I toured Rome with Michael Jackson in disguise, and I remain to this day one of the few journalists able to contradict the rumours that Michael and his sister La Toya were the same person: I'd had dinner with them both at the same time. I worked with Linda McCartney and Cynthia Lennon on Beatle-wife memoirs that were banned from publication. I quizzed Frank Sinatra exclusively in LA, despite the fact that he famously never gave interviews. I whispered carelessly with George Michael, did the Fandango in Cuba with Carlos Acosta, and revisited rehab with Stevie Nicks. I was both propositioned and abused by Marco Pierre White, and was serenaded in a limo by Gordon Ramsay, while our sons were pupils at the same school. I declined a fortune offered by John Hurt in exchange for my unborn firstborn. And I raised three unusual children single-handedly while working as a freelance feature writer and author, after my ten-year marriage collapsed in appalling circumstances.

I contribute to documentaries for British and American TV channels these days. In some of them, I am called upon to discuss the cult of celebrity and what makes artists 'tick'. After so many years spent living and working among them, I believe that all artists suffer from a permanent inner disquiet. This is not merely part of the territory, it is the element that drives their art. Almost every great artist experienced some sort of childhood trauma: something that triggered their creativity. It is as if each new thing they produce is created specifically to assuage whatever is gnawing at their brain. I have never met a highly successful entertainer who is not like that. Art is always a symptom of deep inner pain. To attempt to cure the torment may well kill the art.

As for me. I have long thought of myself as something of a cut-price Gloria Gaynor. I have survived: skin cancer, peritonitis, meningitis, life-saving surgery, the last rites, miscarriage, swine 'flu and a shattering divorce, culminating in the death of my gutsy, polished London barrister Mark Saunders, who was killed by police marksmen in 2008 during the

Markham Square siege. I was held at gunpoint in Tobago, kidnapped in LA, and Susan Boyle landed me in clink.

Writing a memoir is nerve-wracking. It prompts the same cold sweat as that brought on by the thought of going outside in the nude. I have begun and abandoned this many times over the past decade, never certain that I wanted to put it out there. I forced myself to finish it in the end, partly because I was determined to find some missing pieces that might join my past to my future. I wanted to gather together and reconsider all the Lesley-Anns that I had been. I was keen to face a few home truths, and to own up to some wrong-doing. I longed to revisit and re-experience those misspent days, to feel the fear, to forgive myself, and to work out what I would have done differently, if only I were allowed that time again. I wanted to hack back through the gnarled forests of childhood and family, gash open old wounds, and find ways of coming to terms with the things that went wrong.

Above all, I wanted my three children to know what my life was once like. I longed to introduce them to the girl I was before I had them. They know me as the bitch in the kitchen, the stay-at-home mum, she who went shopping, got breakfast, laundered their sports kit, ran them to and from school, cooked endless dinners and was always there: unglamorous in Uggs and leggings and without make-up, dishevelled and sleep-deprived. The woman who had relinquished a thrilling career to have them, and who would do that again in a heartbeat, because they are, cue cliché, my greatest achievement. How could Mummy-Madre-Madge-Mamma have worked in that cesspit, flown all those miles, met all those people, lived that mad life? I did, and I needed them to know about it.

And then there's the other reason. Time passes. I had put the past on the back burner. The pot was beginning to boil dry. What if one day I found myself no longer able to recall the detail of this assignment, that splash, all the life-affirming and life-threatening encounters? What if the faces faded, the names disappeared, and an entire eccentric era that was already less than a whole memory simply evaporated, silently, and ceased to exist, because I could no longer remember it?

More time passes. The years die page by page, paragraph by paragraph, semi-colon by semi-colon. But these stories are stories that my generation of journalists know. The generation down will not know them.

Unless we tell our tales to our own children, they will never truly know us as we were. They will never be able to imagine us as energetic, full-of-it, glittering young things with our whole lives ahead of us, with risks to take and with everything to play for, as they themselves now are. There will never be a reason for them to know that Fleet Street once shuddered to the beat of colossal printing presses beneath its pavements, nor that the smut and the scent in its air were ink, nor why newspapers even mattered – for they won't for much longer. They might find themselves wending their way from Ludgate Hill past St. Bride's, the Sir Christopher Wren church where my three babies were baptised and confirmed, where my ill-fated marriage was blessed and our vows were renewed, and past Child & Co, the country's oldest bank. They will perhaps feel a flicker on passing through ghosts, and pause to wonder: did my mother waste the best years of her life here? No, I would tell them, and no again, because it wasn't a waste. All human life really was here, and in some ways still is. It was here that I learned about psychology, behaviour and relationships. Where I discovered how to make mistakes. Maybe one day they'll follow in our footsteps on a Fleet Street pub-crawl, from the Old Bell to the Harrow to the Punch Tavern to Ye Old Cheshire Cheese to the Tipperary to the Wig and Pen, falling into El Vino's and out again; perhaps they'll wonder in passing about the 'Black Lubyanka' and what that imperious building once was, and about the Royal Courts of Justice and the Temple; they might even attend the odd wedding at St. Dunstan-in-the-West or at one of the so-called 'Island Churches', Saint Mary-le-Strand, or St. Clement Danes – the church of the Royal Air Force – where my ex-husband married his first wife on my birthday, divorcing her several years before he and I met.

The past as we lived it will still be lost, and no one will care. Yet journalists care. I find myself at funerals with alarming frequency these days, another big Fleet Street name having bitten the dust. The services are often held at St. Bride's, the journalists' church. My church. The turnout is always impressive. Ask not for whom the bell tolls. We pitch up, brushed and booted, not only out of respect and in loving memory, but to see who is left. The hacks we hung with then, we hang with now. The chat at the back afterwards and in the dusty, sagging saltlicks we once frequented, with the same flags, foreign bank notes and lost neckties drawing-pinned to the walls, is in shorthand. It is a language that we still understand. It is loaded with criticism, self-deprecation and gallows humour. There is but one theme: the good old days. We talk scams and scoops and outrageous expenses, always expenses, and about the ones that got away.

Perhaps this is not rooted in that good old alley called Fleet Street at all, nor in a handful of crazy stories that have been or perhaps ought to have been forgotten. Perhaps it is about regret and lament and longing, about one for the road with our younger, more courageous selves. About heydays, both collective and individual. About who we really were behind the bylines, the datelines and the grinning bravado, getting away with it. About who we still are. For, as long as we can still lie on the floor without holding on, as an old crooner called Dean Martin may or may not have once said – we still are.

PART ONE

1. DON'T SHOOT THE FOX

Elvis Presley was dead. Not newly, recently, latently benumbed, but comprehensively lifeless. As dead as a doornail. Under the sod. Think Monty Python's Norwegian Blue pining-for-the-fjords parrot sketch and you get the drift. You are on the right page. Not only was he deceased, but he'd been exanimate for ages. The Pelvis had perished and had been buried, with an extra 'A' in his middle name on the headstone just to make sure, way back in 1977. A hui hou from Hawaii. Elvis had left the building, laydeez and gennlemen. It had been goodnight from him for the past five years.

None of which deterred the boss. God forbid. The Daily Mail's quick-lipped, snake-hipped, pork pie-munching associate editor (showbiz), one of several, with a Basil Brush bark and a pair of rotting elastic-sided boots that he was in the habit of plonking on your desk as you typed like a maniac to deadline, was never knowingly inclined to take no for an answer. He regarded the facts of most matters as little more than a flimsy distraction, a minor inconvenience. Weaned on the diet of dishonesty and downright invention served up by the paper's then Editor-in-Chief, Sir David English – himself no damp-eared novice when it came to the penning of fiction masquerading as veritable news and features – the boss, who performed on a life-threatening cocktail of adrenalin, neuroses, black coffee, booze, sweat and profanity, seemed as immune to the illegality and immorality of the title's more brazen end-of-pier practises as a honey badger to a cobra bite. When cornered, attack, so the showbiz desk adage went. Get in there. Both sets of teeth. Testicles first. The boss had got wind of a rival tabloid's world-exclusive interview with The Man Who Had Been King, and he was after a spoiler. At any cost. Oh, come on. What, I was supposed to hot-foot it to Graceland, dig the crooner up, prop him on a grassy knoll for a few mug-shots and proceed to cram words into his mouth? I had been only mildly aware of the Mail's reputation on the Street as a cesspit of exaggeration and fabrication when I took the job. I had chosen to put the rumours down to envy and resentment. But it was beginning to look as though there might be some truth in them after all.

'Call yourself a showbiz writer?' he raged, bits of pastry spurting from his thin-lipped gob, a porky shred catching me right in the eye and causing me to weep, 'a rock and pop expert?' He gargled the words through an expression of disgust. 'Then get out there and fucking earn some, for crying out loud. Fuck off over the briny and do whatever it takes. And I mean, whatever it takes. Got your passport, LA?', he growled, menacingly. I had it, of course. It was a sack-able offence not to have the wretched document secreted on one's person at all times. In those pre-internet days, one could and did find oneself being despatched at no notice on a potential exclusive on the other side of the world.

'This is a national fucking newsroom, not the 'Blue Peter' studio,' he reminded me, continuing to boil. 'So get to Memphis. Travel are on it. I want fifteen hundred words by Friday.' This was Tuesday.

'But he's dead ...' I stuttered.

'So fucking what!' he screamed, his face now redder than a freshly-caned buttock. 'We're not talking Queen fucking Victoria or Jimi fucking Hendrix!' I failed to follow. Could he be joking? Nobody thought so. I could tell, because every last member of the Daily Mail showbiz department had his or her head down, and was furiously pretending to work.

If in doubt, repair to the Wine Press. We did this every day, at least twice. Late lunch, unless we were off somewhere on yet another wild goose chase, warranted a bottle. At the end of a twelve or fifteen-hour day, we more often than not felt deserving of a second round. Our out-crowd included some of the Mail's most colourful characters and sea-soned scribes: Jack Tinker[i], the finest theatre critic on the Street, whose party piece included a wicked impersonation of HRH Princess Margaret on the subject of the first words her children ever spoke. In a haughty voice, imaginary cigarette holder in one hand, crystal tumbler of G&T in the other, diminutive Jack would cry: 'Mine said "CHANDELIER"!; Then there was Sean Usher, definitive film critic; Baz Bamigboye, chief show-biz writer; Steve Absalom, Geoff Sutton, Pat Hill (R.I.P.) and Anne Bar-raclough, fearless showbiz reporters; feature writer Corinna Honan; and Herbert Kretzmer, who reviewed TV programmes, never giving up his day job while he toiled quietly at home on his lyrics. South African-born Herbie had been Jack's equivalent on the Daily Express for almost twenty years before defecting to the Mail. He never said a lot about his past. We knew he'd interviewed a few legends, Truman Capote, Tennessee Williams and Louis Armstrong among them. He didn't boast about it – unlike the stationery-cupboard-raiding freelance friend of the stars, David Lewin (God rest him). We also knew that Herbie had penned a few songs in the past, including 'Goodness, Gracious Me', a comedy number produced by Beatles guru George Martin which became a Top Five hit for Peter Sellers and Sophia Loren in 1960, and which won Herbie an Ivor Novello award. He'd spent years in collaboration with French crooner Charles Aznavour, writing the English versions of his hits, including 'She' and 'Yesterday When I Was Young.' He was so unassuming about the adaptation of 'another French thing' he was working on that none could have guessed, when it opened in 1985, that it would turn out to be the longest-running musical in West End history. 'Les Misérables' earned Herbie Tonys, Grammys and an OBE. He didn't go on about it. He'd just grin and offer you a bite of his hard-boiled egg.

Missing that afternoon was Lynda Lee-Potter. She was the paper's 'woman columnist', or according to Private Eye, our 'Glenda Slagg'. You'd always know when she was in the house. Lynda's 'angry voice of Muddle England' (sic) entered the Wine Press ahead of her. 'The First Lady of Fleet Street' seemed terrifying, but was a softie at heart. Never forgetting that she had herself once been a rookie (if not a Jean Rook-ie, geddit???*!*!*! Bye-eeeee!), no favour, tip or leg-up was too big an ask. I learned much at her ten-denier knee about interview technique. 'The Columbo question' being one example. Wrap up a routine interview, thank the subject profusely and beat a hasty retreat, only to pause at the door, turn to face your victim, smile beguilingly, hit them with the killer that will catch them off-guard, and score: 'Just one more thing ...'

I adored 'Fanny with the Fringe', as the subs called her. They had a ruder name than that for her too, which decorum deters me from repeating here. She was the first to laugh at her own expense (if not at her own expenses). She was patient and funny. By her own definition, a so-what Lancashire lass. A miner's daughter who got lucky – and who insisted there wasn't a recipe in existence that couldn't be knocked up with no more than an old breadknife and your grandmother's cracked ceramic mixing bowl. It was in the Wine Press, our favourite Fleet Street hostelry, that our gaggle began guzzling at twice the rate of normal consumption that late afternoon in 1985, in an attempt to work out how we were going to save my skin. By the time I returned to my desk for the inevitable confrontation with my tormentor, he was nowhere to be found. At about nine o'clock that night, none the wiser, I wandered off home. The next morning, he was already in the inner sanctum with the Editor when I presented for duty, ready to fly. Then it was morning conference. Travel hadn't

yet come anywhere near me with flight tickets, transfer vouchers or requisite wedge of cash. I maintained a low profile. It was beginning to look
as though I was off the hook. Perhaps I had got the wrong end of the
stick. Maybe it had all been a terrible misunderstanding, or a jape at my
expense, just to keep me on my toes. I had packed clean underwear in
vain. Come the early afternoon, I was on my way to Windsor to terrorise
Elton John. The rival rag ran its lukewarm 'interview' in due course,
'THE OTHER SIDE OF ELVIS,' which might perhaps have drawn a more
appreciative audience as 'ELVIS FROM THE OTHER SIDE.' The vital
spoiler appeared to have been forgotten, abandoned or written off, and
was never referred to again. Not in the office, at least. My colleagues continued to tease me with it well into the next decade, long after I'd left. So
haunted was I, so regularly deprived of sleep at the memory of it, that I
was eventually forced to process the nightmare into a concept for a full-
blown West End stage musical with original songs by 'The Two Jameses',
Nisbet and Graydon, still in pre-production, entitled 'Don't Shoot the
Fox'.

Every Fleet Street hack of my vintage will have perceived its inspiration.

'I regard not finding Lord Lucan as my most spectacular success in
journalism,' said the late, great Mirrorman Garth Gibbs. South African-
born Garth, one of old Fleet Street's most colourful and legendary characters, died in 2011 after a lengthy 'battle' with cancer.

Originally a royal reporter, he progressed to his own daily page in
the best-selling tabloid, 'Gibbs Gossip', before becoming a professional
hunter of Richard John Bingham, seventh Earl of Lucan, on a never-
ending mission and magnificent expenses. No sighting was ever substan-
tiated, which suited Garth fine. Because he had taken as his motto the
wise words of former Sunday Express editor and Mail on Sunday columnist John Junor:

'Laddie, you don't ever want to shoot the fox. Once the fox is dead
there is nothing left to chase' ...

As mantras went, it was incomparable. In other words, seek Lord
Lucan for as long as you deem it profitable ... but if you know what's good
for you, never, ever find him. Its meaning stretched sublimely, to the
greater good of all journalists. The implication being that whenever one
found oneself onto far too good a thing, it was in one's own best interests

to maintain a low profile, keep dark about the finer detail, and run with whatever the story was for as long as one possibly could.

'Of course, many of my colleagues have also been fairly successful in not finding Lord Lucan,' conceded Garth, towards the end of his life. 'But I have successfully not found him in more exotic spots than anybody else. I spent three glorious weeks not finding him in Cape Town, magical days and nights not finding him in the Black Mountains of Wales, and wonderful and successful short breaks not finding him in Macau either, or in Hong Kong, or even in Green Turtle Cay in the Bahamas, where you can find anyone.'

Garth's job was the best in journalism, it being widely accepted that the murderous peer – who in 1974 had killed the family nanny, Sandra Rivett, after mistaking her for his wife Veronica Duncan – had simply vanished. Whether, as rumour had it, 'Lucky Lucan' had drowned himself, having tied a stone around his body and scuttled the powerboat he kept at Newhaven, or had shot himself and had his remains fed to the tigers at his friend John Aspinall's Kentish zoo, he was gone for good. Indeed, despite the fact that Lord Lucan has recently been declared officially deceased, (his financier son George Bingham inheriting the title), no corpse nor any evidence has ever been found.

The Elvis episode returned to haunt me yet again, and much fun was had at my expense, when I was despatched by the Mail on Sunday's YOU Magazine to Los Angeles in July 1990 to interview an American band called Dread Zeppelin. The line-up performed the songs of Led Zeppelin in the reggae style, fronted by a twenty-two stone Las Vegas-style Elvis impersonator. They had to be seen to be believed.

It was a sweat of a drive southwards out of the mad metropolis in a mid-summer heatwave, but that's LA for you. You joined the queue and you melted your way along the packed Pacific Coast Highway. Redondo Beach beckoned: a small, undramatic seaside suburb lined with condos. Three hours later, anyone who was anyone in the music business had followed me there, and the Strand dance club, a smart, sophisticated music venue, was turning them away at the door.

Dread Zeppelin, the latest cult act to take America by storm, were headlining that night. As yet, they'd had no airplay, had never released a single, and their fame had only spread by word of mouth. But whoever was in charge of cheerleading had done a magnificent job. Fans, American music press, an international media representative – me – and even a scout from the Johnny Carson Show were falling over themselves and each other for standing room only.

Another new group? Here we went again. When there is no further virgin territory left to tread (as I wrote at the time), seize the best of what's been done already and do it all again, with a twist. The coefficient is humour. Take none of it too seriously and have a good laugh at your own expense.

There I stood, waiting to be thrilled. The house lights fell, the spotlights flared, and suddenly all hell seemed to break loose. It was him, all right. Baby blue suit of lights shining with appliqués, flared bell-bottoms at half-mast, foil-lined, jewel-encrusted cape, fake-fur sideburns, spangled boots. The King, all three hundred-odd perspiring pounds of him, seemingly burger-filled and out of his mind on prescription chemicals, materialised, complete with treble chin. I was seeing things.

So this was how it was in the good old days, when the fat, feisty, fortysomething Elvis wowed them in the Vegas clubs. As impersonations went, it was a good one. Not only was this guy a dead ringer, but the voice could be mistaken for the real thing.

'A-one, a-two, a-one-two-three-four!' 'Elvis' stamped his Cuban heel, and the band jerked to life. But 'Return to Sender', 'All Shook Up' and 'The Wonder of You' were off the menu that night. Instead, the band – all white except the conga player – dressed in a colourful array of Rastafarian-style outfits – launched into a frenzied reggae cover version of the Led Zeppelin classic 'Black Dog'.

A white reggae band with an Elvis-impersonating lead singer performing Led Zeppelin numbers sounds like the ultimate bad acid trip, I must agree. But believe me, this was little short of sensational. Combining accurate send-ups of the world's most adulated singer and the greatest heavy rock band of all time provided two icons for the price of one. What's more, it worked. The reggae-beat delivery was actually a bonus.

The Zeppelin fans present were in their element. Elvis aficionados were beside themselves. Everyone else was in stitches as the band careered wildly through a set which included 'Hound Dog' and 'Heartbreak Hotel' along with 'Misty Mountain Hop', 'Stairway to Heaven' and 'Whole Lotta Love'.

'Lemme say this one time, and one time only,' gasped 'Elvis'. 'Ahm an innertainer. Ahm here to innertain you folks, and thass all. No messages, no politics, nuthin but pure innertainment.' We got the picture.

Since autographing a lucrative deal with IRS records boss Miles Copeland, brother of drummer Stuart and manager of the Police, Dread Zeppelin were finally seeing stars.

'It all sounded so mad, I just had to sign them,' Copeland told me.

The band had been touring flat out for over a year, and were on the verge of releasing their debut album 'Un-Led-Ed' that month. They were also about to perform in the UK for the very first time.

The band members were only in it for love of the music, they insisted. 'Elvis', aka TortElvis, claimed to have met the others while working as a milkman in Pasadena. Guitarist Joe Ramsey alias the Prince of Peace and Love, had spent a lifetime in and out of groups that had never quite made it. So had Carl Harris, or Karl Jah, an ace-guitarist with zip-fast fingers who seemed to do it better than Jimmy Page. Paul Maselli, aka Fresh Cheese, was a Scientologist. Bruce Fernandez was Ed Zeppelin, conga player supreme. And my favourite, Gary Putman, or Put-Mon, bared his butt at the drop of a jockstrap. The others described him as a closet nudist. There wasn't too much closet about it. Prancing around all afternoon at the soundcheck in the minimum of clothing, his stagewear consisted of a lime green and black thong complete with lace sporran, chain and antenna:

'It stops the other guys getting too close.'

Black leather fingerless gloves and knee-high leopard-skin boots completed the deranged look. With a baby doll tied to his guitar that 'cried' on cue at regular intervals, he stood on a monitor on stage to play, tossing his blond head wildly. He would leap periodically from his pedestal to launch headfirst into a series of eye-watering contortions, usually ending in a back spin with his legs in the air. As he skipped to the front of the stage to take a bow, women clambered over each other to tuck dollar bills into his pants.

During the 'innerval', TortElvis took me to one side, and insisted on regaling me with the 'true' story of the band's existence. He was, he insisted, the 'real' son of Elvis and Priscilla Presley, conceived by an alien from outer space, who was instructed by his daddy on his very deathbed to perform Zeppelin songs in a reggae style: 'the way they were meant to be sung.'

Just nice, middle-class, Mister Average American boys, then.

I remember they really went for it during the second half. Put-Mon twisted his crotch at the ecstatic throng, and flung himself into an uncontrolled Can-Can. TortElvis now had so many garlands wound around his neck, he couldn't get his lips against his Budweiser. He proceeded to kung fu across the stage, and sank into the splits. He couldn't get up again. Two valets rushed from the back to lift him into the wings. Stage left, a row of middle-aged couples – the parents? – were staring on in open-mouthed amazement.

'Laydeez an' gennlemen, TortElvis has left the building,' boomed a voice into the dark arena, thus sending up the King's live shows to the bitter end.

Like the man said, it was innertainment, pure and simple, fer sure. I can't recall what Terry Wogan made of it. But I did read somewhere the other day that Dread Zeppelin have recently celebrated their twenty-fifth anniversary. I did the math, and it didn't quite add up. Still a whole lotta fakin' goin' on.

Herbert Kretzmer, LAJ & Jack Tinker, Joe Allen, London, 1987

Dread Zeppelin, Los Angeles, July 1990

2. THE SOUND OF ONE HAND CLAPPING

There was little in my past to suggest that I would grow up to stalk celebrities for a living. I would sometimes cross-examine the dearly beloved on this theme, longing for clues that might explain what I now understand to have been a quite irrational obsession with the rich and famous. Nothing definitive ever came to light. Not that there was ever any shortage of larger-than-life characters in my childhood.

One fascinating fact that presented itself during those mostly fruitless conversations was that our family's exposure to the madness of the music business did not begin in the late 1970s with me. It came more than half a century earlier, courtesy of Auntie Jane: the sister of my paternal grandfather's brother Shoni's wife, Auntie Annie, if you follow, who was something of a local heroine in her day. Like countless other members of our eccentric family, Jane was blessed with the primary attribute of the Cymric race: an energetic and wildly expansive character. She also seemed untainted by Celtic gloom. By the time I came along, Jane had flourished into an exquisitely mono-bosomed matron possessed of a mock-indignant mien in the drag-Les-Dawson mould. She had once pounded the organ with gusto at no fewer than five services on Sundays. Some claim that this miraculous duty was fulfilled at the Ebenezer Welsh Baptist Chapel in Merthyr Tydfil, while others insist it was in the now-nameless, long-defunct, altogether humbler little house of worship opposite 13 Baden Terrace: the house in which my grandfather was born.

'Dear gosh! Come sit by 'ere and tell me all about it!' was one of Auntie Jane's catch-phrases in her declining years, after she'd relocated from Birmingham to the southern seaside in the late 1940s. Some of the family had diverted to the Midlands during the Second World War, to make shells and bullets in the munitions factories, and (ironically) to dodge the bombs. Post-war, some returned to Merthyr, others remained in Birmingham, while the more intrepid of the clan ventured forth, and settled in Margate.

In Thanet's golden-sanded pleasure resort, daring Jane – who had married her twenty-years-younger lodger Norman Yates in Brum – took in paying guests. To be clear, that's Yates, not Bates. And it was a respectable B&B, with pristine net curtains and crocheted toilet-roll covers, not some crumbling backwater motel, in case you're anticipating a sidestep into Hitchcock/'Psycho' territory. Auntie Jane once rented out her ice-cream-pink-painted Georgian house with glorious sea view to 'The Benny Hill Show' for the filming of one of its beloved 'Yakety Sax' accelerated 'chase' scenes featuring scantily-clad young babes, including my friend Cherri Gilham. This was the myth regurgitated annually around the Christmas tree, at least, after one too many crème de menthes or Warnink's Advocaat snowballs. What actually happened involved not Benny Hill at all, but a Scottish actor and impersonator who rose to fame courtesy of his hugely popular TV comedy series 'The Stanley Baxter Show' and 'The Stanley Baxter Picture Show'. His best-loved impersonation was of Her Majesty the Queen, to whom he referred, on screen, as 'the Duchess of Brendagh'. Old man Stan made Auntie Jane an offer she couldn't resist: the opportunity for the freshly-spruced front of the Yates's boarding house to find fame at last in a comedy sketch on one of his 1970s Christmas Specials. But in the spirit of Old Fleet Street, where much of this memoir is set, why allow the truth to impede a good story? While I'm on the subject of Celtic myths, I should perhaps pause to revisit The Legend of Donny Osmond.

A nebulous suggestion had long been accepted as truth among the Joneses, that Merthyr Tydfil single-handedly originated the Mormon movement. This was undoubtedly stoked by copious cups of Cinzano and lemonade, not to mention the historical fact that, during the late 1840s, severe unemployment in Merthyr happened to coincide with a rise in conversion to Mormonism. Convinced of a bright future in the promised land of 'Zion', as they called America back then, Captain Dan Jones led the first Welsh immigrants to the US in 1849. Thousands followed him to Utah, where they created small Welsh communities under the Mormon wing. Many of them did what they had voyaged long and hard to escape from: they went down the mines.

Twenty per cent of the population of Utah today is of Welsh descent. That includes the all-singing, all-dancing Osmonds: Alan, Wayne, Merrill, Jay, Donny, Jimmy and sister Marie. Their late mother Olive, whose maiden name was Davis, had researched her family tree, but much of it was subsequently proven to be erroneous. When heart-throb Donny took up the cause, and traced his roots to Merthyr, BBC Wales seized upon the opportunity to make a film about his pilgrimage. The documentary premiered on St. David's Day 2005. Not only did Donny talk candidly about his ancestry, which could now be plotted all the way back to 1585; but he had identified his great-great-great grandfather, Dr. John Martin, a respected surgeon in the Merthyr steelworks. Donny had always believed that his Welsh family fled to America to avoid religious persecution. It was actually to dodge a cholera epidemic. The moving film depicted him weeping at Doc Martin's grave, as well as crooning 'Cwm Rhonda' ('Guide Me O Thou Great Redeemer') with the Dowlais Male Voice Choir.

Back in the pre-politically correct day, as indeed now, merciless Mormon-bashing was tasty sport. There was plenty to mock. The Church of Jesus Christ of Latter-Day Saints was blasted for practising polygamy, although they officially gave up plural marriage in 1890. They were said to be 'not Christian.' They are, for the record, although they heed other scriptures in addition to the Holy Bible, including the Book of Mormon. They were said to be banned from drinking alcohol, tea or coffee, to baptise corpses, to get naked in the temple, to persecute homosexuals, to wear 'magic underwear', whatever that is, and to not be allowed to dance. This mythology, like most mythology, was irresistible. When 'Book of Mormon' the musical comedy satirizing their religious beliefs and practices by the writers of 'South Park' opened in New York in 2011, it was described as both 'wildly offensive' and as 'the best thing that Broadway has ever seen'. It picked up nine Tony Awards, including, of course, 'Best Musical'.

As for our particular line of Joneses being directly related to the Osmonds: which impish clan member dreamed that one up? One too many warm Babychams in front of a roaring gas fire on New Year's Eve and the aunties would be frothing at the mirth, swearing to God Almighty that it was true. When young Don returned to Merthyr in 2007 to give a concert at Cyfartha Castle – the 'Donny Comes Home!' special – my Cambrian sense of mischief got the better of me. It was as much as I could do to rein myself back from stalking him to his dressing room door and challenging him with the sentence that is every celebrity's worst nightmare: 'You know we're related, don't you ...'

From the time we could first toddle, my brother Gareth and I anticipated visits to Auntie Jane's with keen desire, salivating at the thought of her exclamation when she heard us coming:

'Get the sweet tin, Norman!'

'Orrrggghh! There's lovely!' she would gurgle, once she'd sat us down before her ample legs, well-fortified by a couple of pairs of American Tan support stockings, in front of the three-bar electric fire in her green-tiled hearth. That fire would be on full-blast all year round, come heatwave or in hail. 'Just the one!' she'd then remind us, shaking her vessel of sickly delights.

A cherished topic among members of the Jones tribe was Merthyr Tydfil: the southern Welsh town at the top of the Taff valley which was the place of my father's, grandfather's, both great-grandfathers' and many other members of our clan's birth. From Merthyr's hillsides, Britain's first-ever coal was gouged. It is said, today, that the best thing about Merthyr Tydfil is the by-pass. Even with roadworks. Not what you'd call a holiday destination, then, despite its close proximity to the ravishing Brecon Beacons. You've seen 'Deliverance'. I've read that life expectancy for an adult male on Merthyr's Gurnos Estate is lower than in Afghanistan or Haiti. That estate has its own police station. Enough said.

I haven't been back to Merthyr for a dozen years. There are only graves to visit there now. But this ancient Glamorgan settlement, built over Roman remains, was once the largest town in all Wales. It was named for Saint Tydfil, an early Christian convert and martyred princess. At one time the arrhythmic heart of the south Wales coal-mining community, and lauded as the 'centre of the earth' when its nineteenth century iron mining industry was in full swing, Merthyr was, during the aftermath of both wars, a pretty desperate place. Rumour has it, it still is. To my ebullient elderly relatives, however, who hardly ever went back there, and who peered into their collective past through rose-tinted specs over thimbles of Harvey's Bristol Cream, it was a fabled corner of the land of their fathers, the green, green grass of home. Cue the mellifluous melodies of the Pontarddulais Male Voice Choir, crooning 'Men of Harlech', 'The Old Wooden Cross', 'We'll Keep a Welcome in the Hillside' and 'All Through the Night'. There are none so Welsh as Welshmen who live elsewhere.

Sometimes, when my brother and I were little, we would all go 'home' to Merthyr, though neither my brother nor I had actually been born there. (For the record, the stork delivered me to Gravesend hospital in Kent, while my brother was dropped off at Lewisham General, south London.) But Welsh-ness was ineradicably in our blood. We'd been raised to have pride in our roots; to revere Richard Burton as the most formidable Shakespearian actor of all time; to give thanks for the howlings of Shirley Bassey and Tom Jones; to give it up on a Sunday night for Harry Secombe on 'Songs of Praise'. Though we didn't much care for the flavour of laverbread or leeks, we sported daffodils on St. David's Day, committed chunks of 'Under Milk Wood' to memory, and learned to laugh in all the right places while assembled around the Dansette, revisiting Max Boyce LPs. So off we'd trek 'home', Mum and Dad in the front of the Ford Cortina, Dad driving, and Gareth and me in the back. Never once did I make that journey without a bucket between my knees. Invariably, I vomited all the way there. Car journeys were, for the first seventeen years of my life, a dreaded ordeal. Not until I learned to drive did motion sickness subside.

Dad remembers how he'd exit the motorway at Newport and continue on up to Abergavenny, then west through Brynmawr and Tredegar to reach Merthyr Tydfil from the brow at Dowlais top. The whole town spread out before you there. From that distance, he says, Merthyr was much as visitors saw the place when they caught their first glimpse of it a hundred years ago or more.

Not that we kids could imagine it. But Dad could. What Merthyr must have been like before the depression. A seething hell of furnaces and coke ovens. Tormenting, blood-curdling sounds, both mechanical and human. Vast volcanic torrents of waste, which solidified into giant ridge-backed dragons silhouetted against the slopes. Though the foundries and the collieries were long gone by the time my brother and I were born, and the grass was by then a lot greener, my father claimed you could still hear the echoes of Merthyr's merciless past. The place had once been a cesspit of shanty towns, a hotbed of misery, an enclave of immorality and murder. A place where infant mortality was less a feared possibility, more an accepted way of life. The land of my fathers, lovingly sighed over by our grandparents, aunties and uncles in faraway Margate as they clinked tiny tumblers of Tío Pepe and reminisced about the olden days, was at one time described as the hardest place on earth. An oft-repeated Merthyr legend told of babies born so angrily into the world, they had clenched fists.

My great-grandfather William Daniel Jones and my great-grandmother Granny Annie lived in the Merthyr mining village of Penyard. Their 'ag lab' (agricultural labourer) forbears had been drawn in the mid-1800s by horse and cart from Llanfihangel-y-Creuddyn, Ceredigion, (formerly Cardiganshire), west Wales – 'the fag end of creation, the very rubbish of Noah's flood!' – where our family's names dating back to 1775 are inscribed in the parish register of St. Michael's church, to find work in the industrial south. William Daniel, known as 'Big Daddy' despite being little more than five feet tall, was an iron miner. He was also an autodidact. He'd left school at thirteen to work down the pit. He'd have starved, otherwise. But he was reluctant to abandon his studies. A remarkable man by all accounts, given his poverty-stricken beginnings and lack of secondary education, Big Daddy taught himself the Esperanto language, and practised it while toiling underground. Esperanto had been invented by a Polish-Jewish opthalmologist in the late 1800s, to enable people from different countries who did not share a common first language to communicate – presumably because they didn't have the patience to apply themselves to Greek, Latin or the confusing Lingua Franca. He built himself a radiogram out of bits of scrap, so that he could tune into political broadcasts. He owned few books. The Holy Bible, in Welsh, and Karl Marx's 'Das Kapital', the communist bible of politics, philosophy and economics that was published in 1867, were two of them. Big Daddy was nothing, so legend goes, if not wildly obsessed with the exploitation of labour as the motivational force of capitalism. A fervent follower of Scottish socialist politician James Keir Hardie, he became a founder member of the Independent Labour Party, and in 1926 was banned from working in every pit throughout the valley in perpetuity for being a 'dangerous agitator' during the General Strike. So passionate were his convictions, it was said that, with the benefit of formal learning, he would have made it to the House of Commons. As it was, with a dozen mouths to feed, he took up a profession favoured down the years by various of his ancestors, including Daniel 'Jones the Barber', who had a shop at 9, Victoria Street, Merthyr during the 1850s; and Josiah Jones, who appears on the 1871 census for Llanelli, Carmarthenshire, as 'Hairdresser and Tobacconist'. Big Daddy attached a red and white-striped pole to the wall of his terraced two-up-two-down cottage, installed a creaking, leather-padded, oak swivel chair in his humble parlour, and set himself up as a barber. It was the perfect front for the political salons he would proceed to chair in his own front room.

Big Daddy fathered ten children. Five of each. Following in the footsteps of their clean-living, starch-collared patriarch, all five sons dropped daily into the coalmines for shillings a week from the age of fourteen, and suffered withering hardship. By some inexplicable miracle – their father had never kicked a ball in his life, so they weren't exactly looking to emulate their elder – they found their way out of the pits and back into daylight by taking up football. No one could ever explain where their talent came from. One by one, the five brothers – Will John ('Shoni'), Ivor, Emlyn and Bertrand Russell (named after the great philosopher, of whom Big Daddy was an ardent fan) – were sold to First Division English clubs. My grandfather, Emlyn, known as 'Mickey', went to Everton, before becoming a star at Southend United between 1929 and 1936. My petite, pretty grandmother Nancy was swooned over there. Applauded each time she tip-toed out into the stand, behatted, gloved and glamorous, she was one of the game's first-ever WAGS.

My great-uncle Bryn, five years my grandfather's junior, became the world's most expensive player in 1939 when he was sold by Wolverhampton Wanderers to Arsenal for £14,500: about £6.9 million in today's money. That (at the time) unimaginably huge transfer fee knocked talk of war and the Great Depression off the front pages and incited a riot in Downing Street, while disgruntled fans burned down the goalposts at the Wolves ground, Molineux, in protest. Serving with the Royal Artillery in Italy and North Africa while still playing games for Arsenal and Wales, Bryn was capped seventeen times and starred in eight wartime internationals. Despite the fact that he even appeared in 'The Arsenal Stadium Mystery' that same year, one of the first motion pictures to feature football as its central theme, fame never went to Uncle Bryn's head. Always a quiet, lonely man, he was troubled by the glare of the media spotlight. He married Mavis, had two children, Bryn and Margaret, and remained clean-living and modest throughout his life. Pre-mega-millions product endorsements and advertising contracts, a First Division footballer's wages were hardly lavish. In 1949, Arsenal set off on a tour of Brazil. During a game against Rio de Janeiro's Vasco da Gama club, spectators invaded the pitch. Uncle Bryn was hit on the head accidentally by a Brazilian policeman. So serious was his injury that his doctors insisted he retire from the game. He coached Norwich City for a couple of years, until 1951, after which he ran a small newsagent's and sweet shop near Arsenal's Highbury ground. He died a forgotten hero, alone at home, in October 1985.

Family history repeated itself in the Sixties, when our Joneses again produced the world's most valuable player: my father's cousin Cliff. Because they had been raised as brothers, and even shared a bed as boys, we knew him as 'Uncle.' Cliff was bought from Swansea Town for £35,000 by Tottenham Hotspurs. Capped fifty-nine times for Wales, he was famously part of Spurs' 1960-1961 Double-winning side during the team's 'Glory Glory Days'. He married his teenage sweetheart Joan and had four children, Debbie, Steven, Kim and Mandy. (Debbie was later lost to breast cancer). Once hailed as the best left-winger in the world, Uncle Cliff collected three FA Cup Winners' medals and the European Cup. He moved on to Fulham, and ended his playing career at King's Lynn. After his retirement, he became a P.E. teacher, coached the football team at Highbury Grove School in North London, and acquired a share in a butcher's shop. A White Hart Lane 'Legend', he recently published 'It's a Wonderful Life', his second volume of autobiography. They call Gareth Bale 'the new Cliff Jones' today.

My father Ken followed his father and four uncles into professional football, playing for Southend, Swansea, Gravesend and Northfleet and Hereford, before suffering an inoperable injury which ended his playing career. He became a football writer on the Daily Mirror, in those days a remarkable newspaper, in 1958 – the same year that Uncle Cliff went to Spurs. He rose to the position of chief football writer within four years, became the Sunday Mirror's 'Voice of Sport', and was poached by the Independent at its inception in 1986. A respected columnist, author and television and radio pundit – gathering round our tiny black-and-white set to watch Dad on BBC Grandstand on a Saturday afternoon as my mother stood ironing was a fixture to set your watch by – he covered ten World Cups, eight Olympic Games, spent a decade on the road with Muhammad Ali, and attended more boxing title fights than I could keep up with. We saw our father on television and in the newspapers more than we saw him at the kitchen table. In December 1992, on his way home from a drinks do, he fell under a train at London Bridge station, and lost his arm.

I am trying to find the words here. It was a long time ago, but the cliché is true: we relive the horror of such incidents as though they happened yesterday. I had just returned from an interview assignment in Los Angeles. I was watching bed-time TV with my eight-year-old firstborn, Mia, at home in Sevenoaks, Kent, when the phone rang. It was my mother, Kathleen. 'Your father's been in an accident,' she said calmly. The 'five Ws' fell out of my mouth before I could take a breath.

'I know as much as you do,' she replied. 'I'm not there yet. I want you to stay at home – I want you all to stay at home – and I will call you as soon as I get there, as soon as I know any more myself.'

By 'all', she meant the four of us: my brother Gareth, my younger sisters Beverley and Samantha, and the eldest: me. Needless to say, by the time she reached Guy's Hospital at London Bridge, every one of us was there. We sat in an eerily-lit waiting room, white-faced. Nobody said a word. Our father was in emergency surgery that would last all night. All we knew was that he had fallen under a train, and that it had taken fire-men hours to cut him from the wreckage. We knew nothing of the extent of his injuries. We did not know whether he would survive. With that de-layed realisation, the tears came. Slowly at first, just a trickle of moist emotion, but building into uncontrollable floods.

Dad was the Independent's chief sportswriter at the time. He was making his way home from the office Christmas party. He'd done the sensible thing: he had left the car at home. A number of homeward-bound trains from London Bridge station that evening had been can-celled. There was a lot of hanging-around, and a prevailing mood of im-patience. The concourse was packed with pre-Christmas revellers, their hangovers beginning to kick in. Suddenly, a last-minute platform-change was announced. A stampede up the stairs ensued, over the bridge and down the other side. My father, a compact and relatively fit sixty-one, was swept up in the maelstrom and hurled down onto the rails, just as the train was pulling in. That they managed to drag him free was a mira-cle. What was left of his right arm, and his writing hand, were left behind.

He still hears the voice of the nameless ambulance man who talked him into holding on, into clinging to life. To this day, he suffers searing phantom pain in the arm that isn't there. He has lived for a quarter of a century with this. He never moans about it. He continued to travel the world well into his seventies, covering major prize fights, football match-es, and summer and winter Olympic Games. He only retired when they made him. He could still kick them senseless for that.

Ken in his eighties is as sharp as a scythe. He is bored, much of the time. When you've worked for a lifetime in a profession that still defines you, it is often the case – because you are not doing it anymore, but your name and reputation remain connected to it. On a good day, we still have fierce bouts over politics, news and sport. He'll always have several books on the go, everything from Ancient Rome and Shakespeare to modern biographies, and ever the poems of Dylan Thomas.

My father lost a part of himself, that bitter night. But he became somehow more of himself because of it. In many ways, utterly random and brutal though such catastrophes are, his was the making of him. I've been looking at that raw, tragic stump for two and a half decades, now. It still shocks me to recall what happened, longer ago than the births of my children. It breaks my heart. But then I remember, he's still a whole dad. No less of a complete, confounding jigsaw of a man, for want of a single absent piece.

Come Christmas, as you might imagine, I'm all over the kids about stations. Run for the shadows. Never for the train. Never, ever, run for the train. If all else fails, grab a cab. Or I'll come and pick you up. And when you're standing on the platform, hang back from the edge. Stay behind the line. So what if you don't get on it, this time. There will be another one along soon. You might not be as lucky as Grandad. Which is the way he sees it. He always has. It must be what saved him.

My father carried on writing. People would ask him all the time – they still ask him – what on earth became of the beautiful game? We know what happened. Money happened. Football gave in to monstrous corporate investment and the attempted gentrification of what remains, essentially, a working man's fun. To the thousands of miners who once toiled in the valleys my family hailed from, their flat-capped trudge to the weekly match was their solitary light relief, a reward for an honest week's work. There was once dignity in a game of football. I'd like to hear them say that now.

A former chairman of the Football Writers Association, Ken is one of only two non-American writers to win the Nat Fleischer Award for excellence in boxing journalism. He was honoured by the Welsh Sports Hall of Fame in 1991, and published his definitive account of the England team's World Cups, 'Jules Rimet Still Gleaming?', in 2003. He retired from newspapers in 1998. He continues to contribute occasionally, as a freelance pundit and commentator.

'There was no beginning in that I did not set out to write about sport or ever imagine being at the ringside in New York and Las Vegas and all those other locations,' he once wrote, in an overview of his life in newspapers.

'Life can be like that: you take off in one direction, a destination clear in your mind, only to be diverted somewhere else.'

My father was diverted in ways he could never have imagined. He got knocked down. He got up again. Survivors make their mark in personal ways. What would he make of my gauche attempts to follow in his footsteps?

Kenneth Powell Jones & Nancy Jones, LAJ's father & grandmother, 1935

Daddy's girl: LAJ & Ken

The Jones Boys: Back: great uncle Bryn, grandfather Emlyn.
Front: Bryn, Uncle Cliff, father Ken

The 'Thanet Aunts': Jane & Annie

The Joneses: Sam, LAJ, Gareth, mother Kathleen, Ken, Beverley

Muhammad Ali & Ken Jones in 'Fighter's Heaven': Deer Lake, Pennsylvania, where Ali trained for the Rumble in the Jungle, 1974, and the Thrilla in Manila, 1975

LAJ, Ken & Gareth, Atlantic City, New Jersey, 1992, when Ken was awarded the Nat Fleischer Award for Excellence in Boxing Journalism by the Boxing Writers Association of New York

3. ALL THE HITS AND MORE

It was Hyacinth Money who introduced me to David Bowie. Hyacinth was Lisa's mum and Lisa and I were best friends at Oak Lodge County Primary School. Her mother, a self-taught musician, artist and photographer, had arrived in England from India at the age of eighteen. She married her first boyfriend, and had four children.

Hy was probably the only Asian in our ordinary white town, which was still stuck in the Fifties. She was racially abused there. When we danced through the streets dressed in the contents of her dressing-up box, other mothers shooed their children indoors.

Shortly after her youngest child started school, Hy began taking pictures for a local newspaper, the Beckenham Record. She would eventually make a name for herself as the UK's first female sports photographer at Crystal Palace Football Club – but only after having fought off male rivals who complained to their union and tried to get her banned.

Hy's fame was a few years off when, one Sunday afternoon in 1969, she took Lisa and me to a performance by Lithuanian sitar player Vytas Serelis, at the Three Tuns Folk Club in a pub on Beckenham High Street. She was there to photograph him. Marc Bolan and David Bowie were there too. Lisa and I were none the wiser.

David Bowie co-founded the Beckenham Arts Lab at the Three Tuns soon afterwards and was suddenly, thrillingly, in the news, his enigmatic single 'Space Oddity' having been chosen by BBC television to accompany their coverage of the Apollo 11 moon landings. Lisa and I progressed to different secondary schools. So with my new classmates from Ravensbourne School for Girls, I set out to discover where David lived – which was in an imposing arts and crafts house on Southend Road, Beckenham, named Haddon Hall. We started door-stepping him and his new wife Angie after school. Angie dished out signed photographs, for which we were always grateful. But the best thing she ever did for us was to be out one day when we called. David answered the door himself in a lemon silk embroidered kimono, clutching a bottle of black nail varnish. He invited us in for tea, which we drank black after he discovered that they were out of milk. We sat cross-legged on the floor and discussed 'Space Oddity', his unsuccessful acting career, and UFOs.

David Bowie and I bought our records from the music department in Medhurst's, a large store on the Market Square at the top end of Bromley High Street – but I had to save up to buy mine. You could try before you bought there, in special listening booths.

'Top of the Pops' on BBC1 was unmissable. It's hard to believe but the 30 minutes on a Thursday night were about the only way to see any music in the days before the internet, DVDs and streaming. It was all we would talk about in the playground the next day. We all saw David Bowie perform 'Starman' on 'Top of the Pops' on July 6, 1972, but we were less than blown away by it. The belief that he walked on water was still to come. 1973 was the game-changer for me: the year when music began consuming my life. Out went the childish magazines I'd been devoted to: 'Bunty', 'Jackie' and 'Girls' World'. In came the 'Melody Maker' and the 'New Musical Express'. Up in the loft went the Thunderbirds, and the Sindys with their outfits that my mum had painstakingly hand-sewn for them. Into the bin went my moth-eaten gonks and trolls. In came vinyl. I even swapped my Lady Penelope pink Rolls Royce for a record player, and my National Health specs for coloured contact lenses.

It was all happening in the wider world too. Edward Heath was in Number Ten. Richard Nixon and the Watergate scandal dominated America. Britain joined the EEC – which soon became the European Union. My sports reporter father went to Jamaica to cover George Foreman almost slaughtering Joe Frazier to take the heavyweight world boxing title at the 'Sunshine Showdown'. The new London Bridge opened, generating huge excitement, as did the ill-fated World Trade Center twin towers in New York – at the time the tallest buildings in the world. A year later, as part of a schools exchange programme with Stella Maris High School on Long Island, I stood with my friends on top of the South Tower in the Top of the World observatory, never imagining what would happen there twenty seven years later. Her Majesty opened the Sydney Opera House, which had taken longer than my lifetime to build.

Significant singles that year were Tony Orlando & Dawn's 'Tie a Yellow Ribbon Round the Old Oak Tree', Sweet's 'Ballroom Blitz', Elton John's 'Crocodile Rock' and Roberta Flack's 'Killing Me Softly'. Elvis Presley's TV special 'Aloha from Hawaii via Satellite' (which Auntie Ann, my mother's youngest sister, loved) was the first worldwide telecast by an entertainer. It was viewed, perhaps perversely, by more people than had watched the 1969 moon landings. And David Bowie's chum Lou Reed was bitten on the bottom by a fan during a gig in Buffalo, New York. These were the factoids I relished, recording them for posterity in exercise books – for an entire year – in purple and orange mirror-writing with Spirograph patterns down the sides. Virgin Records arrived, with Mike Oldfield's 'Tubular Bells'. The Everlys broke up – bye bye love. Queen released their debut album, its stand-out single 'Seven Seas of Rhye'. The Who brought out 'Quadrophenia', and Roxy Music launched 'For Your Pleasure'. Pink Floyd produced 'Dark Side of the Moon' (which I didn't buy until about five years later). Bowie collapsed with exhaustion at a concert in Madison Square Garden ('Gimme your hands!'). And I was at Hammersmith Odeon on July 3, for the retirement of the Spiders from Mars.

I have a list in the back of my purple diary from that year, of the albums I added to my collection in 1973. As well as the Beatles' 'Red' and 'Blue' albums (I got to the Fab Four party late), I bought 'Aladdin Sane', 'The Rise and Fall of Ziggy Stardust and the Spiders from Mars' and 'Hunky Dory'. I also bought 'Red Rose Speedway' and 'Band on the Run' by Wings, my other great loves at the time. For Bolan, it was as good as all over by March 1973, when he released his single '20th Century Boy'. I chucked him for Bowie, and never looked back. At least not until I wrote his biography in 2012.

David Bowie was our epiphany. People like him didn't exist in our semi-detached, prize-dahlia-cultivating, elderflower cordial-making, melon-seed-necklace-making, 'Opportunity Knocks'-watching, spaghetti-on-toast-scoffing world. Had it turned out that he really was from a parallel universe, I doubt I would have been in the least surprised. He was twenty-three, still a boy, and yet married. Mortal, flawed, a scrawny chancer, and yet apparently enchanted. And I had met him. I knew what he was really like. Which was friendly enough. Indifferent. He was a preener and a posturer. He'd sit around nattering and giggling, rolling and popping his lips as if having just applied lipstick. He'd pick at his cuticles, flick his locks, bat his eyelashes, hug his knees. Perhaps he was posing as one of us, mirroring the behaviour of gawky young teenagers. Trying us on for size, seeing what quirks he might pilfer. He was a 'bird of paradise with a broken wing,' I wrote later. 'Perfectly beautiful, except for the awful teeth.'

Androgynous get-up and posing aside, the lasting, paradoxical impression was of how normal he was. That complicated, contradictory, cheeky, charming, disarming Bowie-by-Bromley – I was to find, over the years to come, never really changed.

I remember him quizzing me about my hair, mere tufts at the time. It was taking ages to grow back after surgery. I had suffered a post-operative condition called Telogen effluvium, which meant that my hair had fallen out from shock. I'd spent much of the previous year in hospital and then convalescing at home. My appendix had ruptured, a few days before the Easter holidays. They operated on Good Friday. My condition worsened. I was diagnosed with life-threatening peritonitis. Our local vicar came to visit me in the Intensive Care Unit of Farnborough Hospital. I was not expected to make it through the night. But I survived, a freak: scarred, skeletal and three-quarters bald. The cool girls at my new school kept their distance. I made three friends, and I know them still. David was sympathetic. He too, he said, had undergone painful surgery at Farnborough Hospital, just across the road from where my parents still live, after a punch in the eye that apparently resulted in the most distinguished look in rock.

'My cousin saw you in Margate,' I remember blurting. 'She's still got the ticket.' I cringed at such a lame line.

'Margate!' he grinned. 'I'm very fond of down there. Oh, I do like to be beside the seaside! It's that great look-out-there-nowhere-longingness.'

What on earth did that mean? I didn't dare ask. I scribbled the phrase in my rough book as soon as I got back on the bus, but I never did find out.

'Maybe I'll move there one day,' he mused. 'It'd be a great place to bring up kids. I do feel an affinity. I have a real fondness for the old seaside schtick, all that music hall end-of-pier stuff. It's very real. My Nan was a nurse at the Seabathing on the front, before the First World War. She used to sing me little ditties. One of them was about Margate. 'A breeze! A breeze! Who sails today the ocean's swelling waters,' he mock-warbled, crooking his elbows and rocking his arms in time, like something out of Gilbert & Sullivan's 'H.M.S. Pinafore'. 'I wish I could remember how it went. My grandparents got married there, and lived there for a while.'

'Mine still do,' I told him. It was true. My own grandmother, Nancy Jones, worked with her brother and sister-in-law, Gladys and Glyn Powell, at their guest house on Westbrook Bay. Auntie Jane and Auntie Annie were there. My grandfather Emlyn ran the putting green opposite the beach, just down from Margate station.

'I've potted a few balls there in my time,' David nodded. 'I'm such a kid, I never can resist a round of pitch and putt!'

There was once a tendency to pour scorn on kiss-me-quick Margate. Look at her now. The old Royal Seabathing Hospital, which once nursed sufferers of tuberculosis, has been transformed into a development of smart apartments, with beachfront 'huts' selling for half a million apiece. The Tracey Emin-supported Turner Contemporary art gallery, harbour development and renovated Dreamland amusement park have put the resort back on the map. Margate had been a quiet fishing village until restorative sea bathing became a popular pastime in the early Eighteenth Century. The landscape painter J.M.W. Turner went to school there from the age of eleven, and returned to sketch and paint as a young man. From the 1820s, he was a regular visitor. His landlady Mrs Booth became his mistress, and is immortalised as the 'Shell Lady' statue at the end of the harbour wall. More than a hundred of Turner's works, including celebrated seascapes, were inspired by the sea and the storms at Margate. By the 1900s, the town was well-established. By the early Sixties, it had acquired the saucy-postcard kitsch that epitomises the English seaside resort; the end-of-pier fish-and-chip-ness that David said he loved.

In 1965, he was the lead singer with a Margate Mod band, the Lower Third. Back then, the town was a primary destination for Mods, who would pour in en masse on scooters, especially on Bank Holiday Mondays. Brawls with Rockers on motorbikes would ensue, as they also did in Brighton and other seaside towns, which scandalised the country for a while. The Lower Third had a regular slot at a local hotel. They played nine or ten gigs throughout the summer season at Cliftonville Hall, as well as a string of other engagements around the country. Had I been a few years older, no doubt I would have seen them play. I'd spent every half-term and holiday with my grandparents in Margate since I was little. The memory shimmers with seemingly endless summers of rubber buckets, choc-ices and donkey rides on sand; of the Margate Caves and the Tivoli Park circus, the shell grotto, the Winter Gardens, the pier – lost to a storm in 1978 – and the penny arcade.

I fantasised for days after that visit to Haddon Hall. I dared to imagine growing up to be like David Bowie. Fat chance. I was plain and four-eyed, hardly what you would call artistic, and never in a million musical. We didn't have the money for lessons. I longed for so much in life that was never going to happen to me. Fleet Street might be a more realistic ambition, then. Perhaps, I dared hope, it was in the genes.

Years later, while a modern languages student, I ran into David one December in Chartier on the Faubourg Montmartre in Paris. In those days, Chartier was a budget brasserie and a short walk from my digs. David was, by then, an international star. But here he was, flat-capped, unadorned, unaccompanied, barely recognisable. He seemed on the edge of a cold. He was scoffing cassoulet and swilling vin blanc de table. I sat and had a glass with him.

'The barnet made a comeback, then,' he grinned. Nice pun. Incredible memory, too, I thought. And still making a joke of everything. But wasn't he afraid of getting mobbed, in a place like this?

'Nah,' he said with a shrug. 'They don't know it's me.'

'I knew it was you.'

'You knew me before.'

'Before what?'

'You know. Before the madness. They'd never expect to see me in here, so they're not looking for me, if you know what I mean. I keep my head down.'

'And your hat on.'

'And me 'air on. Very me, don't you think?'

'No.'

He doodled houses, trees, starbursts and wings with a black BIC biro on the paper tablecloth. I wish I'd kept it. I have the menu, at least. I noticed that he was left-handed like me. It was another thing we had in common (and probably a 'sign': which everything is to a teenager, when every emotion is exaggerated and almost unbearable). He chain-smoked Gitanes, removing one from the packet with his teeth, lighting it with a match, sucking down a few drags, tapping the ash into a tin ashtray before grinding the half-smoked fag there, and lighting another.

He'd been at some awards event, he told me, and was on his way back to Geneva to spend Christmas with the family at home in Blonay, a village above the lake near Montreux. He'd nipped to Paris to find a few presents in the Galeries Lafayette on the Boulevard Haussmann, a less than ten-minute walk from where we sat.

Our encounter concluded. We wished each other a Merry Christmas … 'and a Happy Blue Year.'

'Ta-ta,' he said, touching his cap. No kiss goodbye. Not even a handshake. I left him standing there on the pavement in the cold as I turned to go, enveloped in unfathomable sadness.

By the end of my three-year stint at the Polytechnic of Central London (since re-invented as Westminster University), I'd been in and out of love; had got engaged to and subsequently disengaged from a fine chap who is still my friend and has a lovely wife and family; was as good as fluent in French and Spanish; had begun classes in but soon got fed-up with so had jacked in Danish and Italian; could at least order drinks and dinner in five languages; could type at a speed of about eighty words per minute, and was ready to take on the world.

Inspired by my maternal grandfather Charlie, a former merchant seaman, I thought I'd give life on the ocean wave a go. I applied to both Cunard and P&O to train as a purser (what was I thinking?) and was granted interviews, but was rejected as 'unsuitable' by both. What did they know. Undeterred, I turned my attention to the United Nations in New York, where I thought, somewhat deludedly, that I might land a dream job as a simultaneous interpreter or translator. I didn't even get a response. I signed up with a temp agency in London's West End, who sent me on a string of dead-end assignments: typing up reports for a building company on Tottenham Court Road, PA to the art director of an American incentive company overlooking Marble Arch, assistant to the creative director at a long-deceased advertising agency in Covent Garden. It was only on the off-chance that I eventually fell into an internship (which in those days we called 'work experience') at Capital Radio.

I could barely believe my luck. I loved that radio station. I listened to it round the clock. I carried a transistor around in my schoolbag and tuned in whenever I could: on the 119 bus on the way to and from school, in the playground at break over my buttered Rich Tea biscuits, in the toilet block, and during the lunch hour while other girls were doing sensible things like playing netball. Graham Dene, Mike Allen, Dave Cash, Little

Nicky Horne, Greg Edwards, Peter Young (R.I.P.) and Kerry Juby were legends of the airwaves. I knew their jingles by heart. Michael Aspel made your morning, he made your day. Gerald Harper had a 'Sunday Affair'. Kenny Everett's lunatic sci-fi series 'Captain Kremmen' ('Carla, you're a country member.' 'Ok, Captain, I'll remember.') Maggie Norden's 'Hullabaloo' and the annual 'Help A London Child' appeal (I once bid for Bonnie Langford's doll) were essential listening. No-nonsense Anna Raeburn with Adrian Love on a Wednesday night had the answers to all your problems. Operation Drake, a two-year round-the-world venture under the patronage of Prince Charles, offered opportunities for Capital listeners to join the jaunt as Young Explorers. My college pal Sandy Evans pitched up for the Kenyan leg as a newly-qualified marine biologist, and never came back. Then there was 'The Best Disco in Town' at the Lyceum Ballroom off the Strand, with your actual airwave DJs spinning the discs. For a couple of years, it was the centre of the Earth to me.

My favourite DJ bar none was Roger Scott, who by then had been at the station for ten years. Millions of Londoners who grabbed a little piece of heaven from three 'til seven daily, and who cruised with him on his Friday night Oldies show, found him addictive. He took me under his wing at Capital. Nurturing my inclination to write rather than broadcast, he devised an unofficial role for me as 'interview assistant'. I'd transcribe the tapes for the Capital archives, which I was then able to borrow back as the basis for magazine profiles that would simultaneously promote the station. This was all perfectly legit because, thanks to Roger, I had genuinely met the subjects. I am painfully aware today that I didn't come close to appreciating the enormity of this favour, nor the privilege that it conferred. Thanks to Roger, I met Rick Wakeman, my friend to this day. I also met Freddie Mercury, Brian May, Roger Taylor and John Deacon for the first time, in 1981, together with David Bowie, at Queen's Mountain Studios, Montreux, where they were working on 'Under Pressure.' Roger and I interviewed David together at the Birmingham NEC in 1983, where we also interrogated Lionel Richie. We quizzed Kate Bush at home, Prince at the Roof Gardens, Spandau Ballet's Gary Kemp around a snooker table above the Groucho Club, John Taylor of Duran Duran at Tramp, and Mick Jagger in the gloomy recesses of the Ship public house on Wardour Street. One of the most instantly recognisable rock stars in the world, Jagger blended into the background and wasn't bothered by a soul. I found this fascinating. It just went to show that a superstar would only be mobbed if he or she went looking for it. David Bowie had been right.

In Los Angeles, where Roger signed a coast-to-coast contract with Westwood One Radio to syndicate his coals-to-Newcastle all-American shows, we hung with his ultimate hero Bruce Springsteen and conducted the last-ever interview with Beach Boy Dennis Wilson. Perhaps the most musical Boy in the band, drummer Dennis confided that the greatest love of his life had been Fleetwood Mac's Christine McVie. He drowned at Marina del Rey shortly afterwards, hammered, in December 1983. His 1977 solo album 'Pacific Ocean Blue' was one of the most cherished pieces of vinyl in Roger's collection.

In Florida we caught up with born-again Christian Dion diMucci, the Fifties/Sixties teen idol who'd found his calling singing a capella on downbeat street corners around the Bronx. Roger idolised Dion & the Belmonts, whose debut hit 'I Wonder Why' had established them rock'n'roll pioneers. Dion survived the plane crash that killed Richie Valens and Buddy Holly in 1959, He sobbed his way through a conversation with us about it. His solo hits 'Runaround Sue' and 'The Wanderer' were Roger Scott classics.

In New York, we accompanied Billy Joel to 142 Mercer Street, SoHo, where his record company had shot the cover image for his rock heritage tribute album 'An Innocent Man', and interviewed him while sitting on the front door step. In New Orleans, we immersed ourselves in the Neville Brothers. Keith Richards introduced Roger to the group. The Stone would play on their 1987 album 'Uptown'.

It was at Roger's suggestion that I applied for a job at Chrysalis Records, the successful independent label run out of elegant offices on Stratford Place, close to Bond Street underground station in London. He had a friend who knew someone there who was looking for an assistant.

A gift for David Bowie at 155 Hauptstrasse, Schöneberg, Berlin
(his old apartment) in 2017

LAJ & Roger Scott, Miami, Florida, 1989

4. METAMORPHOSES

Landing the lead in Oak Lodge Junior School's summer production 'The Witch of Nettles', in which I was transformed from villain into multi-petticoated Good Fairy with the flick of a black silk cloak made by my wicked-with-a-needle mother (as were the black gloves, with externally-attached five-inch fingernails made from bits of Ready Brek boxes and spray-painted silver) had given me a taste for the thespian life. I soon scuttled into panto (oh no you didn't, oh yes I did, and it's behind me), having hastened to audition for the West Wickham Pantomime Society. Performing a solo as the jester in 'Humpty Dumpty', and as a dancing villager in 'Mother Goose', I convinced myself that I had what it took to Make It on the West End Stage.

My plans took a slightly more Sybil Thorndike-ish turn, however, once I reached Ravensbourne School for Girls. There, the great classical actress's influence on our démodé English and Drama teachers had us straining credibility in productions of George Bernard Shaw's 'Arms and the Man', Sheridan's 'The School for Scandal', and Peter Ustinov's take on the greatest Shakespeare tragedy, 'Romanoff & Juliet': a comic spoof of the Cold War, in which I played the female of the star-crossed lovers as a spoilt American in a turquoise cheesecloth frock. We won rave reviews in local newspapers. Ok, they didn't think much of me. I wasn't about to walk into RADA on a full scholarship, put it that way.

Besides, there was now fierce competition for press attention. Ravensbourne was buzzing with news of the arrival of a pair of sisters, the like of whom we had never seen before. During the late Sixties into the mid-Seventies, our school, like virtually every other English suburban school, had been hitherto exclusively white. Keep your hair on, that's just the way it was. Then into our midst were catapulted two winsome South African 'picaninnies' (let's not be afraid of the words, folks; people really used that term in those days), with coiled locks and 'watermelon smiles' (as people also said back then, long before Boris Johnson was forced to apologise for racially offensive language).

Naomi and Mpho were the youngest two children of Anglican cleric Desmond Tutu. Their father had studied for his bachelor's and master's degrees in Theology at Kings College London during the Sixties. In 1972, when he was appointed vice-director of the Theological Education Fund of the World Council of Churches, he returned to the UK with his wife and family in tow. The World Council was in those days based in Bromley. Thus were his daughters enrolled at our school. They remained full-time pupils until 1975, when the family returned to Soweto. During their tenure, these beauties were known as 'the Tutu Two'. And then they took up ballet ...

Their father, of course, subsequently became the first black Archbishop of Cape Town. As one of the world's best-known Christian leaders, he would win the Nobel peace prize in 1984 for his contribution to the struggle against apartheid. He campaigned fiercely for the ordination of women. How devastated he must have been when his daughter Mpho, who had followed him into the church, was forced to give up her priest's license when she married another woman, Dutch atheist academic Marceline van Furth. The challenges of growing up black and female in apartheid South Africa had set the tone for the selfless futures of both women. Naomi, now a human rights activist who, as a teacher and public speaker is in demand all over the world, maintains to this day her motto 'I will not die an unlived life.'

Having applied to the Central School of Speech and Drama, the Rose Bruford College of Theatre and Performance, and, dear dog in a bucket, LAMDA, and having trawled through my homely outfits to find something suitable in which to perform my auditions, I lost my nerve. I knew, in my heart, that I didn't have whatever it took to be an actor. I sheepishly put aside theatrical ambition thereafter until 1982, when I found myself unwittingly cast by a friend in a pop video for a duo who had recently failed to win the Eurovision Song Contest. Bardo were Britain's 1982 hopefuls, with their song 'One Step Further'. Sally Ann Triplett, a presenter on 'Crackerjack', and singer Stephen Fischer, were the favourites. Both Terry Wogan and John Peel loved them. But on the night, their dance routines were denounced as distracting, and they came in only seventh. Bardo were managed by Nichola Martin, the woman behind the previous year's winners Bucks Fizz. Galvanised by the chart success of Bardo's single, she decided to keep them going. Their follow-up cut, a melodic offering called 'Talking Out of Line', featured a mock-up trial in a Californian courthouse. Peer intently and you will see an awkward, bespectacled stenographer hammering away in one corner on a shorthand machine.

I was coerced into this quite possibly Oscar-worthy cameo against my better judgement, by my lifelong friend Charles Armitage: a partner in the famous Noel Gay agency that had been founded by his father Richard. He had championed my cause since the day we first met, at Fino's wine bar off Charing Cross Road in 1980. We remained close friends for thirty-seven years.

At Charles's first wedding in 1987, I was nine months pregnant with the firstborn. Charles took the precarious precaution of seating me at the right hand of actress Jane Seymour's obstetrician father, John Frankenberg. 'Dilated to meet you!' cried the eminent physician. 'And I suppose you paint the hallway through your letterbox,' was my riposte. A gyne romance. It was all downhill from there. I laughed so much, I gave birth two days later.

Charles and I were often to be found tucked away in snug corners of shabby bars and restaurants, a Japanese lunch here, a French supper there, putting the vile world to rights. He was always talking about 'the business', and about his grandfather Reginald, aka Noel Gay, who had founded the company which his father Richard lifted to glory, and upon which he and his brother Alex had built, to immense acclaim. Their revival of the musical 'Me and My Girl' starring newcomer Emma Thompson won them transatlantic attention. Alex's famous stutter generated irresistible yet not unkind mirth. A story frequently told (and laughed at by Alex himself, God bless him) recounted his debut negotiation on behalf of his client Rowan Atkinson: 'The fee's a thou.. a thou.. a thou.. five hundred quid.'

We called him 'Paschimodo'. Any comparison to Lon Cheney's portrayal of the protagonist of Victor Hugo's 'The Hunchback of Notre-Dame' was deliberate. Not that our leader was visibly deformed. Nor did he have a giant wart covering his left eye. He was neither hideous nor a creation of the devil. Not in any way that we could tell. He was, as my Grandad Charlie would have described him, 'a tall, upright man who walked with a stoop.' He was a creature of habit: he loped off, alone, to the same restaurant every single lunchtime. We knew, because we were bastards, and we followed him. His canteen of choice was a doll-sized fish and chip shop off Marylebone Lane.

John Pasche's professional lair was the top floor of a grand old house at the top of Stratford Place, off Oxford Street, which for some years had been the home of Chrysalis Records. John's claim to fame was that he had created the most recognisable image in the history of rock and pop, which became a symbol of brash rebellion for almost half a century.

He designed the Rolling Stones lips and tongue logo while studying for his MA at the Royal College of Art (RCA) in 1969. Legend has it that Mick Jagger himself went to the RCA, seeking a fresh young artist to come up with cool images for the Stones. Paschimodo got the job. He later identified his inspiration as Jagger's own face, explaining that the first thing you noticed upon meeting him was 'the size of his lips and mouth.' He was paid about fifty quid for the design, which was originally used on the 'Sticky Fingers' album. Years later, when the Stones copyrighted it, John had to fight them through lawyers for a meagre share of the royalties. Notoriously parsimonious, the group appear to have stumped up a slice. John later sold his rights for a modest lump sum. And in 2008, when he put the logo's original drawings up for sale, the V&A unexpectedly stepped in, paying just over £50,000 to their creator to preserve them for the nation. John declared that he sold them to pay his eleven-year-old son's private school fees. Go Paschimodo.

John, who had also drawn and coloured-in Stones' tour posters during the Seventies, and also created the promo sticker for the 'Goats Head Soup' album and the single bag for 'She's So Cold', progressed to work with many other artists, including Paul McCartney, the Who, the Stranglers, Dr. Feelgood, Jimi Hendrix, David Bowie, Judas Priest and Van der Graaf Generator. Oh, and the Bay City Rollers. Just keeping things real. Between 1981 and 1991, he was the Creative Director of Chrysalis, who had poached him from United Artists. During his time with the butterfly boys, he designed sleeves for the Art of Noise, Go West, Sinéad O'Connor, Steeleye Span, Jethro Tull and Living in a Box. Sometimes, although the practice was privately frowned-upon, an artist or band would insist on using their own independent artist or designer instead of our in-house team, as was the case with Ultravox. This highly stylish and somewhat pompous line-up (except Midge, who was normal) demanded the artistic skills of graphic designer Peter Saville. Saville found fame designing sleeves for Factory Records, notably for Joy Division and New Order. He also designed for Duran Duran, Wham!, Orchestral Manoeuvres in the

Dark and Peter Gabriel. At his studio across town, he worked with a high-ly-strung dogsbody called Brett Wickens: a British Canadian who became a pioneer of Canadian electronic music (I'm not making this up), and who 'famously' designed the logotype for HBO's 'The Sopranos'.

Saville was notoriously late with everything. It was my job to chase his artwork, and to get it in to Chrysalis in time to make the printing deadline. This was easier said than done. So much easier said than done, in fact, that I kept a list, regularly updated, entitled 'Best Excuses from Peter Saville and Brett the Brat (and Gary at Uptons)', drawing-pinned to the cork-board behind my desk. I still have the list. I reproduce it here for your delectation.

Typesetters let us down again.

Ultravox office didn't give us the credits.

Lost the key to the darkroom.

The band have added a couple of credits, and I had to redesign the whole bag (album sleeve).

We're not a corporation, we don't have the money to send bikes.

Had to get the band to approve it: you know what it's like trying to get hold of them.

How do you expect us to Red Star it up to Bedford?!

We don't know which way up the ads are (!!!)

I'm the other side of Hyde Park.

The cheque's in the post.

The train was derailed from Birmingham.

I'm not married, it's my sister's ID card.

Dot gain (!!!)

I'm telling you, I'm in Brighton for the print run.

I clearly remember the particular spring morning when Ultravox's lead singer, the reasonable and ever-cheerful Midge Ure, stood chatting in front of my desk and sipping the coffee I'd just made him. He suddenly stopped, mid-slurp, and leaned forward, the mother-of-pearl buttons of his pale sage shirt grazing the top of my backcombed barnet as he strained to read the dog-eared list with the words 'PETER' and SAVILLE' in the title. His initial reaction was a snort of disbelief. He was soon cack-ling so hard that tears were bouncing off his face, whence they made their leap of faith into my parched bouffant. By the time he reached the bottom of the list, Midge was wetting himself.

It was a time of loaded innocence, and the heyday of the Chryalis era. 'We' had created the first-ever music video album, a VC with music promos for every track on Blondie's 'Eat to the Beat' album, released simultaneously with the record. We had Pat Benatar, Leo Sayer, Huey Lewis and the News, the Michael Schenker Group, and Fun Boy Three. Not only all that, but Chrysalis was at the vanguard of the UK's New Romantic 'movement', with bands such as Billy Idol's and Tony James's Gen X and Spandau Ballet. We were closely involved in the whole Ska revival, thanks to 2 Tone Records, the Specials and the Special AKA. Scary Jerry Dammers, who became an anti-apartheid campaigner, wrote 'Free Nelson Mandela' in 1984 about the then jailed ANC leader in South Africa ('are you so blind that you cannot see?') with its evocative lead vocal by Stan Campbell, and dear, departed John Bradbury on drums.

The Chrysalis label was the creation of Chris Wright and Terry Ellis. Chris had once managed newsreader Anna Ford, during her Joan Baez-wannabe days, and had booked acts for the Students Union while at Manchester University. Terry had been a social secretary at Newcastle University, and had written about music for the college paper. They had first crossed paths as competitors, but eventually agreed, in their early twenties, to pool their resources and know-how. They formed the Ellis-Wright Agency in London, blending Chris's first name with Terry's surname to create a telegram 'address'. That new name eventually morphed into 'Chrysalis'. To begin with, they operated out of Ellis's flat, before finding offices off Regent Street. Their first taste of success came courtesy of Ten Years After. They were soon representing Jethro Tull, Marc Bolan's Tyrannosaurus Rex and the Nice. They expanded the operation to become a production company as well as an agency, and in September 1968, decided to launch their own independent record company to rival Chris Blackwell's Island Records. By the time I went to work for them during the early 1980s, they were a mega-successful operation with branches in cities all over the world. They very nearly signed David Bowie, too. At least they bagged his song publishing.

It would be disingenuous of me to describe my time at Chrysalis as 'work'. Not only was it not 'work', it was like going to a party every day. We certainly dressed for socialising rather than for business. There was usually a gathering or a bash, and at least one if not two gigs to go to, every single night. They were exuberant, excessive and thrilling times. They were to get even more thrilling, the day I was apprehended by a fabled record producer in Reception.

George Martin, who was as good as God in the music industry, ran AIR Studios from ground-floor offices in our building. The recording business he'd co-founded owned a huge facility overlooking Oxford Circus, and had been acquired by Chrysalis for a mint. My leather mini skirt, shredded tee shirt and battered pixie boots were no match for his pristine appearance. The Beatles' guru, then into his fifties and still an upright 6' 2", sported a crisp striped shirt and navy tie. Grey hair fringed his collar, and his crinkled blue eyes shone.

'Come into my office and see someone you know,' he grinned.

John Burgess, Managing Director of AIR and former producer of Freddie & the Dreamers and Manfred Mann, had once played football alongside my father in the charity soccer team the Showbiz X1. The team consisted of former athletes, entertainers, agents and managers. Sean Connery, Jimmy Tarbuck, Des O'Connor and David Frost turned out for them during the Sixties, when the crowds routinely topped thirty thousand. George and John had been colleagues for years, having met at Abbey Road Studios as employees of EMI. I hadn't set eyes on John since I was small.

George and John promptly took me to lunch. Typical George, treating management and minions as equals. At point-blank range, he was just as I'd imagined him. Quietly funny. Endearingly shy. John was the crowd-pleaser. They were quite the double act. It emerged during the meal that George and I had something else in common: we had attended the same school in Bromley, Kent. He'd gone to the boys' school, while I (without any choice in the matter) had attended the girls'. Peter Frampton and Billy Idol had been pupils there too. George even recalled our school motto (which was more than I did) – Dum Cresco Spero: I Hope When I Grow.

We talked about John Lennon, who had been murdered in Manhattan in December 1980. George had weathered with dignity endless vitriol from the former Beatle during the Seventies. Lennon belittled their producer's 'influence' and input, while Paul, George and Ringo 'were always sweet.' Implacably loyal, George had of course been distressed by the news. There had not even been a funeral at which to pay his final respects. So he'd gone to Montserrat, where he had opened his dream residential recording studio the previous year. He sat staring at the ocean and listening to Lennon in his head, he said. The studio complex and most of the island would be flattened within the decade by Hurricane Hugo.

After I left Chrysalis, I submitted several interview requests to George over the years. He never turned me down. I hadn't seen him for ages when we convened at the BRIT School in Croydon, South London in September 2011. George was a founding governor of the school that produced Amy Winehouse, Adele, Katie Melua and Jessie J. My daughter Mia had been there during the same era, as a drama student. The opening of a state-of-the-art studio in George's name to mark the BRIT's twentieth anniversary was about to take place. Then the fire alarm sounded. Everybody out. George and I caught up with each other in the car park. It was just like old times.

The last time I ever saw him was at the Savoy Hotel, for the Gold Badge Awards in October 2012. Doddering, deaf, a very old eighty-six, George was honoured by the British Association of Songwriters, Composers and Authors for services to the music industry. For the man world-famous not only for the Beatles but for film scores, Bond themes, orchestral arrangements, best-selling books, thirty Number One hits – his final chart-topper was Elton John's reworked 'Candle in the Wind' in 1997, his tribute to the late Diana, Princess of Wales – innumerable albums and almost half a century in the studio with more household names than any other producer in history, it seemed an understatement.

'I've had a great innings,' he said. 'I know I look decrepit and past-it. But the brilliant thing about growing old is that while you fall apart on the outside, you don't feel any different on the inside. Is it the Irish who say we all have an age at which we 'stop'? I have been thirty years old all my life. I'm with George Bernard Shaw: "We don't stop playing because we grow old; we grow old because we stop playing".'

It was in 1962 that Brian Epstein delivered The Beatles to George at EMI. It was a last-ditch endeavour on the part of the tenacious manager, who had been shown the door by every other record company. The match was obvious. George always declined credit for having 'created' the group, dismissing the notion that he was ever their 'Svengali'.

'A lot of nonsense was written and said,' he once remarked. 'It was a myth that they were uneducated guttersnipes and that I was this toff who knocked them into shape. In fact, the Beatles and I came from very similar backgrounds. I went to the same sort of schools. Musically, we were all essentially self-taught. As for our accents, mine was as working-class as theirs before I became an officer in the Royal Navy. You can't hang around with such folk without absorbing a bit of posh. I had also belonged to a dramatic society, which helped. As for the music, I muddled through. I experimented and learned on the job.'

His chemistry with the Beatles arose from the fact that they were enthusiastic Goons fans, he revealed.

'They worshipped Peter Sellers, and knew that I'd recorded him. They weren't exceptional when we began. The magic wasn't instant, it had to emerge. But when they hit the jackpot, it was chaos.

'I've been so lucky, I really have,' he concluded. 'I've worked with and enjoyed relationships with great people, and not only pop stars. And I've never worked for any length of time with anyone I didn't like. Life really is too short.'

Technology was marching on. Likewise, I was about to. Although we didn't yet have personal computers or mobile phones, by 1982 we had compact discs. CDs were launched by Philips and Sony that year, marking the death of cassettes and the beginning of a temporary end for vinyl. The televisual world was also getting a lot more interesting. Until 1982, the UK had only three terrestrial TV channels: two licence-funded BBC channels, and a single commercial network, ITV. Then, that November, Channel 4 was born. Originally a subsidiary of the Independent Broadcasting Authority, it would eventually be owned (as it is now) by the Channel Four Television Corporation. Its early remit was to provide alternative programming to the offerings of the existing channels, particularly programmes of interest to minority groups. That included music. I was about to find out what Andy Warhol had meant.

Sir George Martin, LAJ & Jonathan Morrish,
BRIT School, Croydon, London, 2015

'Don't put your daughter on the stage ...' LAJ,
West Wickham Pantomime Society, 1975

Chrysalis Records boss Chris Wright & LAJ, 1983

5. CHEEKY TELLY GIRL

Most people understand the phrase 'Fifteen minutes of fame' to mean a moment in the media spotlight, a short-lived burst of unexpected publicity, or the sudden rise (and subsequent, equally expeditious fall) of a person, incident or circumstance. What Andy Warhol actually said was, 'In the future, everyone will be world-famous for fifteen minutes.' These words were inscribed, in 1968, in the brochure for a Stockholm exhibition of his coveted artworks. A string of apparent imposters subsequently laid claim to the quotation. I never got to ask him about it, as I never met Andy Warhol. He would die in February 1987, aged fifty-eight, before I got the chance. I'm inclined to believe that both the observation and the succinct articulation of it were unequivocally his own. The very words, one might say, were distinctly Warholian.[ii]

Little did I know that I was about to experience my own Andy-esque quarter of an hour, when I auditioned for a presenting job on a new Channel 4 music magazine series called 'Ear-Say'. The first series of the Saturday evening prime-time show was set to air for twenty-six weeks. Now that we are routinely blinded by science in the fast-forward digital age, with thousands of television channels both satellite and terrestrial accessible at the press of a thumb around the clock; and now that a high proportion of programming falls into the 'Reality TV' category, every Elvis-impersonating car wash operative and his fleabag poodle, every one-legged, partially-sighted, psoriasis-blighted barmaid with an addiction to prawn cracker-flavoured crisps and a secret penchant for re-runs of 'The Incredible Hulk', believe themselves to be in with a chance of fame and fortune acquired by national and even international television exposure. Back then, in the mid-Eighties, there were just four channels. And I was up for a job on one of them. I only attended the audition because I was dared to for a laugh by Tef 'n' Dave, my designer boys in the art department at Chrysalis. There are various idioms of improbability that I could deploy here, none of which would perfectly do the job. But if I tell you that not for a New York minute did I think they'd give me the gig, you'll understand how seriously I was taking this process. You could have knocked me down with a plume from a Norwegian Blue's posterior when they sent me the contract.

I will state from the outset that what I knew about television presenting could be transcribed onto the back of a used postage stamp. I'd
watched my father do it competently for a number of years, on BBC
'Grandstand', various important-looking sports documentaries and
equivalent, and had long admired his cool self-possession on screen. He'd
speak in a rich, Burton-like voice at odds with the quieter and lower-key
version I was used to hearing at home. I once read his accent described as
'transatlantic Welsh'. That phrase conjures luminous images. He hung
out with 'TV personalities', as we called them in those days, such as Michael Parkinson, David Frost and Des Lynam. I had always presumed
that their compelling characters and indefinable to-camera skills had
passed osmotically or indeed magically into my father. Thus, on the
threshold of a glittering new media career, I took Dad down the White
Horse opposite Farnborough Park for half a lager, and asked for his advice.

'You can't learn it, that's for sure,' came his crushing response. 'You
either have it or you don't. You can do it or you can't. All these hopefuls
on Media Studies courses with stars in their eyes are wasting their time
and money if they think the ability to do it can ever be taught.' But how
did he do it? He seemed stumped. We had another half.

Anyway, how hard could it be? Back in those heady days of a whole
new fourth channel and opened-up opportunity for all, the world and his
panda were having a go. It seemed churlish to refuse. I thought, why not?
I wasn't a big telly-watcher at the time. I started devouring everything, in
the hope of picking up tips. I studied newsreaders and weather girls assiduously. Every curl of Jan Leeming's gleaming lower lip, every lopsided
Wincey Willis pout, was pored-over and practised before a well-lit bedroom mirror after everyone else had gone to bed. I pondered ad punctum
vanitati, but could never quite work out what the elusive 'skills' were. I
guessed I'd just wing it.

Not even when I was well-immersed in the studio routine down at
the Ewart TV complex near Wandsworth Bridge was I any the wiser. I'd
get picked up from my Islington flat at an ungodly 7 a.m. by a cab that
already contained my co-presenter Gary Crowley (Little Nicky Horne,
once one of my Capital Radio idols and the somewhat caustic third man
in our terrible trio, would make his own way there in a nippy sportscar).
I'd sit in a make-up chair getting bouffed and improved by a pair of lovely
ladies for half an hour; fall asleep next to Eartha Kitt while having fake

eyelashes applied (I Kitt you not); review the script, photocopied on yellow A4 sheets, which had been written by someone else and finalised the night before; confirm, and underline in red felt pen, the bits of copy that I had been assigned to say. I'd head back to my dressing room, the door of which bore a little red plaque with my name engraved on it, and wriggle into one of the not-entirely-me outfits the wardrobe mistress had selected and accessorised on my behalf. When I was called on set, I remembered to sit still, keep my hands and elbows down, look brightly into the correct camera and try not to blink too much, there's a good girl. I'd make extra-nice with the floor manager, who (I was warned) could get you sacked; and with the lighting crew, whose job it was to make you look good (and who could just as easily do the opposite). In between, I'd scoff more than my share of bacon sandwiches, hang with the stars in the Green Room, go drinking with them afterwards, then wend my way to whichever West End venue my notorious Friday Club friends had selected, and set about misbehaving until we got chucked out. That misbehaviour was born of boredom. I found camera work frankly tedious: endless lolling around in your dressing room waiting to get into the studio, where the most exciting bit was reading from autocue some bland, pointless sentences which somebody else had been paid a packet to write, but which I was perfectly capable of making up myself.

The by-product of the job, I soon discovered, was the aforementioned fifteen minutes of fame. Out of nowhere, virtually everything I did was apparently of interest to tabloid reporters and the compilers of popular rags. I'd go out for a couple of White Russians and an aloo gobi with Radio 1's Mike Read, for example, and the next day the Sun would splash exclusively that we were 'engaged'. My mum was forever ringing me up to check. I could bore for England on this. Suffice it to say that such intrusion soon got very tedious indeed. It came to a head one night at the opening of Tony Roma's, a new rib-shack-style restaurant on London's St. Martin's Lane, where one minute I was exchanging witty backchat with Jackie Collins and Mel Brooks, and the next I found myself cornered by the Sun's indomitable showbiz editor John Blake. I'd like to report that I interviewed him very politely about his decision to exclusively announce my forthcoming marriage to Rolling Stone Bill Wyman on his pages – a move that caused Lord Billiam of Stone to despatch a bag marbles to John's office on Bouverie Street, EC4, with a note: 'Dear John, I think you've lost these.' What happened next was a classic example of anger and frustration fusing in a nanosecond of descending scarlet mist. Reaching for a nearby wine bucket filled with water and ice, I hoisted it over John's blond head, and drenched him. His poor, furious wife Diane failed to see the funny side (we are friends these days). The snappers and hacks rushed in. Poor, dripping John appeared on the front page of the Sun the following day. The crime was assigned to a 'Cheeky Telly Girl'.

It wasn't long before the paper's fierce editor Kelvin MacKenzie was chatting me up on the dog and bone, suggesting a weekly girl-about-town column in his rag. The offer was timely. I'd had my fill of telly for the time being. Not that I hung it up altogether. I went on to front a few documentaries in the UK and USA; presented the London strand of 'Hard Copy', for America's 'Entertainment Tonight'; appeared as a pundit on all sorts of shows, including quizzes, and on what turned out to be my favourite, a programme on which you had to make up limericks on the spot, with the likes of Sally James, Lance Percival (real name John Lancelot Blades) and a pre-megafame Carol Vorderman. Years later, I would be hired by Canis Media as showbiz editor of ShowBiz TV, broadcast on Sky channel 266. There, I would earn my first credit as a screenwriter and co-producer, with 'The Last Lennon Interview', starring former BBC Radio 1 DJ Andy Peebles, and masterminded by acclaimed pop video producer Scott Millaney. In between, by some questionable quirk of fate, I wound up at Vintage TV... where I learned, once and for all, how not to launch a TV channel...

Among the strip joints, topless bars and seedy bookshops which define its Soho location, my favourite private members' club (which I've promised not to name) exudes an aura that makes it alluring to the average outsider. Its mildly louche, seductive atmosphere, the ever-changing landscape of its bars, have long attracted international celebrities. They pitch up for everything from a Queen album launch to Madonna's birthday party to Nigella Lawson's first wedding reception. I was present, at all of these. I can even remember them. Packed with eccentrics true to type, its cast comprises the most colourful creatures in London. Outcasts, mis-fits, wanna-bes and have-beens. A fabulous revolving in-crowd all its own.

Who is hiding in the toilets from their publisher? Who is penning reviews about books he hasn't read? Who is downing the Radio 2 presenter's share, now that he's off the juice? Who's that brawling behind the piano with Kate Moss? This fabled watering-hole, of which I have long been a member, is nothing if not a latter-day Rick's Place in 'Casablanca', with a never-ending theme tune of exuberance, glamour, intrigue, anger, fantasy, money and sex.

As such, it is a microcosm of the UK media and entertainment industries of the last three decades.

It also served, not that it had any say in the matter, as the backdrop to the tale of Vintage TV: a niche channel launched in September 2010, which set out to present music from the Forties to the Eighties and thus entertain our cash-and-time-rich over-fifties, of which there were said to be some twenty-one million and rising in the UK. The channel appeared on the Sky and Freesat platforms. It took most of us who helped create it to the brink.

I thought I was seeing things, the other side of my nightmare experience with this channel, when the man who masterminded it walked into my club sporting a nuclear suntan, and boasted that he had just returned from the Caribbean.

On holiday? On what? Didn't he still owe brand designer John McFaul more than £4,000 for personalised stationery, business cards and presentation folders, for which John paid from his own pocket after talking his printer into a rock-bottom deal? What about the cash owed to Chief Operations Officer Clare Bramley, including £6,000 shelled out from her personal savings account to cover a documentary shoot with Paul Gambaccini in New York? The fees, around £15,000, still due to Richard Hughes and Transparent Television for interviews filmed with Cockney Rebel's Steve Harley and Tony Hadley of Spandau Ballet? Don't get me started on what he owed me. Nor on expenses and shareholdings. Although David Pick once threatened to sue me if I talked about it, I've always known that the truth is my defence.

I joined Vintage TV for all the right reasons. I brought the channel many of my music business friends. While it was not my fault that what was meant to be a stylish celebration of their art turned into such a shambles, I could not help but feel awful that so many famous people were so fed-up because of me.

Not that they blamed me for what seemed like a fantastic opportunity: the chance to resurrect real music (their own, in many cases) in a sympathetic and reverential setting; to revive the values of traditional entertainment; to work with all our old friends again, and to have much fun in the process. Just like the good old days. Who wouldn't have jumped at this? A team of us leapt as if from a smoke-filled 747 into a glistening blue lagoon. We came to rue the day that we forgot our oxygen masks and lifejackets. But you can't have everything.

'You can afford to swan off on a luxury holiday, but you can't afford to pay your bills?' I spluttered. Pick didn't flinch. Seizing his luggage, he turned, flashed a freshly-licked grin on others present, and made a bee-line for the stairs. My dinner date was ruined. Play it, Sam. I beckoned another shot, and dared to look back.

In the beginning, the man had seemed a visionary. Charismatic and convincing, he appeared to sleep even less than Lady Thatcher did while ensconced at Number Ten. He presented with personal qualities on the Messianic spectrum, especially after a few Pinot Grigios. Did he also walk on water? Believe it or not, this was asked. As a gag, no doubt, but you have to wonder. David Pick's idea seemed a no-brainer: to bring back classic rock and pop music to the very listeners who had loved it in the first place. Essentially the golden era of radio, but on television, it would rely heavily on the rotation of videos. The fact that the video age only began in 1975 with Queen's all-time classic 'Bohemian Rhapsody' (so the story goes) was a minor consideration. For the many tracks which had been hits too early to have videos, Pick would create these retrospectively, using news archive stills and footage, mainly black and white, from BBC and ITN sources. The balance of his programming would be acquired: old documentaries, and concerts such as the Monkees and Billy Joel, with the added attraction of the Celebrity Vintage Video Collections (VVCs) and 'Me & Mrs Jones': the interview show which I conceived, and of which I became the host.

Pick's original vision was all the more impressive for him being a broadcast virgin. While he'd had a go at a few TV commercials over the years, he had never made a single show in his life, let alone launched an entire channel. Now, armed with his programming formula, he would boldly go and persuade the over-fifties to join the MTV generation.

Paul Gambaccini certainly rated Pick's invention. The respected BBC radio presenter, so-called 'Professor of Pop' and chosen 'Face' of Vintage TV, had no qualms about describing it publicly as 'something of quality'.

'The over-fifties,' Paul told me, 'remember programmes of a particular vintage, like 'Whistle Test' and 'Monty Python'. They are looking for programmes of the same quality: not because they are older viewers, but because those were better programmes. While television and commercial radio is searching for the younger listener and viewer, it's the over-fifties who have the money and who are spending'.

I joined the channel after being introduced by my friend of thirty-odd years and occasional co-author Phil Swern, the celebrated radio producer, songwriter and question-setter who is responsible for Radio 2's most popular shows: Ken Bruce's daily Quizmaster, Pick of the Pops, and Sounds of the Sixties. Phil is also a renowned music collector who built, from scratch, probably the biggest private record collection in the world. Boasting some three million recordings, including every Top 40 hit single since the charts began in 1952, and updated daily, the collection is available commercially through music and technology company I Like Music, run by the brilliant Andy Hill. I Like Music provided Vintage TV with its original continuous soundtrack. I agreed to write the website content, scripts, commercial documents and press releases two days a week. For peanuts, but on a promise of a formal contract and regular pay after the channel's September launch.

Within a short time, Pick had built an impressive team of professionals at the top of their game. As well as Phil, billed as Programme and Music Consultant, and a new Showbusiness Editor (me), there was Business Development Director Clare Bramley, a ball-breaking Emmy Award-winning producer, media consultant and former Head of Broadcast Media at BT; and creative genius John McFaul, responsible for Design and Brand Identity, whose previous clients included Nike, Virgin Atlantic, Audi and Microsoft. With such talent on board, you might have thought, the channel could not fail. Yet less than a year after launch, viewing figures were flagging, the stellar management team had departed, and most of the original household-faces had vanished. Many who contributed in the beginning are still owed money. Others, including me, were left bereft as the dream turned into a nightmare. We were used.

To understand how it came to this, we should begin at the beginning.

A copyright and branding lawyer who had once served at EMI, Chichester-based Pick, then fifty-eight, claimed to have hit on the concept while out training on the South Downs for a marathon. It had supposedly dawned on him – only later did we learn that the intellectual property of the concept may not reside with him after all – that while ticket sales for West End musicals such as 'Mamma Mia', 'Jersey Boys' and 'We Will Rock You' had never been better, there was no televisual outlet for the five decades of pop that still resonate with music-lovers.

'I started looking at what was happening in the charts,' he said, in one interview.

'The music that was selling best was from a different era. Last year (2009) there were significant sales for the Beatles, Michael Jackson and Vera Lynn. They were going through the roof at a time when we were being told that CD sales were falling because of downloads. The possibilities started keeping me awake at night.

'I looked at the music television landscape, and it was all much of a muchness,' he added.

'There was nothing for the older market.'

I remember as if it were yesterday the day I first met him. First impressions are lasting, sang The Impressions back in 1975. Perhaps that's why the hypnotic, polished Pick was able to enthral us for so long. There was 'something about him.' Not that most would find him physically attractive. He was trim, but on the short side, and Napoleonic with it, as I would learn. Fogey-ish style. Bad shoes. Close-cropped, balding, sweaty head. Gallic breath. He talked a plausible talk, exuding culture, entitlement, and five-star tastes. He banged on plummily, as if it were a rock credential, about his interior designer/lay magistrate wife Juliet having attended art college with Adam Ant. He spoke abstrusely of his 'Jewishness'. He boasted, did he mention this already, that he had put his son and two daughters through Bedales: his youngest was still at the trendy Hampshire public school where Ted Hughes and Mick Jagger had sent their kids, and which also 'produced' (Pick's word) Lily Allen. As he sat impressing me with his plans for Vintage TV, and outlined how I could become part of his vision, his brown eyes danced as might Maltesers on the bosom of a matron legging it for a bus. He expressed exuberant, slathering interest in my contacts book. I introduced many celebrities to the channel, including Strawbs and Yes keyboard wizard Rick Wakeman, pop star Kim Wilde and former Tiswas star Sally James, all of whom became presenters of 'VVC's (Vintage video clips). A visual version of 'Desert Island Discs', our celebrity would select ten or twelve favourite tracks, and relate to camera their colourful anecdotes and personal memories about each song and its artist. The video was then played.

VVCs were filmed in a variety of bizarre locations: a back room at the Institute of Directors for Rick Wakeman. The corner of a once-trendy members' club for Kim Wilde. A former East End crack den for Imagination front man Leee John. These were low-budget, usually two-camera shoots filmed by guns for hire, as we could not afford a dedicated crew. Others, including the Searchers' bass player Frank Allen, Spandau Ballet frontman Tony Hadley and Cockney Rebel's Steve Harley, all personal friends of mine, were guests on 'Me & Mrs Jones'.

Such was Pick's inexperience and lack of awareness that he failed to understand why he wasn't allowed on set while the cameras were actually rolling, and once tried to break a door down during a shoot.

Former Radio 1 star DJs David 'Kid' Jensen, David Hamilton, Ed 'Stewpot' Stewart and Tony Blackburn also joined our roster of presenters, most of them introduced by Phil Swern. As slick and professional as they had ever been, their shows were on such high rotation that they soon lost their sparkle, as they would be the first to admit. Former stars such as Janice Long, Nina Myskow and Mick Brown got in touch. A few faded luminaries wanted to pay us to return to the limelight. Managers, agents and promoters began emailing and phoning in droves. Sir Cliff Richard, Chris de Burgh, Katherine Jenkins, Elaine Paige and Russell Watson all generously agreed to appear, and were booked. All were subsequently cancelled by Pick, who couldn't fathom why we should give such 'has-beens' publicity. But surely 'has-beens' were what his channel was all about!

Allan James, a former top record promoter and one-time EMI staffer who numbered among his long-standing colleagues and friends Deep Purple's Jon Lord (R.I.P.), Toyah Wilcox, Fleetwood Mac's Christine McVie, Blondie's Debbie Harry, the Moody Blues' Justin Hayward, and Alice Cooper, met with Pick at my introduction with a view to becoming the channel's fixer and booker – an indispensable role. Pick's reluctance to afford Jamesie's monthly retainer – 'we can get all these people ourselves' – was the first indication that our CEO might not want to play the game by the tried and tested rules. The second was that he refused to deal with agents. What we knew, but which none of us wanted to admit at the time, was that anyone who avoids celebrity agents does so for one reason only.

And yet, the word was on the street. If we build it, they will come, as a phantom baseball star cracked in 'Field of Dreams'. This was precisely the channel the industry had been waiting for. A chance for a galaxy of legacy acts to glow again.

For all their global reach, the media and entertainment worlds remain small. Everybody knows each other. We look out for and scratch the backs of our own. Anticipation had begun to thrum more urgently than Jimmy Page's guitar solo on 'Stairway to Heaven'. Bigger and better investors started to bite. After Pick raved about Vintage over lunch one day to my youngest child's godfather, the boxing promoter and music fan Frank Warren, Frank said that he'd like to invest in Vintage TV. Frank's friend Carl Leighton Pope, who promotes Michael Bublé, did too. A chance meeting in reception led to Pick and me joining agent Neil Warnock (his international company The Agency representing everyone from Status Quo and The Monkees to Liza Minnelli and Pink Floyd) at the Dorchester. Six glasses of champagne, two each. That drinks bill cost Pick £600, hilariously. He couldn't stop going on about it. But it turned out to be money well-spent. The industry defers to Warnock as a man of his word, and he didn't disappoint. His share was in the Vintage bank account by Monday.

So far, so rock'n'roll. Early indications suggested that Vintage TV was set to be a huge and profitable success. Favourable reports began to splash across the media. We were all over television, radio and the internet, and were written up in everything from the Times to PR Week. How Pick preened. Meanwhile, thanks to my series 'Me & Mrs Jones', I was a cover girl again!

Things could only get better, to paraphrase Professor Brian Cox and D:Ream. Week by week, as two days' commitment turned into five, then five into seven, and as we began finding ourselves too frantic and in constant demand by Pick to continue with other professional interests, we began to live, breathe and sleep (if we were lucky, at the Pick country abode) Vintage TV.

The bubble burst much sooner than we could have anticipated. Despite its infinite potential, the project ended in tears for most of us. How on earth could this have happened? One explanation is cash. More to the point, lack of it. As Clare Bramley says, 'Anyone can launch a TV channel. Anyone with over a million pounds, that is. That's how much you need just to cover all costs for the first six months before day one of launch. David Pick went on air under-funded, and he knew it. That was when the problems began'.

Costs, for the uninitiated, included £100,000 to Sky for the purchase of the EPG slot (electronic programme guide): in the case of Vintage, channel 369. In addition, some £20,000 up-front charges fell due to Sky, with a further £85,000 per year to broadcast. Freesat (515) wanted £35,000 for a year in advance. An Ofcom licence (from the regulatory authority of the telecommunications industries) is compulsory. It came in at £2,500. BARB (Broadcasters' Audience Research Board) were charging just under £35,000 for the year following start-up. Satellite bandwidth – the actual space on the satellite, for which you pay through an agent (in our case, Globecast, a division of France Telecom) was quoted at more than a quarter of a million a year. To that, Globecast added their play-out costs, in excess of £60,000 per annum. Last, never least, is production: the making of new programmes, plus acquisition of existing shows. The budget should have been in the region of £830,000 in the six months prior to launch, with an annual spend thereafter of a million. Add to that the cost of staff – pre-launch, to set up, circa £158,000, and another £750,000 a year from then on. David Pick had under-estimated or tried to cut corners on most of this. He had done so by paying a little while promising the earth. He got away with it, too: few suppliers or individuals had contracts.

The other explanation is Pick's extraordinary behaviour. A nonpractising barrister who lived in Chichester, he maintained neither offices nor secretarial staff in London, but operated instead out of – guess where – one of my own private members' clubs, on a membership which I had arranged for him. Having muscled in on my hiding place, he then claimed squatters' rights. 'Rick's Place' became 'Pick's Place'. Of all the gin joints in all the towns in all the world.

His professional past was cloudy. It featured, my painstaking research told me, no fewer than thirty-one failed company directorships. Though his marriage was intact, and his affection for his three children sound, his reputation was nebulous. His manner with those whom he regarded as beneath him was mercurial and offhand. He barely comprehended how to behave in a restaurant – he once stormed out on me midmeal at Langan's Brasserie – let alone how to conduct a routine business relationship without allowing emotion and hubris to get in the way.

Our confidence in him began to wane when we witnessed ways in which Pick was treating those he suddenly deemed surplus to requirements. First, John McFaul, whose branding was in use all over the TV screen and website. Then producer/Head of Acquisitions Stephen Kahn. An especially shameful demolition, this, given that Kahn and Pick, friends since Youth Club, went back forty years. This was all suspiciously at odds with Pick's initial seduction campaign. A sinister pattern was emerging. Each of us had experienced his undying adoration. You should see some of his gushing emails to me. We had been 'promoted', and had been assured of future pay rises. We had signed meaningless A4 sheets on a promise of generous share-holdings. He lauded us as indispensable, until the moment came when he'd sucked us dry. It was vampirical. The next step was the negative campaign, focusing on what Pick perceived to be an individual's Achilles heel, or on some personal and/or irrational dislike. The most excruciating example of this was Paul Gambaccini. Having been championed as both 'Face' and 'Voice' of the channel, he and Pick had not so much as spoken since launch date, despite the fact that Paul had filmed a remarkable exclusive interview at her home with Dame Vera Lynn. This was arranged, set up and exec-produced by me through Vera's daughter Virginia. To this day, it has never aired. Out of courtesy and respect to Dame Vera, it should have been.

When challenged by a colleague as to why he and Paul were no longer speaking, Pick's alleged explanation had us in shock. The story was that he'd met Paul for lunch, and that during a difficult conversation, Paul had become agitated. He had allegedly slammed his own wine glass on the table, causing the contents to spill and the stem to break. With broken glass, he then allegedly threatened Pick in the face. That can't be true for a start, I thought. Gambo never drinks. Why on earth would he be holding a glass of wine?

One by one, as it dawned on us that our desire to see Pick's business succeed, and Vintage TV triumph, was being taken advantage of, we either left (as in Clare's and my case) or were dismissed – exhausted, financially compromised, and utterly, spiritually drained. I walked primarily because he cancelled my show after only six episodes, declaring that viewing figures were insufficient. In reality, he had not given the series a chance. It takes time to build an audience on a new niche channel, and to settle on the most appropriate transmission slot. This in turn takes trial, error, and a huge amount of research. It was far too early in the process to tell which viewers at what time of day or night would favour which programmes.

The likelihood is that he found my show too expensive to film. Even though it was made by my friends, on less than a shoestring. And no, they never got paid. Despite this, and despite the fact that he does not own the intellectual property of the show – it belongs to me – Pick continued, after I'd left, to air every programme I made. He even sold my series on the international TV market.

While several of us were forced to instruct lawyers to respond to Pick's litany of increasingly imaginative accusations about our 'incompetence', not at any point did he stand up to be counted in terms of his own shortcomings and oversights. Nor has he ever given any interview or public explanation as to why none of his original management team or celebrity presenting team continued to work for him.

Wisdom with hindsight is predictable. You must remember this. Of course we believed in David Pick. Why? We really wanted to. A part of us actually needed to. Because what else is there, halfway through the game, beyond keeping our old electric dreams alive?

Time goes by, croons the old guy in the movie. Would we do it all again? You're asking me? When the old team gets together, which from time to time we still do, we always wind up agreeing that we would have to. Despite the fact that we feel a bit stupid for allowing ourselves to be duped, we admit that Pick's judgement was sound. Not least with regard to the management team he selected. We would say that, wouldn't we.

Revenge being the dish best eaten cold. Late in 2018, eight years after its inception, Vintage TV collapsed, owing a fortune. But, with nearly £5 million to its name in shareholders' funds, how on earth could the channel have disintegrated so thoroughly?

Head Gear Films, one of the UK's most prominent investment and production companies, had lent David Pick a further £1 million, giving him £6 million to play with. They stand zero chance of being repaid.

There are no assets other than those original shows, all of which have been fully exploited.

Before any creditor receives anything, the administrators will seize at least the first £100,000 in fees.

Their Canada operation has lost £638,000 of Vintage funds. How interesting. Call me suspicious, but don't blame me for smelling a rat.

The only up-side is that I cannot see David Pick ever re-surfacing, or doing this to anybody else. He must be finished, now. That's a long list of serious shareholders who are set to be upset for a very long time. There can't be a bank in existence who would now give him credit. Even better, his list of creditors probably includes everyone he would need in order to start again. Next.

Gary Crowley, LAJ & Nicky Horne, Ear-Say for Channel 4, 1984

David 'Kid' Jensen, LAJ, 'Diddy' David Hamilton, Sally James,
Ed 'Stewpot' Stewart, Tony Blackburn, Vintage TV launch,
Groucho Club London, September 2010.

Paul Gambaccini, Dame Vera Lynn, Vera's daughter
Virginia Lewis-Jones, LAJ, 2010

6. STREET OF SHAME

Television presenting requires a certain switching-off of self, a suspension of the ridiculousness involved in talking to a camera as though it were a real-life person, while trying not to imagine the thousands, millions of folk in front rooms, back rooms, bedrooms and kitchens all over the land (and nowadays the world), making the erroneous presumption that they sit Superglued to their sets and are dangling from your every word. They do not. They've got fishcakes to grill and rabbit cages to clean out. You'd need an ego the size of Bulgaria to con yourself into thinking that it matters. Which is probably why my heart wasn't in it. I never really had the stomach for television. I might be better at it now that I no longer have the face for it. I continue to contribute to the odd documentary, when lured by the lucre, about Freddie Mercury, George Michael, David Bowie or whoever. Keeping my hand in. But my default thought, whenever I'm asked to do it, is 'I'd much prefer to be doing this on the radio.'

There prevails an impression that working in television is the most desirable, glamorous and best-rewarded job in all media. We can thank Bridget Jones for that. Or Piers Morgan. Or the salaries of Simon Cowell and Ant and Dec. You have only to observe members of the general public falling over themselves and each other in desperation to lever their frames into the auditoria of live or pre-recorded TV shows to appreciate how powerfully seductive the medium remains. In reality, the television industry is a sewer clogged with three-faced fiends and ogres from the depths, obsessed with stoking their own bank accounts while stamping the life out of the ambitious-minion pretenders to their thrones. I witnessed more manic depression, more alcoholism, more chain-smoking, drug-taking and other life-threatening behaviour in television than I ever came across in the music business. And then I went to Fleet Street.

I have gone undercover as everything in my time, from hospital nurse to London Zoo-keeper, in the quest for a sensational story. I once even dressed as a hotel porter and hung around the tradesmen's entrance of the Dorchester Hotel, lying in wait for Madonna while she was out on a run around Hyde Park. I got the interview, despite the fact that she saw right through the disguise. Probably because I was six months pregnant at the time. The as-yet-not-re-christened Her Madgesty did at least see the funny side. She was generous with her congratulatory bouquet.

I've observed to my dismay in recent years that the role of journalist (we of Her Britannic Majesty's Press Corps, old-school, made loose use of the term) is not what it once was. Few of us in my era were formally trained. Some had left school at sixteen to acquire the skills on the job within the comparatively sheltered confines of local newspapers, such as the fabled Stratford Express. They might write a splash which would get picked up by one or two of the nationals, who might then invite them in to work a couple of shifts. If they proved hungry, eager and accurate, and if they consistently got results, they might eventually be offered a full-time job. Others had graduated from university with degrees in a wide range of subjects, and had entered the training schemes offered by specific newspapers or publishing houses. A number were accredited, having passed National Council for the Training of Journalists exams in the requisite skills, shorthand and typing among them. But everybody knew that the fundamental requirements had little to do with Pitman speeds. The vital qualities were imagination; great contacts; an ability to travel, work and deliver, alone and under pressure, at times in life-threatening circumstances; supreme communications skills; and, never least, a blinding, nimble and natural way with words.

In March 2016, I attended the marriage blessing, at St. Bride's Church, Fleet Street, of press baron Rupert Murdoch and reformed honky tonk woman and ex-supermodel Jerry Hall. Outside the north door of the church, the hack pack were piled high. Many were perched atop telescopic stepladders. Every one of them was frantically taking photographs and notes, and shooting video footage, as well as audio-recording proceedings. Not one of them was over thirty years old. They were all pretty shabbily-dressed. What happened to the collar and tie, the neat dresses and pearls (yes!) of yesteryear, I found myself lamenting. We'd never have been allowed in the office looking so dishevelled. Then again, I instantly corrected myself, this breed of hacks rarely go near their offices. They are always, round the clock, away on a job.

They are required to do at least five jobs, in fact. Often simultaneously. As reporters and feature writers, they research, interview, write and file copy by email: no more dictating (point, new par!) from public phone boxes on bleak street corners. As film makers, they not only video-record goings-on, and edit their own footage, but they upload it instantly onto their news organisation's website. They also record digital audio files – podcasts – which they edit and upload, for the title's subscribers to listen to. They have been trained to the hilt to do all this and more, on dedicated degree courses such as those offered at City University London. IT and social networking skills are compulsory. And the pressure is increased by so-called 'citizen journalists', competing for ever-diminishing inches in newspapers and magazines, and for airtime on TV and radio. Not to mention bloggers. And who needs critics? They are now obsolete! The population of the world, and their husbands and wives, are all journalists now. It's enough to make you want to lie down. It wasn't anything like this in my day. We didn't go concerning ourselves with 'ethics', either. There weren't any.

To observe that I entered Fleet Street via the back door would be a first-degree understatement. A national newspaper editor saw me on television, perceived me as an up-coming girl about town with a picture by-line-friendly face and regular access to the rich and famous, must have envisioned an infinite stream of explosive interviews with rock and pop stars, and offered me my own column – regardless of the fact that I had less than an hour's worth of experience to my name. I was paid the then princely sum of three hundred pounds a week.

I was at long last following in my father's footsteps: the very thing that, all along, I had set out to do. The route had been, to put it mildly, circuitous. Many a mind-blowing distraction had lured me from the beaten track. But here at last I was, thanks to the Sun's vulgar, terrifying editor Kelvin MacKenzie. Murdoch's 'little Hitler' (as Rupert called Kelvin, not unreasonably) was the author of such edifying headlines as 'FREDDIE STARR ATE MY HAMSTER' (he didn't), GOTCHA! (to 'celebrate' the sinking of the Belgrano during the Falklands conflict) and 'HOP OFF YOU FROGS!' (when France decided to ban the sale of English lamb). This was the heyday of showbiz coverage on newspapers, mid-Eighties to mid-Nineties, when every tabloid had at least one 'rock and pop correspondent', and when we travelled together as a pack: striving constantly to out-do each other with news stories, features and interviews, but also sharing, bartering, bargaining and occasionally thieving when the pickings were lean.

While I relished the job, and still look back on those years with wistful longing, it is fair to say that I started out with absolutely no idea, and therefore no right whatsoever to even be there. Perhaps because of or even in spite of that, I got way more than I bargained for. So much more, in fact, that I was forced to compromise myself at every turn. I was at first relieved when the Daily Mail poached me from the Sun after a year or so of doing grim MacKenzie's stern bidding, identifying an escape route from his ruthlessly-flaunted 'Shock and Amaze on Every Page!' ethos.

I assumed that the Mail would be a doddle, compared. How wrong can you be. What I was subjected to at Northcliffe House was almost indescribably worse. The ostensibly charming but shouty bully of an Editor, David English – 'the outstanding editor of his generation' (which didn't say much for the rest) – had himself once invented an entire interview with Betty Ford, when her former US President husband Gerald Ford was considering a return to politics. Betty was an alcoholic. English perhaps concluded, upon putting pen to paper, that she would never remember not having talked to him. He was also infamous for having written a minutely-recalled eye-witness account, on one particular anniversary, of the assassination of President John F. Kennedy, despite the fact that he had been nowhere near Dallas at the time.

At the Daily Mail, such invention was sport. 'We haven't got a splash? Come on, over the Wine Press,' some editor would command, 'let's put our heads together. What can we think of? I know: Princess Margaret is having an affair with Elton John. LA, get to Windsor and doorstep the old poofter. Find out if he's there first. Steve, call Dickie and get a statement. Do it!' The following morning, they'd have an exclusive all right:

'Buckingham Palace denied last night sensational reports of a secret romance between Her Majesty the Queen's sister HRH The Princess Margaret and millionaire rock star Elton John.

'The alleged ongoing relationship between the Rocket Man, 38, and the Countess of Snowdon, 55, is said to have started last Christmas at the princess's Caribbean hideaway, Les Jolies Eaux on Mustique...'

The classic Who/What/When/Where/Why in the first two pars. (While the 'Why' is undefined, it is lurking between the lines). What you might call text-book journalism: note pointed use of the word 'alleged'. Except that it was complete and utter fabrication. We were, at that stage, years ahead of the Press Complaints Commission. The Press Council had been founded in 1953 with an aim to maintain good standards of ethics in journalism. But standards had slipped during the 1980s. Not only were newspapers routinely breaching standards, they were practically getting away with murder.[iii] It will come as no surprise that the Daily Mail was among the worst. I was put to work on endless stories that were essentially untrue, no more than the product of some ambitious or desperate editor's imagination. 'Never let the truth get in the way of a good story' was a motto muttered countless times each day. Every innings proved an ordeal of interminable battles with my editors (there were several) to get unadulterated copy and genuine, legally-acquired interviews into the paper; to protect showbiz and media friends from being turned over; and to preserve at all costs my precious contacts book. I succeeded on more occasions than I might have expected, looking back – often thanks to having promised celebrity interviewees guaranteed copy approval, which I wasn't supposed to do, but without which they would have run a mile and refused point-blank to talk to the paper. But I would often find that my efforts had been subsequently ruined and the artist's wrath incurred by some disastrously insensitive or offensive headline, or compromising photographs. I couldn't win.

When I found myself unexpectedly pregnant, was abandoned by the father, my long-term boyfriend, but decided to keep my baby (Papa don't preach), it became glaringly obvious that I could no longer do the job I'd been appointed to. But not even the Mail could sack a woman for being pregnant. So they mounted a campaign to get me to resign. I thought I was hearing things when I first learned of it – from a late, heavyweight, long-suffering deputy editor over a G&T in the Harrow, our two hundred-year-old local on Whitefriars Street. A number of staff members were in on it, he admitted. Even showbiz-desk stalwarts whom I had long considered to be my friends. Why was he telling me this? He felt sorry for me, he said. Inwardly distraught, I felt obliged to keep smiling regardless, and to maintain an inelastic upper lip. The episode culminated in my being despatched, reluctantly, to lurk on the domestic doorstep of the outgoing BBC director General Alasdair Milne, whose suspicious resignation (did he jump or was he pushed?) followed a turbulent five-year term during which there were arguments about everything from coverage of the Falklands war, the broadcasting of 'The Thorn Birds', an interview with IRA leader Martin McGuinness and a disproportionate increase in the Corporation's licence fee. I was to remain on the threshold of the Milne residence throughout the night, or for as long as it took to get an interview with him.

We're talking 1987. Mobile phones existed, but were not in general use. That assignment from hell involved tramping through the snow snow to a phone box at the corner of Holland Park every hour on the hour, to call in to the news desk with updates. It happened during the most severe spell of winter weather the country had seen since January 1740. Mr Milne's divine wife Sheila came regularly to their front door with mugs of cocoa and Garibaldi biscuits, expressing her concern for 'a slip of a thing in your condition' and urging me to hasten off home. She must have known that I'd have been sacked for pulling myself off the job without the night editor's permission. So it was that I continued to trespass, that snowy, starry night, in my brightly-coloured puffy get-up that yelled 'In the Tyrol!' The only part of the sad ex-DG that I managed to glimpse through the brass letterbox were his sensible brown lace-up shoes. I never got the interview, and I never saw either of them again. Sheila died less than five years afterwards, in 1992. Her husband lived on for twenty-one more years, succumbing in January 2013, aged eighty-two.

A newspaper could be sued to hell for such abuse of a pregnant reporter today. In those days, however, if you didn't like it, you knew where the fire exit was.

My eventual escape, post-birth, was to YOU magazine, the colour supplement of the Mail's sister and rival paper, the Mail on Sunday. YOU's recently-appointed new editor Nick Gordon had grudgingly admired my features on the Mail, and called me in ('bring the baby with you, it's no skin off my nose!') to offer me a rolling contract. It would still mostly be about celebrities. But Nick's was a better and much classier brief. Thus did I find myself bagging two cover stories out of four, some months. On YOU, our interviews were not doctored, nor edited sensationally against our will. The headlines always enhanced the copy. I had almost five exhilarating years there. Then they fired the editor. Dee Nolan, Nick's replacement, a golfing pal of Associated Newspapers' proprietor Lord Rothermere, dispensed with Nick's favourite scribes. Noleen, as the antipodean-born Ed was dubbed, proceeded to redesign the magazine into something unrecognisable.

The consolation prize wasn't bad. Piers Morgan, then at the helm of the News of the World and at twenty-nine the youngest-ever Fleet Street editor, invited me to come and work for him. I had a hair-raising run at Wapping, penning the weekly 'Lesley-Ann Jones Big Interview' until Piers left 'the Screws' to edit the Daily Mirror. The new editor, Phil Hall, would offload Piers's favourite writers. It was the normal 'Fleet Street' way of things. Except that 'Fleet Street' had now been reduced to a mere metonym, and no longer defined the newspaper industry's geographical location.

Rupert Murdoch's 1986 revolution had kick-started the exodus, when he took on the print unions, sacked the workers, got new ones in at Wapping where he had acquired cheaper manufacturing premises, and moved News International, publishers of the Sun, the News of the World, the Times and the Sunday Times to a shiny new home. Associated's titles, including the Mail and Mail on Sunday, departed for Derry Street, off Kensington High Street. The Express titles vacated their magnificent Grade II-listed art deco Daily Express building, to which Private Eye always referred as 'the Black Lubyanka' after the Moscow headquarters of the KGB, and set up shop in an unimpressive new edifice over Blackfriars Bridge. The Guardian and the Observer moved on up to Farringdon Road. And the Mirror Group titles, the Telegraph and the Independent were off to Canary Wharf, with the Telegraph subsequently shifting again, to Victoria. Desk by desk, expense claim by expense claim, our brawling, squalling, seethingly exquisite community vanished. When I think of it now, it can still prompt a proper sob. I experience the memory as a sliding one, as if viewed from a speeding bus.

I'm often on Fleet Street again these days, making my way to and from St. Bride's. There is a melancholic beauty about the old drag, though it wears an air of nonchalant ennui. I step on it outside El Vino's and keep my head down until I reach Ludgate Circus, occasionally pausing in the vicinity of what was once the Wine Press. Trying not to. For what was then is not now. The pavement no longer vibrates to the rhythms of the presses that once roared beneath it. The all-pervading smell of ink is but a memory. Yet the street itself lives. It breathes, and is vibrant. The casual spectator will see and hear only what exists there now, while past headlines still evoke their noiseless magic. The stories, always the stories. Today's scandal is nothing more than tomorrow's fish'n'chip paper, right? Wrong. Good stories never fade.

St. Bride's Church, Fleet Street, London EC4

The former Northcliffe House, once home of Associated
Newspapers, Whitefriars Street, London EC4

The Harrow public house, former haunt of Daily Mail journalists

The Sun columnist & the heartthrob

Exclusives

More Exclusives

The Hack Pack: with (among others) Craig MacKenzie, Mariella Frostrup, Gill Pringle, John Blake, Linda Duff, Nick Ferrari, 'EJ', David Hancock, Garry Bushell, David Wigg

PART TWO

7. TUMBLING DICE: BILL WYMAN AND MANDY SMITH

Some memories torment us in perpetuity, despite our best efforts to for-get them. We all harbour regrets. The if-onlys, the why-didn't-Is and the wish-I-never-hads can be ignored, most of the time. We park the mis-takes, the poor choices and the lapses of judgement, and we move on. We might wince from time to time when a misdemeanour rears its head, but we shut it down and try not to think about it. The trouble is that wounds are silent. Left untreated, they fester. They become cancers of the con-science, and holes in the heart. Bad things happen when good people say nothing. My guilt is hinged to the things I never said, but really should have. I did not identify the banker drugging members with Rohypnol at a private club in New York. I knew about, but never had the guts to speak up about, a rape in the cloakroom at a members' club in London, the vic-tim of which remains broken to this day. And I knew a grown man who was having sex with a child. He was, in those days, my friend. His girl-friend was under the age of consent. The law on this in the UK is clear: if an individual over the age of eighteen engages in sexual activity with a person below the age of sixteen, then he or she can be charged with a criminal offence which may result in a fourteen-year prison sentence. I was aware of this at the time. What did I do about it, given that I knew what was going on? I did nothing.

Hollywood feigned surprise when film mogul Harvey Weinstein was exposed as a sex abuser. As if Hollywood didn't know. It opened flood-gates. Actresses, models and ordinary women – and men – from all walks of life rushed to join the movement that sheds light on the sexual mis-conduct of powerful males and declare #METOO and #TIMESUP. When Kevin Spacey was exposed, his glittering career disintegrated in a heart-beat. Bill Cosby, media icon, national father figure, philanthropist and world-renowned paragon of virtue who for decades had used television to influence millions of fellow Americans on the subjects of class, race, mo-rality and his own gigantic importance, was at last found guilty of sexual assault after a years-long trial during which he tried to make liars and fantasists of some sixty victims. We asked questions. Why did it take so long for these poor people to be believed? How many wannabes were conned into considering the casting couch normal? And how many millions in myriad other industries yielded to predators after only one thing, because they didn't know they were allowed to say no?

But it was Roman Polanski who took the biscuit. In May 2018, during a Polish interview with Newsweek Polska, the fugitive child rapist denounced the #MeToo movement as 'mass hysteria' and 'total hypocrisy'. He made these comments after the Academy of Motion Picture Arts and Sciences announced that it was at last expelling him and Bill Cosby. Polanski was forty-four years old when he raped thirteen-year-old Samantha Geimer in Los Angeles. She was not, allegedly, his only victim. He admitted part of the crime, and was convicted of unlawful sexual intercourse with a minor. But before he received full sentence, after having spent forty-two days being evaluated by psychiatrists ahead of sentencing, he fled to Paris. He never returned to America, where he could have got fifty years. He subsequently won six Oscars: three for 'Tess', starring Nastassja Kinksi, and three for 'The Pianist', with Adrian Brody and Emilia Fox. It is still hoped that he will be extradited to face re-trial. Meanwhile, will they now obliterate his star from the Hollywood Walk of Fame?

Though we have grown accustomed to the paunch, the sagging chins and the silver hair, there was a time when Bill Wyman was relatively ravishing. The octogenarian former Rolling Stones bassist was once rock's most prolific shagger. Three or four a night on the road, he was wont to boast. Three at a time, sometimes. He wasn't fussed. Bring it on. Women threw themselves at him. He'd have been an idiot to say no. He once said he'd slept with more women than Willie Nelson and Julio Iglesias. That's a lot. As William Perks from Penge, he'd done National Service in Germany and was married with a son when he found himself involved in the fledgling biggest band in history. He was unhappy at home. He went out for a few halves. It was the Sixties.

I first met him during my fifteen minutes of 'fame'. He saw me on television and asked his PA to contact me. Coincidentally, I knew her: her oldest friend had been a colleague of mine at Chrysalis Records. We went for dinner a couple of times at the Ivy; and then, with Ultravox's Midge Ure, to the British Rock & Pop Awards at the Lyceum Ballroom off the Strand, on February 21 1984. Bill accepted an award on behalf of the late bluesman Alexis Korner, who had died of lung cancer the previous month. 'If Alexis hadn't been there, we wouldn't have been there,' he said in his short acceptance speech, referring to the Stones and their inspiration. And he seemed taken with a couple of young blonde whirling dervishes on the dancefloor, prompting Midge to lean over and whisper in my ear, 'I think you've just lost him.' 'He is not mine to lose,' I said. 'And I'm not his.'

And yet, a friendship emerged. It's all it was, and I didn't dwell on it. I hadn't heard from Bill for a few weeks, and had been too busy to care, when he called to invite me to accompany him to the opening night of a revival of the Broadway musical 'Little Me' starring Russ Abbot and Sheila White, on May 30 at the Prince of Wales Theatre. He turned up to meet me dressed in an odd tan leather two-piece suit. I remember thinking he looked like a sofa. During the interval, he asked if he could hold my hand. He was five years younger than my father. I didn't date older men. Why did I let him? Well, that was Bill. Charming, unthreatening, avuncular, persuasive. It would have seemed churlish to refuse.

The after-show party was back at the Ivy. Bill and I shared a table with TV actress Gill Gascoigne and her partner Alfred Molina. It was a pleasant enough evening. Nothing special. The next time I saw him was at a dinner in Thierry's, a French restaurant below his office/pied-a-terre on the Kings Road. Also present were his PA Karen, a couple of her friends, and the songwriter Ken Gold. The vivacious waitress that night was called Lou. She and Ken became an item, and the gang took to going out on the town together. Our group soon expanded, to include Bill's son Stephen, and two sisters I thought I'd met before, called Nicola and Mandy Smith. Bill had apparently introduced them to a friend of his, who ran the agency Models One. They were accompanied by their middle-aged mother, Patsy.

Mandy quickly emerged as the ringleader. She was brazen and bold, and great fun. She liked to call the shots about places to eat and clubs and parties to go on to, with Bill always picking up the tab. Don't denounce us as gold diggers: we always offered. Mandy's favourite club was Tramp, the exclusive celebrity haunt on Jermyn Street. Bill was friendly with its founder, Johnny Gold, whose business partner was Oscar Lerman – at that time the husband of Jackie Collins. Lisa Vanderpump and her husband Ken were part of that throng too. We knew Lisa from the ABC videos. They called Tramp 'the Office', and it was hardly a thrill. The dance-

floor was a handkerchief. You sat around chatting about nothing of con-
sequence while getting out of it on champagne.

They didn't call Bill the quiet Stone for nothing. He'd survey the
scene as if through binoculars. He was always low-key. He didn't court
attention, nor suck up to fellow celebrities. Neither Mick nor Keith, Ronnie nor Charlie was ever present. He hardly ever socialised with 'the others', he said.

What was magical, for me, was to sit and listen to him talking about
what it was like to be a Rolling Stone. The music, the anecdotes, the es-
capades, their exploits on the road. I liked the fact that he always arrived
on time, and invariably did what he said he was going to do. I didn't care
for his chain-smoking. I didn't make fun of him when he admitted to
buying his clothes from a women's shop opposite his home, called Joan-
na's Tent; nor when celebrity stylist John Frieda came to his flat to dye
his hair. Just to be close to an actual Stone was quite thrilling. It was the
last thing I'd ever expected, let alone to become friends with one and
hang out. What surprised me was Bill's revelation that he, Charlie and
Ronnie were little more than employees of Mick and Keith. Their pay was
mere salary. Jagger and Richards wrote the songs and banked the re-
wards.

When Robin Eggar, Phil Swern and I wrote the best-selling 'Rock
Review' for Sony, Bill contributed the foreword and a new photograph of
himself. He was always willing to do a favour. I liked that about him. 'Tit
for tat,' he said.

'What does that mean?'

'You are my friends.'

Were we, though? Again, I didn't give it much thought at the time. I
get it now: even celebrities had to find friends from somewhere. Our lot
had relatively normal jobs. We lived regular lives and did everyday
things. Perhaps Bill identified with us because he himself hailed from a
humble working-class home. He rarely felt comfortable among toffs and
superstars. He liked the fact that Mandy and Nicola lived on a council
estate. He might have seen us as a refuge of normality. Which of us was
deluded, then: Bill, or us?

Only all these years later must I admit to myself that Bill was gathering a clan to conceal his love affair with Mandy. It is glaringly obvious
now. When his limo approached our chosen restaurant for the evening,
he would say to one of the boys, usually the tall, dark-haired, good-

looking one who grew up to become a famous broadcaster and writer, 'Would you mind walking Mandy in?' He would then take my arm and beam for the photographers, snuggling up to me as we emerged from the car. At the end of the night, when the car dropped us off, it would always be Bill and Mandy left in the back. Just the two of them.

We did know about their relationship, but it was never discussed. What we didn't know – genuinely didn't know – was how young Mandy was. We assumed that she must be about nineteen, twenty, twenty-one. We had no idea that Bill was paying for her education and had transferred her from her former state school in North London, to an expensive fee-paying establishment within walking distance of his Kings Road flat. We might never have known that Mandy was an under-age schoolgirl, had not Bill thrown a party for her birthday. We were all invited. There was only one candle on her cake... Our tall, dark, handsome broadcaster-and-writer-to-be couldn't help himself.

'So how old are you today then, Mand?'

'Fifteen,' she said.

She had been dating Bill by then for more than two years.

'After that,' recalls TDHBAWTB, 'we all just fucked off as fast as possible, didn't we. We knew it was wrong. We didn't do anything about it. We never told anyone. We didn't dare. We were unwittingly used to disguise what was going on. As far as the press were concerned, we were just the walkers. The very second we learned the truth, we scarpered. We were dust. We never challenged Bill about it. We never talked to anyone else about it. The media were never the wiser. But we knew. And we were as bad as Bill or knowing that he was abusing Mandy, and for saying nothing.'

Do I feel foolish and guilty now, for having been dragged into it? What do you think?

It's curious how something can be an obsession one minute and be history the next. The last time I saw them together was when Bill took Mandy and me to lunch at Langan's Brasserie. Bill ordered bread pudding for dessert, and Mandy wrinkled her nose. 'What?!' said Bill. 'I can't marry a girl who doesn't know how to make bread pudding!'

I went to Fleet Street, started travelling, and barely gave them or their bread pudding a second thought. I was in denial. I remember hearing that they'd split up, then that they were getting married, and finally that they'd tied the knot. Mandy had turned eighteen by then, while Bill was almost fifty. I wasn't invited to the wedding. I hadn't expected to be. Like everyone else, I read about the lavish affair in Hello! I was taken aback to hear that Mandy's mother Patsy and Bill's son Stephen had become engaged. That didn't seem right – but why? Because Patsy was so much older than Stephen? Roughly the same number of years, give or take, as Bill had on Mandy? The double standard sickens me now. I later heard that Bill threatened to cut Stephen out of his will if he didn't dump Patsy. His son was his best friend, after all, and Bill was heartbroken by the 'betrayal'. The irony.

The camera never lies, right? Bill and Mandy's was the wedding of the year. All the Stones rocked up. Someone brought Bill a zimmer frame, ha ha. The honeymoon was in the South of France, at Bill's villa in St. Paul de Vence. Mandy invited a gaggle of relatives, as you don't: her Mum, some cousins, her sister Nicola. Bill was outnumbered. He called his secretary Karen, and asked her to come down and keep him company. Rock and roll.

I still see, and occasionally work with, TDHBAWTB and a couple of the others. We sometimes revisit our collective past. We ask each other, what on earth were we thinking? We usually have to conclude that we were not. Neither was Bill. I do believe his defence: that he had no idea that she was only thirteen when he met her. By the time he found out, he was in too deep to withdraw. He couldn't help himself. Because there was nothing 'thirteen' about Mandy. There was nothing to suggest that the girl was still a child, so it never occurred to any of us to question it. She seemed mature and soignée, and she was so beautiful. Breathtakingly so. Total strangers would stop and stare when she walked down the street or entered a room. It was, I can well imagine, like being confronted with Bardot. Mandy was stunning. I was quite content to bask in her limelight. It sounds as though I'm making excuses, doesn't it.

I am.

Because the age of consent exists to protect children from themselves, as well as from predators. The minute that Bill discovered Mandy's age, he should have manned up, controlled himself, reminded himself both of the law and of the possible consequences, and he should have backed off. He didn't, though. He would later shrug off the whole tragic episode as a 'mid-life crisis'. He got away with it. But how? Why?

The marriage collapsed in 1991. They were divorced two years later. 'Mandy went off the rails for a while. She had lots of affairs,' Bill said. 'And she got really ill. Really thin. She almost died.'

They did not remain friends. Mandy went on to marry footballer Pat Van Den Hauwe, but that fell apart too. Shortly after his divorce from Mandy, Bill married Suzanne Accosta, the former girlfriend who may have inspired his hit record '(Si Si) Je Suis un Rock Star'. He quit the Stones the same year. He and Suzanne had three daughters, Katherine, Jessica and Matilda. In 2013, following the sex abuse scandal involving Jimmy Savile, Rolf Harris, Gary Glitter, Max Clifford et al, Bill walked himself into a police station and made contact with the Crown Prosecution Service, inviting them to interview him. He was told in no uncertain terms that there was no case for him to answer. Why not? Because no one had lodged any formal complaint? He had married Mandy, but that is hardly a get-out. Why did our police force go gunning for Jonathan King, Chris Langham, Paul Gambaccini, Nigel Evans MP, DJ Dave Lee Travis, comedian Jim Davidson, Sir Cliff Richard and the rest, while turning a blind eye to a rock legend? Why are some led as lambs to the slaughter while others appear untouchable?

I read a book by that title recently. 'Untouchables' by Michael Gillard and Laurie Flynn, published in 2012, exposes countless cases of dirty cops, bent justice, racism and bribery within Scotland Yard. I recommend it. Mandy declared publicly in 2010 that she and Bill began sleeping together when she was fourteen years old. Her elder sister had called for the Stone to be prosecuted. Nothing came of it. After her second marriage folded, Mandy moved to Manchester, embarked on a relationship with a male model, and gave birth to a son. In 2005 she turned to the church, and began counselling abuse victims.

And we're still asking, all these years later: did Bill groom Mandy? Was all that getting to know the mother and the sister and winning a precocious child's confidence no more than a ploy? Why on earth would Patsy 'sell' her daughter to a rock star? Had the liberties taken by the likes of Jerry Lee Lewis and Elvis Presley fallen on deaf ears?

Loyal Mandy would never have a word said against her mum.

'She was really ill at the time and thought she was going to die – we didn't know what of – and he looked after me,' she told journalist Caroline Phillips. Wasn't it because he was a rich celebrity? 'No, no. We weren't impressed by people.' Why didn't Mandy help the police press child abuse charges? Because, she said, she felt partly to blame.

'It was like it was my fault as well,' she insisted – as Caroline put it, with the classic guilt of an abuse victim. 'I fell in love with Bill. I wasn't a little sex temptress. But I'd feel too guilty getting someone charged for sex abuse.'

Yet in the opening pages of her autobiography, 'It's All Over Now', written with Andy Coulson and Ingrid Millar and published in 1993, the year of her divorce from Bill, she dedicates it:

'... to every woman and girl who has suffered abuse – sexual, emotional and psychological – at the hands of a man.'

It was an illegal and immoral relationship. It was accepted, and blind eyes were turned. The perpetrator was an A-list rock star. I am a mother of a son and two daughters. I turned a blind eye too. I am ashamed.

In 2015, Bill released 'Back to Basics', his first album in decades. The following year, he was diagnosed with prostate cancer. He turned up at the opening of 'Exhibitionism: The Rolling Stones' at London's Saatchi Gallery, to join his former bandmates for their fiftieth anniversary. It wasn't much fun.

He celebrated his eightieth birthday with an exhibition of his own photographs at Proud Gallery, Chelsea. He also committed to co-producing a biographical documentary. There is much to depict. Not only the endless years rolling with the Stones and his own Rhythm Kings, but Sticky Fingers, his rock'n'roll restaurant in Kensington. His many books – including an art tome on the work of Marc Chagall, once his neighbour in St. Paul de Vence, France. His obsessive metal detecting. The diaries he has kept daily since childhood. And his Stones archive, said to be worth millions.

Does he ever pause to reflect how lucky he was? Or does he fear that his luck could yet run out? Because, bottom line, that was never a 'love affair'. It was a scandal from the start. In April 2010, Victoria Coren wrote about Bill and Mandy in the Guardian, and denounced the latter's status as a poster girl for the wild-child generation:

'It was never right ... How was I allowed to believe that this relationship – Mandy's life – was glamorous, cool and aspirational? It was child abuse.'

Even if the law never catches up with him, the greatest punishment imaginable has already been handed down. It cannot be comforting to Bill to know, towards the end of his life, that he will not go down in history for his musical talent, nor for his status as a member of the biggest rock'n'roll band of all time – but for the fact that he abused a child.

In preparation for a documentary for American television not long ago, I read Gregg Allman's New York Times best-selling autobiography, 'My Cross to Bear'. The late Southern rocker jokes therein about an old road manager of his whom he describes as 'the original dirty old man'. The manager kept a chart in his case, detailing the legal age of consent in every US state. He had copies made for everyone in the band. He'd hand them round at the start of each tour, and retained additional copies in case they were mislaid. It begs every question I would like to ask Bill Wyman. And answers them.

With Mandy Smith, 'Willie & the Poor Boys' shoot,
Fulham, London, 1985

With Bill Wyman, 1985 (photo by Hy Money)

With Bill Wyman & Keith Harris, BASCA Gold Badge Awards,
Savoy, London, October 2013

Ringo Starr, Barbara Bach, LAJ, John Entwistle

8. LIVE AID

13th July 1985: the day that rocked the world. I'd stayed with Who bassist John Entwistle and his girlfriend Maxene at their Roehampton, London house the night before, in a bizarre bedroom filled with Max's china
dolls and John's trainsets. This was different from Quarwood, their ram-
bling Stow on the Wold residence, where I'd grown accustomed to doss-
ing among stuffed toy lions or collapsing suits of armour. We had been
friends for a year or so by then, having met at the BPI music awards. I
remember Holly Johnson from Frankie Goes to Hollywood up at the mic
that night, telling gags about 'phone sex with Prince. The revellers were
so drunk, they'd laugh at anything. Even tasteless jokes at the expense of
a 'velvet-clad midget'.

'Beam me up,' groaned an unfamiliar voice behind me. 'I'd have
more fun buried in concrete under a motor-way. Burger, anyone? You
look as though you could do with feeding up.' John prodded me. 'Come
on then, shake a leg, I haven't got all night. Certainly not for this crap'.

We repaired to the Hard Rock Café on Piccadilly, the proprietor of
which was Isaac Tigret. Isaac was the multi-millionaire businessman
boyfriend of John's friend Maureen, who had been Mrs Ringo Starr in a
former life. She was there waiting for us: John and Max, John's Mum
Queenie and her chap, Who drummer Kenny Jones and his wife Jayne,
Bill Wyman, his secretary Karen, and me. It was in Maureen's Hyde Park
front room that we later passed out for the night – me on a pillow under
the piano – after one for the road in Bootleggers on Margaret Street.
Which was John's favourite club.

John, Max and I shared a pathological inability to take anything seriously. I confess that I didn't know a lot about The Who back then, having been but a child when they rose to fame. During the Seventies and
early Eighties, I'd been a Hendrix and Bowie fan, which didn't leave
much room for maximum R&B. The Who, however – sensational at
Woodstock in 1969, and massively popular in the States – were as big as
the Beatles and the Rolling Stones. Their hits, 'Substitute', 'Pinball Wizard', 'Who Are You', 'My Generation' and the rest, were instantly recognisable. But I had never yet seen the band perform live. I owned only one
of their albums, 'Quadrophenia'. I knew that windmilling Pete Townshend wrote most of the songs, that Roger Daltrey was the sexy one, and

that their beloved drummer Keith Moon had died. That was about it. I knew nothing about the big bass guitarist they called 'the Ox', who hung back behind his lipless smile and got on with it. But I really liked him.

Perhaps I was embraced by the Entwistle throng because I got on so well with his mother. They called her 'Queenie', and she lived up to the name. I asked her that first night what John was like as a kid. She didn't mince her words.

'A miserable little bugger if you want to know,' she said. 'Ruined by his Grandad, a real spoilt brat. Academically average, but always very artistic. Always singing and drawing. Singing from the age of two, precocious little rat. I took him to see Al Jolson when he was three. He knew every word of his songs. Afterwards we went to a club called Napier's, and John did a turn. Stood on a table and sang his heart out, then fell off and ended up in hospital having his head stitched. Funny thing, he's never fallen off stage. Though I think he walked off once, when he was blind drunk. Too plastered to notice where he was going. I remember the first guitar he had, when he was fourteen. He made it himself, on his Grandma's dining room table. I think I knew it would all be downhill after that.'

Back to Roehampton. At about nine o'clock on Live Aid morning, I was summoned to John and Max's bedroom.

'Max has got a problem,' declared John. He was lying naked to the waist in bed, wading through the morning newspapers. 'She can't decide what to wear.' All over the bed and hanging around the picture rails, I counted at least fifteen pairs of white shorts. Every pair looked identical. 'Damned if I know,' I said. 'Me neither,' replied John. 'Brandy, anyone?'

We were sober enough as we climbed into John's Rolls estate to head for Wembley Stadium, me into the boot with Fits Perfectly, their giant grey Irish wolfhound. The colour of the car was a bit queasy, I thought. I remarked to John that I'd never before encountered a Rolls Royce sprayed that shade.

'Neither had anyone,' he said. 'I took a plastic Harrods carrier bag to the bodyshop the day I bought the car, and told the paint sprayer to match that'.

There was a time when politicians made great orators. That art form has dwindled in the 21st century. Rock'n'roll, of all unlikely disciplines, remains one of the few professions in which an artist or group can hold an audience in the palm of their hand, controlling a throng of thousands with their voice. Screen actors can't do it. Television presenters don't even come close. It is one of the reasons why the rock superstar is now the last great compelling figure of our times, and even that is mostly Emperor's New Clothes. This occurred to me when I was standing in the curtained wings of Wembley Stadium's vast stage with John and Max, surveying the frenzied scene. We later watched Freddie Mercury perform in sweltering heat for close to eighty thousand people, and for a television audience of ... who knows? A lot of conflicting figures have been bandied about in the ensuing years, but the consensus seems to be four hundred million or so in around fifty countries via satellite. With nonchalance, wit, cheek and sex, old Fred gave it the absolute works. He knew exactly what he was doing. We looked on, open-mouthed. Perhaps he knew, when he addressed the audience out there, that no one could hear a word that he was saying. He wouldn't have cared. Knowing Freddie, he would have scoffed at the ensuing reviews, describing him as having 'a raw power which held us, a power so potent, you imagined you could smell it.' What pompous tit thought that one up? That would be me. Backstage, 'the most legendary names in rock' (as fresh a phrase in Eighties 'rock writing' as 'millionaire rock star') paused to watch their rival stealing the show. They must have felt sick. Yes, it was a global charity effort. But only the disingenuous would refuse to recognise a gigantic commercial opportunity, not to mention the chance to out-do their keenest rivals with practically everyone on earth watching. Queen's quintessential frontman knew exactly what he was doing. For eighteen minutes that seemed like hours, he ruled the world.

We make luck in random ways. Bob Geldof, scribbling in his diary in a taxi one nippy day in November 1984 knew a bit about luck. From the recesses of his throbbing brain, a 'battleground of conflicting thoughts' as he described it, came rudimentary bites of lyrics which would soon build into a song that would 'change the world'. It happened shortly after watching Michael Buerk's shocking bulletin from famine-wracked Ethiopia on BBC News. Horrified by television footage depicting suffering of biblical proportions, Geldof's gut compelled him to get involved. But how? He could only do what he did best, and he was really dicing with death, here: get back to the drawing board, write a hit single, and donate the proceeds to Oxfam. Big deal. His Irish punk band the Boomtown Rats were, to put it kindly, over the hill, having not enjoyed a Top Ten hit since 1980. They'd peaked with 'I Don't Like Mondays', a Number One which came and went in 1979. Music fans, Bob knew, would flock to buy a charity single by an artist or artists who were big enough names, especially at the Christmas-single-buying time of year, at a time when 'Christmas singles' were still a thing. Now that the classics have all been written and committed to the Yuletide compilation CDs that we J-cloth off each December with the arrival of The Tree, no one gives a toss about any new ones. Give me Wham!'s 'Last Christmas', the Pogues' and Kirsty McColl's 'Fairytale of New York' and Chris Rea's 'Driving Home for Christmas' and I'm an even-toed ungulate in excrement. Am I right, pop pickers? Go on then, I'll give you Jona if I can have Slade. So anyway, Bob's dilemma was finding a sympathetic star to record a brand-new song with the potential to become an instant Christmas classic. No pressure. If in doubt, dump the star. Get a galaxy.

Bob called Midge Ure, my old Peter-Saville-tormenting partner-in-crime from Chrysalis Records, whose band Ultravox were appearing that week on The Tube: a Channel 4 rock and pop show fronted by Geldof's future wife Paula Yates. Good old Midge agreed to polish Bob's lyrics, come up with a tune, and even do the arrangements. Bob then got on the blower to Sting, Duran Duran's Simon le Bon, and Gary and Martin Kemp from Spandau Ballet. His balls were now rolling. His galactic line-up expanded by the day. Boy George, Frankie Goes to Hollywood, the Style Council's Paul Weller, George Michael and Andrew Ridgeley of Wham!, Paul Young. Francis Rossi and Rick Parfitt of Status Quo went in willingly. Phil Collins and Bananarama followed. David Bowie and Paul McCartney were otherwise engaged, but made contributions remotely, which were dubbed on later. Sir Peter Blake, who created the iconic artwork for the Beatles' 'Sgt Pepper's Lonely Hearts Club Band' album cover, agreed to design the sleeve. Band Aid was born, the name a pun on a common brand of sticking plaster. The idea was a 'band' which would 'aid' the world.

'Do they Know It's Christmas?' was recorded free of charge at Trevor Horn's SARM West Studios in Notting Hill, West London, on 25 November 1984, and was released four days later. At Number One that week was brilliant Scottish singer and dear friend Jim Diamond, with his sublime, timeless ballad 'I Should Have Known Better'. Although Jim's group PhD had scored a hit with 'I Won't Let You Down' in 1982, he had never had a solo hit, bless him. The music industry was gobsmacked when Jim gave an interview about his chart success.

'I'm delighted to be Number One,' he said, 'but next week I don't want people to buy my record. I want them to buy Band Aid instead.'

'I couldn't believe it,' Bob said. 'As a singer who hadn't had a Number One for five years, I knew what it cost him to say that. He had just thrown away his first hit for others. It was genuinely selfless'.

That was the Jim I knew.

I'd known him longer than I'd known myself. We'd had a regular slot together on Radio Clyde, reviewing the week's new releases on a round-table show hosted by Bill Padley with sublime-to-ridiculous guests, such as Meatloaf and Thereza Bazar from Dollar. We fell in together on those weekly trips, flying up to Glasgow and staying at the Holiday Inn, which, asking for it, had a swimming pool in the lobby. Jim became more than a brother to me. My real brother had stepped out of my life, and Jim had fallen out with his, so we decided to be each other's brother. He knew my best secrets. I knew his. When my life collapsed completely in 2006 (of which more later), it was Jim who dropped to his knees to look for the pieces. A tiny Celt with an estuary of spirit, he was bursting-proud of his Scottish roots. He loved music more profoundly than any musician I have ever known. Jim was music. He'd known his share of heartache. There was more to come. But his voice set him free. His was a more important talent than the industry recognised. They should have known better.

The following week, 'Do They Know It's Christmas' zapped to Number One in the UK, outselling everything to become Britain's fastest-selling single since the chart's inception in 1952. A million copies were shifted in the first week alone. The record clung to the summit for five weeks, selling in excess of three and a half million copies. It went on to become the UK's biggest-selling single of all time, ending the nine-year reign of Queen's magnum opus 'Bohemian Rhapsody'. Where do you top that?

Only in America. The Stateside contribution, by super-group USA For Africa, was 'We Are the World'. Written by Michael Jackson and Lionel Richie, and produced by Quincy Jones and Michael Omartian, it featured some of the planet's most gasp-inducing musicians. They recorded it at Hollywood's A & M Studios in January 1985. 'They' being Diana Ross, Bruce Springsteen, Smokey Robinson, Cyndi Lauper, Billy Joel,

Dionne Warwick, Willie Nelson, Huey Lewis et al. Which kind of knocked our lot into a cocked hat. In all, more than forty-five of America's most revered artists ever took part. A further fifty had to be turned away. When the chosen ones arrived at the studio, they were confronted by a sign instructing them to 'please check your egos at the door'. They were also met by Stevie Wonder, informing them that if the recording wasn't down in one take, he and Ray Charles would be driving them home. The record sold more than twenty million copies, and became America's fastest-selling pop single ever. Not to be outdone – heaven forfend – Geldof dialled his aid campaign up a notch, and announced plans to create the most ambitious rock project in history, of all time, ever.

Because they had been ignored for the single, Queen did not consider themselves an obvious choice for the gig line-up. What an irony that seems now. Despite their fifteen-year career, a ridiculously good back catalogue of albums, singles and videos, royalties into the multi-millions, and having landed most music awards going thanks to musicianship which embraced the lot, from rock, pop, opera and rockabilly to disco, funk and folk, Queen's star appeared to be firmly in the descendant. The band had been away from home for a considerable period between August 1984 and May 1985, promoting their 'The Works' album, during which they took part in the Rock In Rio festival in January 1985, performing live for three hundred and twenty-five thousand fans. But the tour had been beset by problems. There was even talk of them going their separate ways. The New Romantics era was upon us. Spandau Ballet and Duran Duran ruled. The hoary old rock band seemed to have had its day.

After touring to promote their bewilderingly dance-y, guitar-less 1982 album 'Hot Space', Freddie Mercury, Brian May, Roger Taylor and John Deacon had effectively disbanded to concentrate on solo pursuits: notably Brian with Eddie Van Halen on the Star Fleet Project, and Freddie on his own album. In August 1983, they regrouped in Los Angeles to collaborate on 'The Works', their tenth studio album and debut CD. 'Radio Ga Ga' was the first single. The album also featured hard rock number 'Hammer to Fall', the ballad 'Is This the World We Created', and the controversial 'I Want to Break Free', its 'outrageous' cross-dressing video loosely based on a scene from UK TV soap 'Coronation Street'. While the single proved hugely popular at home and in other territories, it had offended conservative Middle America and upset many fans. Get a grip.

Worse, Queen had recently broken the United Nations cultural boy-
cott, as had Rod Stewart, Rick Wakeman, Status Quo and others, to perform in apartheid South Africa. Their October 1984 shows at Sun City,
Sol Kerzner's casino, golf and entertainment resort in Bophuthatswana,
earned the band widespread criticism and saw them fined and blacklisted
by the British Musician's Union. For an African-born musician, which
Freddie was (to the many who still insist that he was Asian, get an atlas,
people), this was a travesty. The situation was not resolved until racial
segregation fell in 1993, a year before Nelson Mandela was elected President. Queen would become major and active supporters of Mandela in
later years.

Live Aid's 'global jukebox' would be staged in two huge venues,
Wembley Stadium and the John F. Kennedy Stadium in Philadelphia.
Organisation proved a logistical nightmare.

'When Bob first came in to my office to discuss this event, I thought
he was joking', promoter Harvey Goldsmith told me.

'In 1985 there weren't fax machines, let alone computers, mobile
phones or anything else. We were working on telex and landlines. I remember sitting in my office one afternoon with a big satellite map and a
pair of old wooden callipers, trying to map out where the satellite was
going to be at certain times. Also, when we went to the BBC, Bob was
thumping the table and saying, 'I want seventeen hours of television'.
That was revolutionary. Once the BBC had committed, we could use that
as leverage to persuade broadcasters all over the world to do it. It was the
first time that had ever happened. And it was my job to pick up the pieces
and make it all work.'

Then came the challenge of persuading rock's biggest names, some
of whom had already contributed to the recording of the charity singles,
to perform and raise further funds. This was blatant retaliation by the
music fraternity at governments around the world which had failed to
act. As Quo's Francis Rossi told me, 'this was the dickheads in rock and
roll, just getting on with it. It does make me angry when I look back. I
believe that if everyone had pulled together – if we'd understood then the
magnitude of what could have been achieved – we could have got the oil
companies, the BPs and Shells and whoever else, to do their bit. We could
have made twenty times whatever it was we raised. Don't tell me the
Government couldn't have legislated to get round the issues with advertising and so on. All big businesses could have got involved, and the re-

sult would have been mega. At the time, it was virgin territory. We think about Live Aid differently today. But still, all credit to Bob. He pulled together something which precious few could have achieved.'

So far, so worthy. On the day, until Queen came on, it was all a bit of a picnic. Which is not to say that they were being calculating or cunning or using the occasion to feather their own nests. They were just doing what they normally did, expecting nothing more than for everyone else to do the same. A number of artists went out and belted their latest single, which was a bit crass. The occasion wasn't meant to be a promotional opportunity for new product, it was all about the hits that people knew and loved. The 'greatest rock performance of all time', as it's often referred to, was actually just Queen being themselves. They were simply a band at the top of their game doing what they did best. Why was the world so amazed? To them, it was another day at the office. But after Live Aid, their entire universe changed.

PR Bernard Doherty was in charge of publicity at Wembley, taking care of all the media on the day. With only eight triple-A ('Access All Areas') laminate passes, but with hundreds of press representatives from many countries to pander to, he had no choice but to effectively rent them out. One by one he said to everyone, 'Right, you've got forty-five minutes in there, get what you can, get back out, pass on the pass. See you in the Hard Rock Café,' of which there was a 'branch' backstage. 'Backstage' was a wagon-train-style scenario, with the artists' portacabins pointing inwards. Elton John was cooking a barbecue to one side, because he didn't fancy the burgers or the chips. David Bailey set his photo studio up in a corner, he wasn't proud. Conditions were not exactly ideal. But it happened. People got into the spirit of the event, and it worked.

What else do we remember about Live Aid? The sound going down on The Who and Macca. Bono getting in the zone, losing the plot and confounding the others by breaking the rules of performance that day. None of the rest of U2 would talk to him after that. They thought they'd blown it. Le Bon did blow it, with the bum note of all time. The fashionistas drooled over Bowie. Phil Collins played both Wembley and JFK courtesy of Concorde, though I think a lot of people wished he hadn't bothered, not least the hastily-re-formed Led Zeppelin, for whom he drummed at JFK. As for Queen, they did exactly what Bob had asked them to do. I watched from the wings, and I was blown away. Because you never know what to expect. Even the greatest acts in the world bomb for no apparent reason. We needn't have worried, though. Queen gave it all they had. So many other supreme performers flooded back into my minds as I stood watching them. Alex Harvey, the great glam rocker of the Sensational Alex Harvey Band. Ian Dury and the Blockheads. Mick Jagger. Syd Barrett. Ziggy Stardust and the Spiders. What Freddie displayed better than on perhaps any other occasion was instinctive star quality, as well as a phenomenal grasp of what constitutes a must-watch show. He conjured the thrill of Vaudeville. It was as if he'd studied and absorbed the best-kept secrets of every definitive artist who had gone before, and sorcered a little of all them into his act. The ultimate peacock, Freddie seduced us all. Everyone backstage stopped talking to watch Queen's set. That never normally happens.

There is a tendency to look back at Live Aid and see it as more than it was. A global gig staged against all technical odds, granted, but essentially no more than a great day out. That it earned a lot of money for the starving millions seemed almost incidental. Which won't have thrilled Bob, but there you go. Who came on before or after Queen? No one remembers. Not unless they sneak a look at the video or the DVD. What I remember is that Freddie Mercury and Queen were the best group, and that David Bowie was the best solo performer. Over all the years since, I have never met anyone who thought otherwise.

With John Entwistle, Four Seasons Los Angeles, 1989

David Stark, LAJ, Jim Diamond, London, 2008

Ken Jones & Jim Diamond, London, September 2015

9. PICK ON MAMMALS YOUR OWN SIZE: RICHARD GERE

Those of a delicate disposition are advised to skip this chapter. While most people are more than aware of Fleet Street's obsession with the sex lives of celebrities, there will be some for whom what follows is an intrusion too far. I make no apology. The story is true, and I was despatched to cover it. I have from time to time pondered the insanity, the momentary suspension of decency and decorum, that convinced highly-paid and relatively respected Daily Mail executives to believe that their decision was a good idea. Did they think it was funny? Were they so blinded by their own mirth that all sense of reason deserted them, or were there darker forces at work? They knew that I was an artless, starry-eyed twenty-something who had probably never even heard of the debauchery involved. To expose me to it was in itself corrupting. A mental rape, of sorts. In today's litigious climate, lucrative lawsuits are launched (and won) in all directions on infinitely less. Your boss's little finger grazed your bra strap? He pinched your bottom? Called you words you never heard in the Bible? You're having a laugh. I have sometimes wondered what my dear, departed, seaside-dwelling Welsh grandmothers and giddy aunts would have made of it. The voice that echoes from beyond, whenever I imagine myself trying to explain it to them, is Auntie Jane's, going, 'Orrrgghhh! By gosh! There's lovely!'

What's the difference between a gerbil and a mole? An outrageously shocking, gargantuan difference, if you happen to be a Hollywood heart-throb in the habit of pissing people off. As was Richard Gere, during the Eighties. A legendarily cantankerous interviewee with a superiority complex the size and temperature of Antarctica, Gere's loathing of and contempt for the print media were all too well-known. Indeed, the collective term 'Scum' had been known to befall his lips in reference to our intrepid globe-trotting clan. Commonly known across newsrooms as 'Richard's Gear', he was the subject of possibly the most monstrous, revolting and undoubtedly untrue conspiracy theory to have hit Fleet Street in modern times. He was a practitioner, so went the barely believable rumour, of 'gerbilling'. Also known as 'gerbil-stuffing' or 'gerbil shooting', the alleged procedure was said to involve the insertion into the human rectum of a rodent (rats and mice could also substitute) to effect stimulation. A variation on the theme involved psychoactive preparation of the pitiful creature by rolling it in cocaine, thus further enhancing the experience. What about the claws? They removed them. The fur? They wrapped the poor mammal in clingfilm. And so on. What a way to go. Gere, incidentally, never confirmed nor denied this alleged penchant for creature comforts and did not even comment on the rumours until twenty-two years later, in 2008, when he referred to it not as a 'gerbil', but as a 'hamster'.

The names of a number of celebrities had lately become synonymous with this alleged practice, which some of us suspected was made-up. It seemed yet another example of 'gay-bashing', which is rightly illegal, but which back then among certain factions was popular sport. The Eighties were the zenith of the global AIDS crisis. The world had hit a shamefully ignorant low point at which 'gays were to blame' for the killer plague. The lengths to which homosexuals were said to proceed in the pursuit of sexual pleasure was held up as 'proof' of the disease's origin. Most of us dismissed it over yet another round in the Wine Press. But a few were emphatic. They seemed fascinated to the point of obsession with the autoerotic diversion. Which begged more questions than I could bring myself to imagine answers to. Moving on.

In December 1986, the hideous hydra once again reared its ugly heads. It was decided, one Daily Mail morning conference, that 'L.A.' (as they called me) should be despatched to New York to interview Richard Gere, and get the story from the horse's mouth. You're really hearing this? You truly, honestly are.

I could see where they were coming from. The hook upon which to hang the excuse for an interview was Gere's latest movie: a lukewarm thriller set in the Louisiana bayous, entitled 'No Mercy'[iv] and co-starring Kim Basinger, who doubled as the leading man's current real-life flame. My modus operandi would need to be a classic example of the 'Columbo Technique': get in, quiz him enthusiastically about his latest piss-poor flick, lull him into a sense of false security then beat it ... pausing at the door to turn, reflect, and skilfully fling the killer dart: 'Just one more thing ...'

Had the Suits selected me for the task because I was the youngest and most naïve reporter on the desk? Because I was a bit butter-wouldn't-melt, not too excruciating on the eye, and because, of all the representatives they could have sent, I was the One Most Likely to get something out of it at least, because I was girlie-girl bait? Even if Gere was deeply offended by the question, would go ballistic and possibly inflict violence? Which, let's face it, most normal people subjected to such lunacy would. Or was this yet another example of their vindictive and tormenting nature, despatching the meekling on the team on an international assignment so shameful that I couldn't bring myself to tell my mother about it, let alone Dad, and which might possibly embarrass me ad abdicatio? It didn't help in the slightest that His Gearness's middle moniker was Tiffany.[v]

I should have protested, stamped my kitten heel and refused to go? Believe me, I tried. I was reminded of inevitable dismissal for refusal of an assignment. In desperation, I gathered my best gay friends for an on-expenses steak, chips and copious Montepulciano dinner at Joe Allen on Exeter Street one pre-departure night, and quizzed them mercilessly on the veracity of the practice. 'Urban', was the guffawed consensus. 'Have another drink, L.A.!' In other words, every person present had heard of it, but it wasn't an actual thing that real people did. Not just not 'normal' people? 'Not any people!' What could be the genesis of the rumour, in that case, and how had it gathered momentum, I wondered. 'Ah,' said my TV producer friend, sagely. 'Apparently, Richard Gere once had a mole surgically removed from his bum. As in, a birthmark-type mole. I believe, in dermatological parlance, that it would be called a nevus.' So a mole incised from our Hollywood hero's cheek led to the exaggerated notion of gerbils projected against their will and better judgement in the general direction of where cherubim fear to tread?

'Hole in one.'

'A hard day at the orifice, dear?'

The gags kept coming.

We were, at this juncture, years ahead of sordid references to the practice on 'South Park', let alone Dawn French's allusion to it on 'The Vicar of Dibley' in an episode which first aired on April 8, 1996. Rating the sex appeal of Richard's Gear, the lusty cleric comments, nudge-nudge, that she 'wouldn't have minded being the hamster.' We were also aware that there was no known, proven, medically-treated case. Not anywhere in the world. Despite which, the establishment said to have assisted Ricardo in his hour of clawed-Khyber had been narrowed down to the Cedars-Sinai Medical Center, Los Angeles. That hospital, world-famous for the deaths of George Gershwin, Frank Sinatra, Elizabeth Taylor, Debbie Reynolds and Carrie Fisher, and for the births of Michael Jackson's and Debbie Rowe's son Michael, Kim Kardashian's and Kanye West's son Saint West and Posh'n'Becks's daughter Harper Seven, seemed to have employed a planet's worth of doctors and nurses who'd had a hand in Gere's gerbilectomy – or who claimed to have witnessed it as part of an observational team. So many, in fact, that the Cedars-Sinai became an edifice of legend, as the 'best-staffed hospital in the world'.

The upside was that I got to spend three hours with the great modern-day sex symbol in New York. (It was supposed to have happened in Philadelphia, the city of his birth, but he changed the location at the last minute. Much more fun. Go, L.A.) This was a rendezvous for which most of my girlfriends would have killed, blissfully unaware as they were of the real reason behind my assignment.

The downside was that, while Gere had made an excellent officer, he was certainly no gentleman. I admit that a part of me had been seduced by his sensuous screen profile in the afore-alluded-to flick. But the outfit slaughtered the allure. He was wearing brown shoes with shapeless grey slacks, a black belt, a blue button-down shirt and a dusty tweed jacket. The impression was of a hungover art director in a Covent Garden ad agency, who had tumbled from bed into the nearest garments discarded on the floor a few nights before. This was the man who performed a near-naked fandango around Diane Keaton in 'Looking for Mr Goodbar', bared all as a sleazy lounge lizard opposite Lauren Hutton in 'American Gigolo', swept Debra Winger off a factory floor in 'An Officer and a Gentleman' (ballsy Winger described him as 'a brick wall'), and won the favours of doll-like Diane Lane in 'The Cotton Club'. Despite these greatly-lauded associations, Gere denied point-blank that he was ever a sex symbol.

'I didn't make my career out of it, lady. How dare you. You made your career out of writing about it! (I had never as yet penned so much as a syllable about him). I don't know what that label even means. I'm an AC-tor. I don't care about it, and I don't bother to read about it. I think it's total crap.'

That told me. Nevertheless, I pressed (playing for time), he could not deny that his sizzling encounters with some of the hottest females in film had earned him his most favourable notices. Gere was no dumb hunk. He presented as an AC-tor who resented the need to rely on a strong female co-star.

'Yeah, I owe a lot to my leading ladies,' he conceded, grudgingly, with more than a hint of sarcasm. He proceeded to deny romantic involvement with any of them, even though we knew he was playing Pin the Tail on the Donkey with Basinger. He admitted to a relationship with Priscilla Presley, but denied carnal involvement with Madonna, though she herself had blurted it.

'I'm approached by women all the time,' he shrugged (Presley, Basinger and Madonna were mere women?)

'It's flattering to be desired, flattering that people accept the reality of the characters I play, but ridiculous to assume that I play those roles in real life. There's a lot of fantasy involved when you're up there on the screen.'

I guessed so. I smiled thinly. And looked at him. There could be no denying that Gere had made a rather nondescript body and an average face work wonders. Half his charm, in those days, was that sexy hip-rolling walk thing he mastered after many months of practice. He was not, after all, the most charming of stars. Perhaps he just didn't enjoy interviews. Few do. But I found him unappealing to the point of being almost threatening. One of the first 'name' Hollywood actors to play a homosexual, Gere had starred as a gay Holocaust victim in the 1979 Broadway production of 'Bent'. It won him a Theatre World Award, but he didn't want to talk about it. 'That was then,' he snarled.

'I'm not a particularly nice person,' he threw in. 'I'm pretty intense, and I stake my territory.'

He was also moody, difficult and downright sulky, ignoring questions he didn't feel like answering and glancing constantly at his watch. None of which seemed very zen. Gere had become a Buddhist in his twenties, and later an active supporter of Tibetan Buddhism and the Dalai Lama. He was involved in the human rights movement in Tibet, and was vociferously anti-China. I couldn't be fagged to challenge him on all of this. It was not what I'd come for. We bade each other faux-polite goodbyes.

But what about the Columbo killer dart? Reader, I confess. I couldn't bring myself.

Back in Blighty, I filed the piece. In those wattle-and-daub days, we typed our quaint 'articles' in triplicate, pressing smudgy sheets of carbon paper between grey pages of A4, into the rollers of Olivetti typewriters the size of Fiat Unos. These were then circulated, challenged, argued-over, torn to shreds, re-written and edited. They eventually made their way to the 'back bench': the production heart of the newspaper, where grim-faced maniacs with inky fingers[vi] reshaped the 'final' copy to match headlines and fit ad-laden layouts that left little room for the less convenient ingredients of journalism, such as facts. What we hacks supplied was merely raw material. It was the job of the down-table subs to eradicate accuracy, integrity and repetition; to take all the good stuff out, and replace it with more important things, such as proper spelling, grammar and punctuation.[vii] The back-bench men (and they were mostly men) were veritable magicians. Few on earth could crystallise, against the clock, words, photos and eyeball-grabbing headlines into real, actual newspaper pages. A journalist's job, at the end of the day, was only finding stuff out.

Less than twenty minutes after circulating my feature on Gere, I was summoned to the Editor's office by David English's secretary, a Sphinx-like creature by the name of Ina Miller, whose husband Harry was a mate of my dad's, and who modelled herself on Dusty Springfield. Ina maintained a lofty, Elnetted beehive, which she checked in a hand mirror she kept in her desk, every time she answered the phone.

Within the inner sanctum, the editor of editors fumed. Never, in the field of human conflict, he thundered, inserting the odd Churchillian phrase and spiral of spit for fearful effect, had it been his misfortune to set eyes on copy so shameful. He was, he declared, 'spiking it'. The expression harked back to the newsrooms of the Thirties and Forties, when a story deemed unusable because it was inaccurate or insufficient in some way would be unceremoniously disposed of by being hammered down onto a long metal spike attached to a small block of wood in the middle of the desk, like an insect pinned to a corkboard in a natural history museum. (These days, we go 'delete'). Mercifully, there was no mention of the fact that my piece contained not the flimsiest reference to the question I was sent three and a half thousand miles in Club class to ask. I can only assume that the Editor didn't read that far down.

I was dismissed from English's wood-panelled lair, and warned on the way out not to submit any expenses.

Back at my desk in the top right-hand corner of the showbiz department, furthest from 'the Bunker' where our editors sat, I rested my head on my hands, exhausted by the mauling. I was soon jolted by the invasion of my space by one of our numerous associate editors, who plonked himself down fatly beside me.

'Why so glum, L.A.?'

I explained that English had rejected my interview with Richard Gere. 'One of the best intros I've ever written too,' I lamented.

'What was it?'

'"The most genuine thing about Richard Gere is his Rolex."'

Whereupon my interrogator collapsed into snorts and yelps so self-suffocating, he had to be assisted back onto his chair. His face glistened with tears.

'That *is* a good intro!'

'Funny why?'

He stood up, wiped his hands in his hair and drew himself to his full five feet eight.

'What you have to understand, L.A., is that David English wears a fake Rolex!'

'What! How do you know?!'

'I was with him in a market in Hong Kong when he paid thirty quid for it! No fucking wonder he chucked you out!'

10. ROCK'N'ROLL BABYLON

My send-off from the Mail was award-winning. Behind my back, the Showbiz boys got in touch with my mum to find out what I needed for the baby. How about a pram? Thank you very much, but we'd already bought one. Carrycot and new-fangled rock-a-tot car-seat? Got it. What about a full-size cot for the flat? Bless their cotton socks, but we had that too. In the end, they agreed a long list of all manner of baby bits and pieces, including cot linen, blankets, bottle-warmers, bath caddy, books, picture frames, nappy carrier, toys and endless must-haves more, which Steve Absalom, Geoff Sutton and Pat Hill bundled off together to buy. The thought of the three must-get-beers, macho boys, hungover as usual, dodging about in Mothercare and Selfridges with bundles of baby stuff under their arms, still makes me laugh. Theatre critic Jack Tinker contributed a Victorian lace baby bonnet which he'd found in an antique shop near his home, down Brighton's Lanes. Herbert Kretzmer donated a 'Les Misérables' sweatshirt and a hardback commemorative book of the show, with a note, 'Precious cargo, LA. Only a few more one-more-days.' I was presented with all this at my leaver's lunch in a restaurant on New Bridge Street, a couple of weeks before the birth, in a spoof of the conveyor-belt finale on Bruce Forsyth's 'Generation Game' ('Cuddly toy! Cuddly toy!') in which the winner of the show got to cart off as many items as he/she could remember and recite after they'd all whizzed past. The boys set this up themselves, complete with theme music. It brought the house down. We arrived at the Wine Press lugging enough gear to start a nursery.

I was going to miss this bunch. There had been scrapes, humiliations, close shaves, wins, losses, fallings-out, sackings, reinstatements, trips, trials, arrests, dramas and cliffhangers galore. I'd been put to work on such stories as I would never face again. I'd been mentally flogged to within a blink of insanity, by anxious editors, in the name of ... what, exactly? A here today, gone tomorrow newspaper which everyone you met and passed the time of day with professed to detest, denouncing it as not even good enough to wrap cod in, but which they all appeared to have read. Perhaps advanced pregnancy had, against all odds, delivered perspective and priority. I could suddenly see past the irrational obsession of my superiors, who in reality ran scared shitless, just like the rest of us;

who were terrified of being eclipsed by a colleague or getting scooped by a rival rag; who were afraid to leave the office until the final edition had dropped, and who would certainly never depart before everybody else had; who crept home after their spouses had gone to bed and were gone again the next morning before they got up. A number of these executives kept framed photographs of wives and children on their desks. I had to wonder how often they saw them in the flesh. I felt a twist in the gut, a hypodermic to the heart. Could somebody be trying to tell me something?

The consolation prize was always the foot soldiers. The gutsy guys and gals with whom I'd sweated, sobbed and occasionally triumphed around that hallowed Showbiz desk, or out on the road, or over the Wine Press. They were precious characters and twinkling stars. I will always remember them.

Nick Gordon's progressive, feminist idea, as we have heard, was that I should let go of rock and pop to write broad-spectrum features for YOU Magazine. I would trawl the globe for stories with a sprog under one arm. Until she had to go to school, that was, at which point we would have to have a rethink. But in the meantime, imagine the calling card. How dangerous can this bitch be: she's lactating! But the plan fell at the first fence. I was despatched to the Middle East, one of the most hostile terrains on earth, where I would be risking my life around the clock in an environment that was anything but child-friendly. Not only that, but the story was about, how can I put this, a rock band. Nick was sorry about that, he said. He at least had the grace to look embarrassed. There just wasn't another feature writer on the desk at the time with the inclination or credentials to take it on.

I was to accompany Hurrah!, a jingle-jangle pop group from Newcastle Upon Tyne, into Iraq, Jordan and Egypt, on a tour sponsored by the British Arts Council. This imperious public body, dedicated to the promotion of British fine arts abroad, was more accustomed to curating visits by the Ballet Rambert, prodigal harpists or classical string quartets than a bunch of stale, unshaven posers with guitars for necklaces. Not that Hurrah! were without promise. The previous year, they had supported both U2 at Wembley Stadium and David Bowie at a German music festival as part of his Glass Spider tour (I was on that trip, too). One of the first western rock bands to perform in the Middle East, the boys would be escorted everywhere by armed troops. As the hack pack were travelling with them, we would be too. This was unnerving to say the least. With the firstborn holed up safely with her grandparents back in Kent, I took a deep breath, found a corner in my kitbag for a bulletproof vest, and joined the Baghdad-bound posse. The band's equipment was being transported by truck, which was taking a precarious route down through Syria. BBC Radio 1 DJ Annie Nightingale and veteran rock photographer Adrian Boot were also on the outing. The performance venues included the two hundred and fifty-seater Al-Rabat concert hall in Baghdad City, and an almost two-thousand-year-old Roman amphitheatre in Amman. What could possibly go wrong?

It was my first-ever trip to a live war zone. Was this Nick's idea of a joke? His way of chucking me in at the deep end? I wasn't about to query it, I didn't want him to think I was wet. We'd be working in countries wracked by religious and ethnic upheaval and violence, in the shadow of Saddam Hussein's suppression of the Shiites and Kurds, the Iran-Iraq war and the assault on Israel. Only a couple of months earlier, Saddam had attacked the Kurds with nerve and mustard gas. Five thousand people had been killed. A further ten thousand had suffered life-changing injuries. Overall, the brutal dictatorship of the man who wore a diamond-encrusted Rolex while watching his people starve, would claim the lives of a quarter of a million Iraqis.[viii]

It was surreal. On the one hand, all the aforementioned horror for a backdrop. On the other, I was in the desert, in the cradle of civilisation, where humans first began to read and write, first built cities and governments, first forged laws by which to live. I was savouring a river Tigris sunset with a Baghdad iced tea in one hand, and hanging around in souks and mosques. In Babylon, I lingered on the banks of the palm-fringed Euphrates, which shimmered (if you squinted) with mirages of hanging gardens and ziggurats. But it wasn't all trashy-tourist-look-at-me posing-at-the-Ishtar-Gate. It was in Iraq of all places that it occurred to me how privileged I was. What other occupation would afford me the all-expenses-paid opportunity to visit lands I knew only from Geography lessons and atlases, to meet history-makers as well as movers and shakers, to observe people living alternative versions of normal? I remembered a book we'd read at school, about a Sumerian family from four thousand years ago. 'The Three Brothers of Ur'. I should read it again. It might make sense, now.

Iraq's economy was on its knees. While the rich were still splashing their wealth (and pitching up at strange rock concerts, if only to see what all the fuss was about), the vast majority were neck-deep in poverty. A cup of coffee cost us the equivalent of forty quid. The gold-painted artisan clay doll that I bought as a present for my mother set me back north of two hundred (at least it's still hanging on the wall in her kitchen), and seemed an immoral purchase (it was). Then again, what were we doing there at all, in a war zone, pandering to a bunch of British Council-funded popsters who barely seemed to know which way was up? Hadn't the Council (or the magazine) given adequate consideration to the appropriateness of this excursion? Did the Iraqi nation really need our pathetic pop culture rammed down its throat at a time when their very existence was on the brink of annihilation? We were flimsy imposters with no right to be there. Arrogant in our ignorance. To our eternal shame we had a laugh at the expense of the local families who attended those gigs, dragging behind them scowling children dressed in scaled-down versions of their parents' middle-aged outfits. One night, the bored crew constructed a mini-Stonehenge which they lowered from the rigging onto the performing band, in a parody of the sequence in 'This is Spinal Tap' (1982): the faux behind-the-scenes movie tribute to the world's loudest rock band. Who can forget the line, 'There was a Stonehenge monument on the stage that was in danger of being crushed by a dwarf'? If the Iraqis even noticed, it went over their heads. Literally.

Annie startled us at dinner that night, by pointing out what would happen if enemy factions invaded and took control. They would seize the radio station, she said. What difference would that make? 'It's the first thing they do when they overthrow a ruling power,' she explained. 'Seize the national or most prominent local broadcaster. Leave the populace in no doubt.' It seems all too obvious now, but it hadn't occurred to any of us before she mentioned it. The thought half-sobered us.

Was this my most bizarre experience ever of rockers on the road? Perhaps not. As I lay in bed allowing my wine-fuelled dreams to waft me again through mis-spent years, I found myself back in Montreux. It was a realm as removed from Baghdad as I could summon. An Alpine Shangri-La, a picturesque haven on the banks of Lake Geneva, a Swiss Disneyland for grown-ups: it was all these things and more. It was magical. The lake's waters were said to be as deep as its mountains are high. Long a retreat for the rich and famous, it hit the headlines in 1971 after a rock fan fired a flare at a Frank Zappa and the Mothers of Invention gig at the casino. The venue burned to the ground. Watching the disaster from a hotel window, Deep Purple's Roger Glover reached for his bass guitar and wrote the most famous riff in rock.[ix]

I'd been to Montreux many times. The first, with Capital Radio's Roger Scott, was to interview David Bowie and Queen while they were jamming together on a track that became 'Under Pressure'. Thereafter, I returned to cover the annual 'Montreux Rock Festival' as it was known, despite the fact that it was essentially a TV extravaganza: the Montreux Golden Rose Light Entertainment Festival. The musical element was only ever intended to be an after-hours diversion for restless delegates, who had been sitting there bored stiff all day. But over time, throughout the Eighties, the music superseded the television convention to become the main event. Pop and rock's biggest stars of the day would converge on the casino annually each May, to perform live in what was then television's greatest pop-tacular, but which translated onto the screen as 'Eurovision' meets 'It's a Knockout'. Despite the cringe factor, these shows were watched by millions in more than seventy-five countries. They were probably what inspired Bob Geldof to give it a go with Live Aid. We saw and hung with the crème: A-ha, the Beastie Boys, Level 42, Whitney Houston, Bananarama, Kim Wilde, Curiosity Killed the Cat, Alison Moyet, Spandau Ballet, Genesis, the Blow Monkeys, Eighth Wonder, INXS, the Communards ...

And guess who misbehaved the most? Whose insane idea was it to capture Peter Gill, the drummer known as 'Ped' or 'Pedro' from Frankie Goes to Hollywood, toss him into a rowing boat and push him out onto the lake? No one can recall. Believe me, I've asked. Not Annette Witheridge, not Dave Hogan, not Gill Pringle, not Rick Sky, none of them. A collective loss of memory has occurred. When a blanket of fog descended and Ped's little boat had bobbed into oblivion, we panicked. The coastguard was yelled for. Ped was eventually found, thank God, and treated for nothing worse than hypothermia. It wasn't long before he was reunited with his band and his drumkit. No permanent damage. But had he vanished forever into the swirling mists, we could have been done for murder.

There was a party on a paddle steamer on the lake that night, hosted by Queen, whose Mountain recording studios now occupied the old casino building. Phil Collins took it upon himself to berate us publicly for our delinquency. He needn't have bothered. We weren't listening. We were already planning the next wheeze. Not that it involved the tossing of television sets from bedroom windows, the driving of Rolls Royces into pools, or any of those other old rock'n'roll clichés. Our mischief was humbler. As soon as we docked, at the end of the bash, we tore to the Montreux Palace hotel, blagged a pass key, and removed the bed, curtains, telly, every stick of furniture, every garment, every lightbulb, every loo roll, even the contents of the minibar from Queen bassist John Deacon's room. We then staged a John and Yoko-style bed-in in the corridor, having dragged a dozen mattresses into the hall. We created a Norwegian wood outside the bedroom door of A-ha's lead singer Morten Harket with pot plants gathered from every floor of the hotel. He popped his head out at one point, to make polite enquiries, and retreated with customary Nordic grace. Fuelled by booze and boredom – no rock stars were misbehaving enough to file words about, and there was nothing else going on (we're talking Montreux, after all) – we felt compelled, for the sake of our salaries, to do it ourselves.

'FRANKIE GOES BERSERK!

Monday May 12, 1986

The rock band Frankie goes to Hollywood went on a £100,000 orgy of wrecking at a pop festival.

'The Liverpool group destroyed the stage and their equipment while performing their first single in two years in front of millions of TV viewers across Europe. Later, members of the band swore at newsmen and fans and caused an extra £10,000 worth of damage at their hotel by smashing glasses and bottles and stubbing cigars out on expensive carpets ...

'Some of the band later gate-crashed a boat party organised by the pop group Queen, and swore at guests while drinking beer from bottles. Teenage girls from a Swiss finishing school, who had been smuggled on board for the party, were shocked to find themselves being manhandled.'

At last! Action! And so on. We should be ashamed of ourselves. Ah, ya know.

In 1989 came the most coveted invitation of all, the opportunity that every journalist worth their expenses aspired to: the chance to star in a television commercial. I could hardly believe my luck. Could Christmases really all come at once? I started checking out weekend cottages in the Cotswolds, and comparing flats with views of Tower Bridge. What could this spectacular ad be, that was certain to consolidate fame and abundant fortune? For some seductive eau de parfum by Gianni Versace or Yves St. Laurent? A glamorous river cruise down the Danube? A five-star sojourn (all-inclusive) in the Seychelles? No, it could not. Mia and I were asked by the mighty Saatchi & Saatchi advertising agency to make a Pampers nappy ad. Don't make me say it again. They weren't looking for actors and models on this one, they explained. They wanted a genuine journalist with her own real-life child. When they found us, their first question was, 'What brand of nappies do you use?' I gave the right answer, evidently. Because this was going be what is known as 'endorsement advertising', the Advertising Standards Authority rules precluded us from being paid. We were to receive 'payment in kind', then: a year's supply of the product featured in the ad. There were not too many Cotswold cottages or Thameside apartments to be had for that.

Our real-life presence in this doubtless soon to be award-winning short was where the 'genuine' aspect of the exercise ended. We shot it over three days, commencing at a rented house in Teddington which was far too grand to be ours. The idea that a single-mum hack would be able to afford such lavishness was laughable. What on earth were they trying to say here? As for the 'styling': they had the hair and beauty police on board, who practically had to hold me down to transform me into a Stepford Wife. I sometimes look at the footage when I'm feeling bad about myself and could do with a laugh. I simply don't recognise me. I fancied myself as a bit of a rock chick in those days, but you'd never have known it from this. It shattered the image. They knotted my hair in a tight French plait down my back, put me in deputy-head outfits and painted on 'Julie Andrews in The Sound of Music' slap. My weakness in those days was buying beautiful baby clothes for Mia on my travels. Not that you'd have known it from the garish chainstore tracksuits in which they kitted out my roving reporter and her chums.

We shot days two and three at London Zoo, with said nursery friends along for the ride as 'controls'. But by far the most priceless sequence happened back in the lab, where I was required to tip test tubes of thin blue liquid into cut-out squares of nappy. This one soaks it up completely, look, while this one's still damp...

This was worse than reading out bits of nonsense script on autocue back at Ewart Television for 'Ear Say'.

A month or so after they began airing the commercial on high rotation on MTV and various Euro-channels, as well as on ITV and Channel 4 in the UK, I went to Milan to cover some A-ha gigs. My new-found, unpaid fame as a pan-European Pampers ambassador had gone before me. And I learned first-hand that revenge really is a dish best eaten cold. Morten, Mags and Pal got their own back at last on the Norwegian wood episode in their Montreux hotel three years earlier. They did so with a wicked parody of me doing the nappy ad, live on stage.

I ran into Morten again in London, some years later. He gleefully reminded me about the ad.

'It proved to us for once and for all,' he laughed, 'That British television really is crap.'

With Simon Mills, Wadi Rum, Jordan, where 'Lawrence of Arabia'
was filmed

Mamma & Mia, Sunset Marquis Los Angeles, 1991

11. MUM'S THE WORD: MADONNA

We are now entering obs-gyne territory. Squeamish males, tokophobic females and anyone inclined to panic attacks, vasovagal syncope or vomiting at the mere mention of needles and blood, please look away now. You are respectfully reminded to remain in your vehicles, keep doors locked and windows closed, and re-join us for a stiffener in Chapter Twelve.

I'd never had cause to imagine myself as a mother of three children. I hadn't expected to have babies at all. I had been pre-warned. During the Eleven Plus year at my junior school, Oak Lodge, I was felled out of the blue by a ruptured appendix. The surgeon didn't catch it before it exploded. By the time I reached theatre, it was almost too late. My bowel was perforated accidentally during the emergency Good Friday appendectomy. Laparotomy was subsequently performed. Peritonitis, or infection of the abdominal membrane, occurred as a result of the untimely nicking of my intestine. Peritoneal abscesses the size of adult jelly fish followed, which had to be siphoned off. The plastic drainage tubes clamped into open wounds required re-dressing several times a day. After the initial surgery, I had not been expected to last the night. Our local vicar, Douglas Watson from St. Francis of Assisi, West Wickham, consequently came to Farnborough hospital to conduct final prayers. I am told that I was despicably rude to him, which was unlike me. I clearly wasn't ready to check out.

My mother and I discuss all this occasionally, and it never ceases to amaze me. I'm not sure how I survived. I emerged scarred, skeletal and three-quarters bald. My hair had fallen out from shock. Extensive abdominal adhesions were impeding my internal organs. Scar tissue was pulling my ovaries and fallopian tubes in different directions, and the tubes themselves were blocked. Adhesions are a common cause of infertility, not that I knew this at the time. My mother and father were just grateful to have me back. The last thing on their minds was a future lack of grandchildren.

I didn't give much thought to any of this in the aftermath. Love and romance were never a priority, although there always seemed to be some boy or other lurking at the bus stop or swinging on the garden gate. A few months after meeting the one I presumed to be The One, I confessed to my medical history and its probable consequences. It didn't appear to put him off. We seemed all set, then. I wondered fleetingly about a wedding reception, maybe a disco in Chislehurst Caves.

Menstruation and enslavement to hormonal cycles had kicked in much later for me than for my school chums, among whom the subject was now a bloodthirsty obsession. I could never fathom the glee with which some of them fell upon Dr. White's wedges each month. The width and depth of baguettes, these 'towels' had to be looped in place on plastic hooks attached to itchy elastic sanitary belts. A rite of passage and tangible proof that we were on the verge of womanhood, certainly. But the practicalities were such a faff. The compensation was a whole new, hilarious language, which came to be known as 'Euphemish'. It was 'that time of the month'. We were 'on' or 'off', 'on the rag', having a 'leak week' or a 'shark week'. Our auntie was visiting. All our aunties were called 'Flo'. Grandma was sometimes stuck in traffic, or we had the painters in. Or we'd been to the 'slaughterhouse' (there was in those days a meat warehouse on the slope behind Bromley South station; we were sometimes obliged to wade through rivers of dead cows' blood just to get to and from school). While the Seventies were not exactly the Dark Ages, things were only just beginning to get sophisticated on the sanpro front. Internal protection (def Euphemish!) did exist, but our mothers insisted they were only for 'ladies who are married.'

You never had to ask who had the painters in. You could tell by the smell. A pungent blend of rotting fungi and ancient steak, it followed a girl around and was a sod to disguise. The school incinerators made things worse. These clanking, choking bung barbecues were mounted on the walls of all the female toilets. How humiliating to creep from a loo stall clutching a scrunched, bloodied fanny hammock wrapped in hard shiny toilet paper ready to post into the stove in front of your mates. But there was no way round it. Customised bins and discreet, perfumed disposal bags were Star Trek-worthy inventions of the distant future. The offending items were as yet completely un-flushable. A plumbing contravention would be called out in Assembly. Imagine the shame. It wasn't worth the risk. There was not yet period paraphernalia with wings, deodorising panels, self-adhesive strips or stay-dri lock-away cores. The only pads available to us were like wearing chunks of lasagne or Yorkshire pudding in your pants. The worst were encased in stringy net, which was always becoming entangled where it hurt most. Walking around with minge mattresses in our gym drawers gave us a Wild West gait akin to a waddle. By that alone, no one had to wonder who was 'on'. We saved our meagre pocket money to invest in our supplies, poor things, never imagining that there would one day be an entire, militant movement for the abolition of tampon tax.

I was almost seventeen when these shenanigans began. It didn't bother me much at first. But into my twenties, I started to experience acute menstrual pain. A consultant's advice was to have my fallopian tubes flushed with dye, to indicate whether or not the discomfort was due to a blockage. I submitted to a Hysterosalpingogram under general anaesthetic, and was told at the time that a high percentage of women become pregnant more or less immediately after having the procedure. I thought nothing of it: my default stance. 'The One' and I were still together.

I'd like to say that the pregnancy was something of a shock. The thing is, I knew. It happened on Wednesday 26th November 1986. We'd been to see Simply Red at Hammersmith Odeon. We went for a gaeng daeng afterwards at the Chaopraya Thai on St. Christopher's Place, and had (for us) a relatively early night. In my restless dream I spied a creature, part-prawn, part-human ear, with cascading Hucknell-esque russet ringlets, squirrelling into a pillowy pile of cotton wool make-up pads somewhere in the vicinity of my uterus. It seemed to be sucking its thumb and crying silently, its mouth gasping open and closed like a goldfish trapped in a parachute. When I awoke, it was the morning after. Stared at my tits and pissed myself with laughter. They wouldn't be Pinky and Perky for much longer. I knew.

A missed shark week later, I found myself researching pregnancy tests. What a subject. Perhaps unsurprisingly, the ancient Egyptians had a relatively sophisticated handle on this. Women who believed they might be pregnant would be encouraged to pee on wheat and barley seeds. If the wheat grew, it meant the woman was having a girl; if the barley sprouted instead, it was a boy; and if neither plant developed, she was off the hook for this month. Yay her. During the 10th century, things had become a little more scientific. The Persian philosopher Avicenna, for example, would test for pregnancy by adding sulphur to a woman's urine. If worms appeared in this appetising cocktail, she was declared to be carrying life. And 16th century Europeans deferred to specialists known as 'piss prophets' (I've known a few) who read urine the way gypsies read tea leaves.ˣ The PPs (see what I did there) claimed to be able to recognise by appearance alone whether the provider of the sample was with child. I was blessed, compared. All I had to do was exchange a few quid at Boots for the duff-kit, allowing me to pee on a plastic stick in the privacy of my own loo.

The One was less than thrilled. An almighty quarrel ensued. The altercation comes to mind every time I see the film 'The Parent Trap' (1998) starring Lindsay Lohan as identical twins (we watch this movie a lot.) That bit where end-of-tether Meredith wades shore-wards in a screaming rage from her sodden mattress on the lake to confront her fiancé Nick (Dennis Quaid) about the appalling behaviour of his daughters, and demands that they be shipped immediately to a distant Alpine boarding school.

'Get the picture? It's me, or them. Take. Your. Pick.'

'Them,' he says.

'Excuse me?!'

'T.H.E.M. *Them*. Get the picture?'

In an angry confrontation a few weeks after the Hucknall hoedown, I was given an equally life-changing ultimatum.

'You said you couldn't ever have children. You lied.'

'I know. No I didn't. I didn't know. The op must have done it. Isn't it wonderful?'

'No it's effing not. I don't want kids. Ever.' (The last I heard, he'd subsequently had at least two).

'You might change your mind ...'

'I never will. It's me, or it.'

'It.'

Get the picture?

I confess: I presented for the consultation and booked a termination. But I couldn't go through with it. I phoned the clinic on the day, lied that my mother had gone down with something, and said that I had to accompany her to hospital. Would I like to re-book? I did so. But when that dreaded day arrived, I again made excuses. She was telling me something. Did I mention? I already knew by then that 'it' was 'she'. 'Loretta', as she was referred to throughout the pregnancy. Close to the birth, I began calling her 'Jordan'. Thank goodness I went off that before I arrived at the Whittington hospital in Islington, however many inches (as we measured in those days) I was dilated. Jane Seymour's dad, where are you? Beyond the terrible tsunamis of contractions, for which I was given no pain relief, only gas and air (a needle in the spine? Don't come near me with that thing, you bitch-freak, stick it in your eye), and come the unendurable moment of final, forceful wrench when she seemed to swim from the flesh wreckage through buckets of blood slashed from a height all over me and the delivery table (severe postpartum haemorrhage, life-threatening, transfusion imminent, step a-way from the table), the midwife scooped and slapped this shaved-seal-looking thing onto my belly with one hand as she jabbed a massive needle into my left thigh with the other, and the baby looked at me and I looked at her, and we recognised each other, and I said ... 'Mia'...

Where did that come from?

'What d'you think you've got there, a cat or something?' bellowed the giant Jamaican midwife, reaching for a mop and bucket.

'Not miaow. *Mia*. As in Mamma Mia.'

I spelled it, and she wrote it on the chart.

I got the picture.

From then on.

For the next eight years.

Just the two of us.

All of which stood me in good stead when it came to interviewing Madonna.

I had long perceived agony and ecstasy on her face. Between the creases she would rather you didn't see. While the laughter lines around her eyes suggest a ballsy babe still well ahead of the game, her jaw speaks volumes about her slog to survive, as she clings to the sagging dreams of vanishing youth.

Sixty is sixty. Whether you've morphed into mutton or are still getting away with lamb chops, the mirror taunts, the decades haunt, and your bus pass beckons with such startling alacrity that you know it'll only be a matter of time. However dairy-free and macrobiotic her lifestyle, Madonna knows this. She knows, even as her 'sensational' latest whatever product is about to hit the stores, even with her ankles behind her ears in an ashtanga pose, even as she pounds the pavement and throws her Pilates shapes. All she can do is knock back the wheat grass and vitamins. She only smiles for the lens when she knows she's getting picture approval. Because for every Madonna portrait projecting flawless beauty, there's a pap-shot of her puckered elbows, scrawny forearms and claw-like hands.

Sixty is sixty. This was not something she could ever have imagined three decades ago when, the biggest female star on the planet, she landed in London on her 'Who's That Girl' tour for a string of European dates.

August 14, 1987. Fresh breeze, blazing sunshine. The day before, she had endured a terrifying Diana-like chase, foreign Paparazzi swarming all over Heathrow and barnacling her limo into town. Still running with the showbiz pack, despite my advanced pregnant state, I checked into the May Fair Hotel where Madonna had taken the penthouse, in the hope of landing an exclusive one-to-one chat.

Fat chance, they said. 'Fat' being the operative. I was nine days off giving birth to Loretta/Jordan/Mia. So not for me the morning jog with the hack pack around glorious Green Park. A little weight-training? I'll wait here while you train. So off dashed Madonna in her tiny black Lycra shorts with her gigantic minders, tailed by a gaggle of pathetic journalists who'd been up all night knocking back Whisky Sours in the May Fair bar. I hung around with a parcel, dressed in borrowed overalls that were supposed to make me look like a hotel porter. Knowing, because I'd been tipped off by a staffer whose palm I'd crossed with a tenner, that she would re-enter the hotel via a delivery door round the back. Ninety minutes later, we had lift-off.

Madonna did a double-take. She knew who I was. She had seen my face at press conferences. Taken aback by my shape and size, my stupid outfit and my cut-glass nerve, perhaps, staking her out and ambushing her in 'my condition', she instructed her goons to lay off. Then she sat down, wiped the sweat off with the towel around her neck, and gave me a brief, exclusive interview. Bingo.

At five feet three and considerably less than eight stone, she was tinier than I'd remembered, but she filled the place. I was massively pregnant. Madonna desperately wanted to be. This was all too clear from the way she gazed at me. She knelt down, and said, 'Is it ok?' She was asking whether she could touch me. Which was sweet: most people didn't even ask. I nodded. Smoothing her hands over my taut Space Hopper belly to feel for a kick, she even pressed her ear to the bump for a heartbeat. It dawned on me that, despite her superstar status, she was no different from any other woman. Devoted to Sean Penn, her husband at the time, she was longing to start a family.

'When's the little one due? Can't be long,' she said, smiling. 'You okay? Real hot today. Still early'.

A little hot to be running around the park, I ventured.

'It's my natural feel-good thing,' she laughed. 'I'm very energetic on stage, so I have to be fit. It goes with the territory. I've always worked out, ever since I started dancing when I was a young teenager. The dieting began ten years ago, when I was nineteen. I landed in New York City, and found I couldn't afford to eat! I couldn't gain weight again now, could I. I wouldn't know myself! It wouldn't be me. But it's dollars in the bank, ya know? It's a tough world, this business. Nobody wants a fat rock star. I have to be in shape. I wanna be in shape. So I do this. What else would I be doing for ninety minutes? Anyway, at the end, I feel great.'

How odd it seems now, to think that I sat there just inside the tradesmen's entrance of London's answer to LA's Chateau Marmont with the globally-adored Queen of Pop, while unfazed porters, valets, delivery men and janitors went about their business around us. The May Fair was Carouse Central during the Eighties. I knew its layout by heart. Short on palm trees and shimmer, maybe, but London's last word in wild. Every night at the May Fair was New Year's Eve. It was modest compared to its Hollywood counterpart. The Marmont had John Belushi's overdose, a riotous motorcycle race by Led Zeppelin through its lobby, and had been immortalised by the Eagles in a song. 'Hotel California' was once the favourite pitstop of we who earned our crusts as showbusiness writers, rousing the ghosts of Garbo, Garland and James Dean as we went. The Marmont oozed glamour like no place else. But the May Fair was home.

A few steps from Berkeley Square and louche Piccadilly, the grand edifice constructed in the 1920s in what had been the Duke of Devonshire's back garden was having its moment again. Transformed from the stuffily elegant domain which had welcomed King Edward V and Queen Mary to its original launch, the May Fair first re-invented itself in 1957, under swashbuckling Hollywood film impresarios the Danziger Brothers. Landing in London to launch the New Elstree Film Studios, they bought and converted the May Fair as a playground for their movie star pals. By the early Sixties, their establishment was the magnet of London's swinging scene, frequented by Lennon, Jagger and Dylan, Peter Sellers and Princess Margaret, Michael Parkinson and Muhammad Ali. Re-inventing itself yet again in the Eighties as a celebrity haunt, its crocodile-and-parrot-infested Beachcomber Club was unfathomable, its casino seedy, its bar a bunfight. The food was average. No one cared. Where else could you get corked with Debbie Harry at the sharp end while chewing the cud with Bowie at the other? Where better to eavesdrop on Rudolph Nureyev gossiping about dancing with the Kirov in Leningrad for the first time in decades since his defection, curling Jack Nicholson's eyebrows with indiscretions about Freddie Mercury? Bryan Ferry and Nick Rhodes from Duran Duran would sit dishing at the bar downstairs, and once or twice bought me a Screwdriver. The king of cool and the suave lounge lizard sported infinitely more make-up than I did. When the bad-asses were in town, they didn't dare go anywhere else.

It was in the May Fair that I had lolled on a bed the size of a boxing ring with Stevie Nicks in the lavish Monte Carlo suite, inhabited that same year by Michael Jackson. The same suite in which Madonna was now staying. Guarded by gold dalmatians in a pungent forest of evergreens and tiger lilies, shawl-clad Stevie had talked me through her makeshift gallery of self-portraits, the ones she painted in oils in First Class on transatlantic flights. I could tell without asking that Madonna wasn't about to invite me up. Never mind. I was getting exactly what I needed right where I was.

'I'm in this game for the long haul,' resumed my new friend. 'I need to do this for longevity in the pop world, and I do it for my husband and for our children-to-be. Of course I want children! A whole houseful of them! I'm that Fifties housewife in the cheesy dress, baking apple pie with babies around my ankles, still swooning over the guy who said 'I do'. Really! I do need a man to look up to, for reassurance, for confidence, for somebody to be the Boss. I'm traditional like that. I sometimes think it's because my mother died when I was five, and I've basically always had to do everything for myself. But also because I'm one of six children, a real close family, a Roman Catholic Italian-American for Chrissakes! But I'm really no different from you. We both do jobs. This just happens to be mine. I'll figure out a way of having children and being Madonna'.

Little did she know of her future as she squatted there, pondering a potential compromise between Penn's Hollywood career, her pop stardom and longed-for motherhood. Within months, her beautiful love affair would be over, and her short-lived marriage would be hurtling towards divorce while she dallied with crinkled playboy Warren Beatty. She had no inkling of those things as she talked excitedly about opening her tour at Roundhay Park in Leeds the next day, and her twenty-ninth birthday party at my club, the Groucho. Four nights later, she performed the first of three sell-out gigs at Wembley Stadium. On August 22, while she was on the plane to Frankfurt, I went into labour and gave birth the following day. The bouquet she sent was the size of my bed. The card read, simply, 'Madonna'.

Over the next thirty years – fluid sexuality, religion versus sex, more marriage, more divorce, S&M, childbirth, adoption, AIDS-campaigning, politics, getting yanked by her cloak off the stage at the London BRIT Awards (deliberate, for global publicity, or a genuine accident? Either way, no jokes, killer telly) – Madonna established herself as the highest-earning female singer in the world. She conceived her daughter Lourdes with her L.A. fitness trainer Carlos Leon in 1996, then married UK film director Guy Ritchie, of 'Lock Stock and Two Smoking Barrels' 'fame', in Scotland in 2000. She became the mother of two sons: giving birth to Rocco with Ritchie, and adopting David in Malawi. She later acquired Mercy, a little sister for her kids. Madge and Ritchie were both Kabbalah devotees. The family shared homes in London, New York and Wiltshire. And then it all went tits. The Ritchies divorced. Madonna carried on adopting children. She added twins called Stella and Esther, and became a mother of six. If her masterplan is to rival the so-called rainbow tribes of American-born French entertainer Josephine Baker and Angelina Jolie, she has made a cracking start.

Musically, we must give her, she has always moved with the times. She has contrived to work with the latest and the hippest. Justin Timberlake here, Timbaland and Pharrell Williams there. And it's always the usual: terrific production, contemporary feel, bland-ish lyrics. Slinky, kinky photography. An image that hangs in my mind depicts her as a corset-clad prize fighter in a ring, binding her hands with black tape. That pugilistic pose reminds us what a calculating exhibitionist she can be. According to one critic at the Los Angeles Times, 'As an exploration of female sexuality in mid-life, it's just depressing'.

What, then, are we to make of Madonna at sixty? That she is great for her age? Is she really? Her obsession with keeping young and beautiful is the very thing that has aged her. Look at Sharon Stone: same age, somewhat chubbier, seems infinitely happier, still as sexy as hell. Deep inside, won't Madonna always be a doting little housewife with a toddler on one hip, a baby at her breast and a fading dream in her heart – that her man, whoever her man is this week, is still crazy for her?

Ageing is not the thing to fear, Madge. It's the desperation of youth that you want to be worried about.

12. ROCK'N'ROLL FANTASY, OR JUST CAMP?

1989 generated more than usual to write home about. Sky television launched across Europe. The Berlin Wall was torn down. Salman Rushdie earned himself a Fatwa (not 'Fat-Wear, so not a Demis Roussos-sized undergarment) for 'The Satanic Verses'. Black Box's 'Ride on Time' cleaned up as best-selling single. That sort of thing. Meanwhile, back in real life, I was the single mother of a two-year-old, living in a flat on Barnsbury Street, Islington, directly opposite the home of two former editors of mine, Nick Lloyd and Eve Pollard. They were, indeed they remain, husband and wife. Within a year, Nick, for whom I had freelanced at the Sunday People, the News of the World and the Daily Express, would be gonged in Lady Thatcher's Resignation Honours, and would acquire the sobriquet 'Sir Lick Noyd'. What a gift! I'd have a knight of the realm and his buxom Lady to go begging a cup of sugar off, not to mention cajole into one last Ovaltine whenever insomnia got the better of me. I felt blessed. I lost count of the times that La Bollard, as she was referred to by the lower echelons of the industry on account of her elaborate embonpoint, and who at that time was Editor of the Sunday Mirror (she soon advanced to the Sunday Express) marched into the Wine Press one debauched evening, tossed her blonded coiffure in exquisite imitation of Miss Piggy, demanded that her husband depart with her 'THISSS moment!' while reminding him on the way out, just in case he had forgotten, that he had a son at home called Oliver. Her daughter Claudia Winkleman's career was at the time no more than a twinkle in her ambitious mother's and step-father's eyes. She was just seventeen. You know what I mean.

That August, Nick Gordon, my Editor at the Mail on Sunday's YOU Magazine, took me to lunch at the Savoy Grill. Over a pleasing repast of liver and bacon on the banks of the glistening Thames, among the ghosts of Oscar Wilde, Marilyn Monroe, Frank Sinatra and Winston Churchill who had been among the establishment's frequent diners, he informed me that it was time to up my game. I had to extricate myself from the clutches of fatuous celebrities, he insisted. Concern myself with more meaningful issues. Now that he and picture editor Harvey Mann were immersed editorially in the plights of two of the world's most endangered species, the African elephant in Tanzania and the silverback mountain gorillas of Rwanda, our supplement was taking a commendably more globally-conscious turn. While its remit was still to entertain with in-depth features that were 'good reads', as well as to complement the great newspaper it accompanied, I should be in no doubt that there were more important things than pop stars. That said and duly digested along with the penultimate forkful of petits pois, Nick issued me with my next brief. He was despatching me to San Francisco to be a backing singer.

Three o'clock in the morning, and it looked like it was going to be another sleepless night. Michael, the blues guitarist with the Schwarzenegger biceps, started it. He picked a fight with Diana, the multi-instrumentalist-cum-vocalist, and now all hell was breaking loose.

He referred to it mildly as a 'to-do', but it shook the entire hotel for two whole nights. The scene of the crime was the Phoenix Inn, a small salmon-and-jade-painted rock'n'roll hotel not a guitar's throw from San Francisco's Union Square. This, you could say, was the genre in the extreme: out of their minds on drink and drugs, the minutest of disagreements between these people became a major war.

The Phoenix had lodged them all in their time: Chubby Checker, Bo Diddley, the Doobie Brothers, U2, David Bowie, Billy Idol, REM. Linda Ronstadt once booked the entire hotel for seventeen nights, at a cost of around $70,000. When you're paying that kind of dough, you could fight all you liked until the cows came home. Nobody was going to bat an eyelid.

But this lot were not real rockers. They were absolute beginners. A bunch of posers looking for cheap thrills and doing their damnedest to live up to the image. Worse, they had paid for the privilege: a hefty $3,500 a head for seven days and nights to bring their rock star dreams to life. Only in the USA could this Greatest of American Dreams be fulfilled. All you needed was money, and you were into the realm of fantasy camps which would transport you beyond your wildest nightmares. It still goes on. American kids are bundled off to summer camps every July because their parents cannot bear the yelping, Coke-swilling, burger-munching brats around their necks for the entire six-week summer vacation. But the kids never kick the habit. Even when they've grown up, thousands of Americans every year pay their money to enlist at baseball camps, where they mix with major league stars and train in their favourite home stadium. It's all realistic enough: players even get fined a substantial sum for turning up late to practise. If baseball's not your bag, you can enrol in a sportscaster camp and be voice-trained by a real TV anchorman; a space camp, where you can do Neil Armstrong impersonations for a fortnight; a muscle and fitness camp, where you can suck steak, or even a cattle-drive camp, as featured so memorably in Billy Crystal's 'City Slickers' (1991). Yes, folks, you too could be Bobby Ewing for one week only. Eat sourdough biscuits and sleep out under the stars. Only $675 with your own horse ($735 without). The concept has crept here over the years, but on nothing like the scale to which Americans are accustomed.

Now, if you were a Springsteen fanatic or a Madonna-be, there was a fantasy camp to suit your needs. Which brings us back to the Phoenix Inn, San Francisco, where nine 'chosen ones' were going for it in a big way. Across the courtyard, the other female singer, Susie, was receiving into her boudoir various band members, groupies and hangers-on. A good deal of perfume was being sprayed about in Susie's room. Far be it from me to suggest the obvious, but it takes a lot of scent to drown the smell of drugs. In the good old days, it was plain old LSD that kept the San Francisco hippies happy. But that was then. By the late Eighties, you name it, they were high on it.

.Sex, drugs, rock'n'roll ...why, they even had religion. The guitarist in Susie's band was a fully paid-up Episcopal priest. That's the American branch of the Church of England to you and me. He swung with the best of them, allegedly. The good father confessed to enjoying more erotic sex since his ordination than ever in his entire pre-holy life.

There had been no shortage of applicants when the world's first-ever rock'n'roll fantasy camp was launched in the summer of '89. Faster than you could say 'sound check', the enrolment forms were pouring in by the thousand. Dudley Moore's then thirteen-year-old son Patrick was one hopeful.[xi] A sixty-seven-year-old grandmother from Detroit was another. Neither was lucky. In the end, the campers were plucked mostly at random from an infinite list. We had the afore-mentioned Michael, a brandy-swilling, loose-tongued guitarist who also blew harmonica, and who was frantically running his construction business from his bedside table. Alan, a chemistry lab assistant, drummer. Frank, a systems analyst, guitarist and vocalist. Father Phil, we already know about. Troy played keyboards and was an accountant. Kevin owned a hydraulic hose supply company and also played drums. Diana was a graphic artist by day, and Susie was a closet mother of two, who admitted to twenty-five but looked thirty-five, and was rumoured to be an actress. All human life was there – including Charles M. Young, a former Rolling Stone star writer who was covering the event for Playboy magazine, as well as contributing on bass. I really warmed to Charles, a very funny man, who had written the first-ever Sex Pistols interview in the US under the headline 'Rock is Sick and Living in London'; and who famously probed Carly Simon for a RS cover story, his subject living to regret forever having sat for the interview while breastfeeding. Unlike everyone else in the line-up, 'Chuck' did not take himself seriously. He was that rare thing, an American with an English sense of humour. We did not keep in touch, and I so wish we had. But it was all so busy in those days. Email did not yet exist. I was sad to hear of his death in New York from a brain tumour, at the age of sixty-three, in August 2014.

San Francisco was the mecca of mind-expanding trips and cerebral liberation during the Sixties. By the time I got there, there were fewer bangles-and-beads acid-heads attempting to remain upright on street corners, but one got the drift. An obsession with things avant-garde, mystical and counter-cultural at a certain level still prevailed. Zen Buddhism, astrology, revolutionary politics – you name it, they were into it, down in the city by the bay. Music in San Francisco – remember Flower Power? – had once seemed a quirky accompaniment to every deep and meaningful happening. What better place to launch the ultimate rock'n'roll fantasy?

The camp was the brainchild of Gilbert Klein, a forty-two-year-old San Francisco nightclub owner and would-be rock star. Once upon a time, he too had been just one of a million kids who gyrated nightly before their bedroom mirrors plucking at air guitars and pretending to be Elvis or Mick. Hundreds of thousands of kids like Gilbert went on to purchase real guitars and join high school bands. Virtually none of them ever became rock stars. The guitars were packed away along with the school uniforms and the baseball kit. The dreamers got on with real life. All of which set Klein thinking. Between 1960 and 1980, his research showed, more than five million electric guitars were sold in America. Where were they now, he wondered. 'Some were stolen, some were sold, but many of them were still lurking in closets,' he told me. It was the closet rock'n'rollers on which Klein had his eye, that Eureka day when he conceived his camp idea. That it ever got so far was a miracle.

So far, so good. De-jetlagged, I pitched up at the appropriate hour on the appointed day and observed the lucky campers as they were briefed, kitted out and divided into two bands, according to musical taste and ability. The groups were dubbed 'Happy Campers' and 'Woodstuck' (sic). Of the named campers, only two were female. This was where I came in. As well as covering the camp for YOU Magazine, I was assigned to do my bit as floating backing singer, alongside a tiny part-time waitress called Calli and a lanky carwash sponger by the name of Jill.

Thus began a frenzied week in which two groups of diverse individuals would stretch and mould themselves into performance-worthy bands. Come the Saturday, they would be staging live gigs to an enthusiastic crowd, albeit comprised primarily of family and friends.

The musicians took it all Very Seriously. Needless to say, I did not. With tongue firmly in cheek, I applied myself to lyric-learning and the practise of shoe moves, arm-waves, waist-wiggles and trout-faces with all the enthusiasm of the Duke of Edinburgh touring a warehouse in Tianjin. As well as a staff of fully-qualified producers and counsellors, a couple of celebrity coaches had been hauled in at stupendous expense to share some real-life experiences and to tell it as it had been. Mick Fleetwood, resplendent in a quasi-cowboy outfit with requisite reptile boots, had them hanging on his every word as if they were pearls of wisdom dripping from the lips of God. He can give the wrong impression, can Mick, as I have found down the years to my cost. But on this occasion he was friendly and even kind. Perhaps it had occurred to him that for these participants, this was a genuine fantasy, not some common or garden ego trip.

'Try and learn all you can,' he advised them. 'In this game, you are learning all the time. You never stop learning. I've been in the business for many years, and I wouldn't be in it if I didn't love it. This is a unique experience which will prove valuable to you all for years to come. If you get a little taste of the magic of rock'n'roll, treasure it.' Which told them a lot. Mick declared Kevin the drummer to be 'exceptional'. He presented him with a pair of his own drumsticks with 'Mick Fleetwood' embossed down the sides. We were suitably impressed.

The next day, in a scruffy rehearsal studio on the frayed edge of town, Starship guitarist Craig Chaquico arrived to impart his version of rock wisdom. He sure looked the part: tanned and muscular, his shaggy brown hair cascading to his shoulders, his lean frame eased into jeans, black vest and baseball boots. He sat plucking meaningfully at a bright yellow guitar. He was planning, he confided, to share tips on what to do if you played a wrong note, or how to deal with your leather pants splitting up the front on stage.

The campers appeared more relaxed with Craig than they had with Mick. They asked questions such as 'Do you still take the croutons off your salad before you eat it?', 'How do you throw guitar picks into the audience?' and 'What do you do when someone in the band gets really out of it?'

'Fire them!' smiled Craig. 'Or try to be totally adult about it, and give them more money.'

He acknowledged the campers' collective predicament with sensitivity. 'You guys are compressing this whole rock'n'roll experience into seven days. It could blow your minds, ya know? Have you had any love-triangle experiences yet? You know, two guys after the same girl?' Everyone looked sheepish.

Back to work. The musicians slogged hard for the money they'd spent. They did a little recording, dubbing and mixing, and attended a few seminars, but for most of the week it was practise, practise, practise. Then the big day loomed, and was suddenly upon us.

Come Saturday, Susie was in the doghouse for missing most of the dress rehearsal, having swanned off to buy an outfit for her big night. The camp administrators were furious, and forced her to apologise to each band member in turn. The new dress, mysteriously, never showed up. Susie wound up performing in the same studded bra that had seen her through all but the dress rehearsal.

That night, the Full Moon Saloon was alive and kicking. Hundreds of rock fans who had won tickets in a radio competition converged on the venue, along with rock scenesters and the obvious family and friends. There was all the usual paraphernalia of the live gig: monitors, amps, mics, security hunks on the doors, the lot. Even a free bar. For a fleeting moment, at least. Back at the Phoenix, nerves were tuned to breaking point. Both bands (including your friendly, hapless neighbourhood pretend backing singers) were to travel to the gig in the same limo, one after the other. Suddenly, yay, some real rock politics kicked in. Frank and Susie of the Happy Campers had a scrap on the back seat, with Frank insisting that he'd be the one to get out last, and Susie claiming the same privilege. In rock mythology, last one out is leader of the pack. When it was their turn, Woodstuck played out the exact-same scene. Not only did Diana, newly fetching in a little black number she had stitched herself, insist on alighting last, but she made the chauffeur help her.

The end result was fairly predictable. Diana, despite being so highly-strung, rose to the occasion, gave a relatively thrilling performance, sang the best songs (can I remember what they were? Not really), and was by far the most professional. Sure, she jumped up and down a bit, but only in her own space. Susie, on the other hand, was utterly obnoxious. She bounced, she strutted, she crouched – to peer at her lyrics which were taped to a monitor, mostly. Post-gig, she would even have the front to admit it: 'Why waste your time learning lyrics when you can tape them to a monitor?' Calli, Jill and I found ourselves wishing that we'd thought of it. Not that we did too badly at BVs on the night. We'd had zero experience, remember. Badass Susie just ignored us. She was too busy teasing, nuzzling, undressing and hogging the limelight. All of which she did rather well. She even stood centre-stage during the drum solo, until the stage manager managed to knock her off-balance by flicking ice cubes from the wings right at her breasts.

Oh what a night. The grand finale saw both bands on stage together led by Gilbert Klein himself, who was living out his own extraordinary fantasy. He seemed almost carried away by the excitement. 'It's his heart, poor thing,' someone muttered. As if two sets of the most obvious covers had not been enough, the bands and Gilbert launched into 'Wild Thing', and almost went berserk trying to outdo each other.

And so to the farewell breakfast. Much hugging, kissing, back-slapping and mutual admiration, genuine or otherwise. Even those sporting the most serious hangovers had made it. Only Father Phil was missing. It being Sunday, he had three sermons to preach. The vision of him ascending into his pulpit with 'Back in the U.S.S.R.', 'Not Fade Away' and 'Purple Haze' ringing in his ears will stay with me for life.

Gilbert, meanwhile, was eagerly taking bookings for the following year, watching dollar signs rotating before his eyes. This year San Francisco, tomorrow the world... 'One good question I was asked was how we'd decide which band would get top billing on the night,' he said. 'I was trying to be cute when I answered it, but I only understood what I was saying about halfway through the sentence. I responded that we'd have to decide that at the rock'n'roll managers' camp ...'

For the campers, it was back to reality armed with cassettes, videos, tour jackets (I still have mine), laminated passes, beer mats, pens, and every imaginable souvenir. Always something there to remind them. It had been a hard day's night, they had worked like dogs and had paid heavily for the privilege, but without exception they thought it had been worth every cent. My own reluctant fantasy had quickly run its course. Singing in front of a crowd (if they could call it singing), imagining myself making people feel as so many others had made me feel: crikey. Who was I trying to kid? It didn't inspire me towards a career change, put it that way. It was an alley I would not revisit again.

But isn't that the point of a fantasy: that it should never become reality? Isn't the longing sweeter than the having? Isn't it always better to travel than to arrive? What was that line of Joan Cusack's to Melanie Griffith in 1988's 'Working Girl'?

'Sometimes I dance around my apartment in my underwear. Doesn't make me Madonna. Never will.'

Looking back all these years later on that wildest of weeks, I finally get those people. I was too young and inexperienced to understand them at the time. Now I know that there was nothing wrong with them, and that I had no right to ridicule them. They simply had a dream, which they were trying to fulfil. We all have dreams, don't we? We deserve them as much as the next guy. As Marilyn Manson wrote, 'When all of your wishes are granted, many of your dreams will be destroyed.'[xii] In other words, some dreams ought not to be pursued. Because fantasies always end happily ever after. Reality rarely does. The dice keep on tumbling.

The rock star fantasy is a classic. It has little to do with becoming an actual rock idol, being brilliant and revered by millions around the world. It is a simple plea for acknowledgement and appreciation. In real life, as close personal relationships become our adult reality, such fantasies should fade into the backdrop. They should become memories that we can take down from the top shelf of our minds once in a while, like the threadbare rabbit we once hugged ourselves to sleep with every night, and indulge in for old time's sake. But they must no longer be a dominant, forceful need.

13. THE HEAVYWEIGHTS OF HARMONY

I had to wonder about some of the stories I was sent on. They knew my strengths and weaknesses. Were they testing me or sending me up? Having left behind the vindictiveness and dishonesty of the Daily Mail, and having stepped off the freelance misery-go-round to take my chances with Nick Gordon at YOU – who had expressed a wish to 'raise my game' and get me writing about anything but pop and rock – I was sometimes baffled by their unconventional choices. It wasn't all Nick. There were at least a dozen commissioning editors around the table at YOU, fielding demands from PRs, setting up the un-set-up-able, pestering the Palace, placating Richard Branson, freaking out Number Ten, dropping the phone on Janet Street-Porter, bombarding the White House, briefing feature writers, tweeking travel arrangements and assigning the right photographer for the job. All this was a bustling industry in itself: just one of many competing colour supplements. Suffice it to say that we were never bored. Although I was always briefed, I was often none the wiser as to what I was off to get. There were times when it wasn't until after I'd done the research, travelled to the destination, pitched up to conduct the interviews, transcribed the tapes and taken an overview of the material that pennies dropped and I got the point. They were moments to cherish.

Olga the Argentinian masseuse had never seen anything like it.

'My table, she is groaning under the weights,' she lamented as she pummelled the life out of me. 'These are big womans. *Big* womans. I guess maybe I think they need much fat to sing.'

Olga was referring to the legion of females who had descended for the week on the luxurious spa hotel where she earned her living.

'They swept through here like a heavyweight hurricane. The bulk were buying in bulk,' quipped a slender sales lady behind the perfume counter in Bloomingdales. You could say that Miami didn't know what had hit it. One minute it was business as usual for the capital city of the state they refer to as 'God's waiting room', Florida's population tending towards the geriatric. The next minute, like Olga's massage bench, it was wheezing beneath the weight of some eight thousand extra females.

This was the forty-fourth international convention of the Sweet Adelines, American womanhood's answer to the male barbershop quartet movement. The name is taken from a barbershop tune popular many moons ago: 'You're the flower of my heart, sweet Adeline.'

The girls' version was founded in 1945 in Tulsa, Oklahoma, by a bunch of housewives who wanted to sing 'chord-ringing, fun-filled, men-only music.' By the end of that first year, they had eighty-five members. The ball was rolling. They had their first chapter. Two years on, the debut national convention was born. From that moment on, God help us, Sweet Adelines Inc grew in leaps and bounds. By 1989, when I joined them in Florida, there was a devoted international membership of over thirty thousand, with chapters in Australia, Japan, the UK, Canada, New Zealand, the Netherlands, Panama, Germany and Sweden, as well as in all fifty American states. Prospective chapters had begun forming in such far-flung corners as the Cayman Islands and Peru. They even had their own monthly magazine, The Pitch Pipe.

Barbershop harmony, in case you're wondering, is unaccompanied vocal harmony sung by four voices: lead, tenor, baritone and bass. The songs tend to have simple lyrics and accessible melodies. Local chapters were divided into choruses, some with up to two hundred members. The choruses divided down into individual quartets. Both choruses and quartets would compete and entertain nationally and internationally. I'd been despatched to Miami to see what all the fuss was about.

10am and the temperature was rising. It was hardly surprising. These women were so hefty, the lagoon-shaped pool had stretch marks. They were practising in, of all places, the water.

'The more you drink, the better they sound,' mumbled somebody's husband. All eyes on him. He was that rare thing, the spouse who dared to accompany his wife on a Sweet Adelines convention. Most of the dames were there solo. It was, after all, their once-a-year opportunity to get away from him indoors and the kids. Most self-respecting husbands would not have been seen dead there.

'We've saved up all year round to be here,' said the ladies from the Great Lakes Chorus, Sterling Heights, Michigan. At an average of £600 per housewife – back then – this was no mean feat for most of them. Money was raised by 'doing' personal appearances and performing at local events back home. When choruses were competing, the money was pooled for the common cause. A fulsome five from Great Lakes gathered for an individual practice session in the shallow end of the pool. They had all had their hair done in readiness for that night's big night, when all the choruses were to perform for each other. They didn't even attempt to swim, in case their beehives got a soaking. They simply splashed around a bit while they sang.

Over at the Tiki bar, all dolled up in red and black and raring to go, Karen, Kerri, Sheri and Cindy from Beaumont, Texas were flashing scarlet lips and bright blue eyeshadow.

'Give us a song!' yelled a bare-bellied grandad from a side-table. The ladies obliged without further ado, with 'The Boogie-Woogie Bugle Boy from Company B.' None of them needed asking twice. Should anyone express the slightest interest in their singing, they were up on their feet and at it with 'Mr Sandman' before you could change your mind.

12.30pm found Pearl and Marianne from Chicago in their best polyester frocks, indulging in a late breakfast or an early lunch. They couldn't decide which. Being Queens of Harmony – that is, one-time members of a quartet who had won the international convention contest and had ascended to the grandest chorus of them all, the Coronet Club – they were entitled to wear their tiaras at all times. And wear them they did: in the cafeteria, on the street, on the beach, in the pool ...

'I'm the only one in this entire organisation who has never missed a convention,' seventy-six-year-old Pearl told me proudly. 'We won our first back in 1949.' She waved a hand at her companion, eighty-year-old Marianne, a part-time movie extra. 'These past forty years have been the happiest of my life. Everywhere in the world we go, we meet new friends.'

3pm, and the choruses were lining up for a quick few scales before they queued for the buses that would transport them to the concert hall. There were Phyllis, Marje and Durene from Minneapolis in frothy pink frocks, searching everywhere for the rest of their chorus. And there were Bev and Judy in pink, black and white gowns that vaguely resembled piano keyboards, from the River Blenders chapter, Missouri. Linda, Dee, Chris, Nonie, Ewlie, Midge and Gerry, resplendent in buttercup frills and turquoise garters, hailed from Eugene, Oregon. Another bunch calling themselves Sterling Affair from Massachusetts were done up like so many Roy Rogerses, with neckties and blue silk shirts. They looked, when compared to the thousands in sequins and frills, rather butch.

'Between us, we four have been married for ninety-two years,' confided Claire, their tenor. 'This is the great escape from our old men.'

It was much more than that. It was a mass annual hen party, the ultimate Girl Guide camp. A gathering of gentle, like-minded females, most of them at least middle-aged, who had never been able to shake off the need to belong to a club.

'Sweet Adelines can be the best thing to happen to a woman,' reasoned Bev, a painted doll. 'You're making her dress up, make up, perform a little, dance a little. You're getting her to look at herself in a different way. It's a huge challenge, and an enormous confidence boost. It gives a new outlook to the woman who normally only bakes cookies, does the laundry and does what her husband tells her to. As women's roles are changing in the world today, the Sweet Adelines must change with it.'

Every night was Ladies' Night here, but that night was a bit special. It was the Coronet Club's performance, every past winner for the price of one. And it was harder to bag a ticket than a Miami Beach hotel room. The crowd at the Steven Muss concert hall was 'capacity'. The de rigueur look was 'spangled': sequins, Lurex, chiffon and diamanté in tide-turning amounts, with false eyelashes and hairspray compulsory.

Along the hall in the Poodle Lounge, a few sweet hours short of dawn, the sleek black entertainer who used to be a Platter but was all right now was getting on down to 'My Way'. He sported a grubby white tux, was a little frayed around the edges, and they were charging double for drinks. But it was either that or 'Rhapsody in Blue' split four ways and punctuated with sequins and giggles. 'My Way', hands down.

But it was ignorant of me to dismiss the Sweet Adelines because the sound they made was not to my taste. I cannot sing and I have never played any instrument, so what do I know? All these years later, now that I've learned to appreciate music properly, I find all genres of it much more fascinating than celebrities. In barbershop, the lead sings the melody, the tenor and bass harmonise from above and below, and the baritone completes the chord. The most distinctive element in this form of music is the 'overtone', also known as 'expanding sound' or the 'ringing chord', in which sound waves interact with each other to create a fifth voice over and above the basic four. The overtone is sometimes referred to as 'the angel's voice'. All four voices are equally vital to produce the fifth. Leave out any of them – lead, bass, tenor or baritone – and the magic fails to happen. It demonstrates, simply and perfectly, why barbershop can be regarded as a metaphor for life. You get out more than what you put in, if you take time and trouble enough to do it right.

Sweet Adelines International are today one of the world's most recognised singing organisations for women. In October 2009, they set the Guinness World Record for the largest singing lesson in history, in Nashville Tennessee. 6,651 singers took part.

14. THAT OLD GREY MAGIC : FRANK SINATRA

Francis Albert Sinatra never gave interviews. True, there were a few kicking around in the archives and cuttings libraries, such as the famous 1963 Playboy Magazine encounter that people still talk about. But even that's a fake, having been ghosted by a publicist who never sat down with the crooner to quiz him face to face. The public doesn't always get what the public wants.[xiii]

Frank made no secret of the fact that he despised the ladies and gentlemen of the press. This despite a youthful yearning to become a sportswriter. Who knew. According to my father, who should know, Frank had once worked as a copy boy on the Jersey Hudson Observer, a small local paper in his home state; and, in 1971, was briefly a card-carrying sports photographer for Life Magazine, covering a globally-anticipated Ali-Frazier brawl. One of his photos even made it onto the cover. The achievement was not enough to convince him of the merits of a complete career change. After decades of rumoured Mafia involvement, fearsome feuds and murderous conduct aided and abetted by his one-time back-street abortionist mother Dolly, aka the 'Queen of Hoboken', he had discerned that it was in his best interests to hang below the parapet when not on stage. Plenty to hide. Plus, it wasn't as if he needed to flog himself to the media. His tickets and countless albums sold themselves.

'We need to get an interview with Sinatra,' said Nick Gordon.

Was he off his rocker? My war-zone survival hadn't been enough for him? I'd obviously celebrated my escape from the Gulag too soon. Once a Mailman, always a Mailman. Nick appeared to have made a seamless transition from associate editor on daily rag to highly-rated colour supplement chief without too much bloodshed or psychiatric interruption. But the madness was still simmering beneath the surface, clearly. He had failed to shed the absurdity and irrationality which had infested him over there. A brilliant, visionary newspaper man – some called him 'a chip off the old David English block', but he was better than that – he should have risen to become Editor-in-Chief of a national, not been put out to grass on a mag. As generous and encouraging as he was to me at a time when I was finding my feet as a working single mother with an international remit, he was also unpredictable, mercurial, and at times hideously behaved. I adored him, but honestly. Out of the frying pan, then. 'How on earth are we going to do that?' I said.

'Ask him.'

'Come on, Nick. You know the answer. His management and publicists take great delight in saying no. Unless they're feeling generous that day, in which case they just tell you to fuck off.'

'This is not a polite request, by the way.'

'How unlike you.'

'Ever met him?'

As it happened, I had. The first time was in September 1980, at the Royal Albert Hall in London. Frank strode out onto the stage at the start of the show, ambled across to the orchestra stalls where my father I were applauding from our front-row seats, and sang the opening verse of 'Fly Me to the Moon' straight at me. It's true. Ask my dad. Old Blue Eyes locked with Young Green Eyes, and that was it. I was sold. It had long been a habit of Frank's, I would later discover, to zoom in on some random female in a concert audience to sing the first song to. Thanks to my parents, I had grown up on his voice. I knew the albums by heart. Something crystallised in that moment, the night our eyes first met. I had long appreciated Sinatra. I was now a fan.

His love affair with England was still in full bloom. Like elderly ex-lovers meeting under the clock at Waterloo once a year for old times' sake, it was a relationship he could never quite let go. London had been under his skin since the early 1950s, when hysteria among the bobbysoxers first earned him a place in the pantheon. Information about Sinatra in the UK until the early Sixties was scant. The result was a British music-loving public hungry for news about a singer they couldn't get near. Sinatra fan clubs began mushrooming all over the country long before his records were released here. Every import became an instant collectible. Those fans remained loyal for life, converging to catch him in his acclaimed Royal Albert and Festival Hall concerts. He thanked them with the only Sinatra album ever made outside America, recorded in London. 'Sinatra Sings Great Songs from Great Britain' featured gems by the British composers he most admired, including Noel Coward's 'I'll Follow My Secret Heart', Ivor Novello's 'We'll Gather Lilacs in the Spring', and Ross Parker's and Hughie Charles's enduring war-time rouser for Vera Lynn, 'We'll Meet Again'. The recordings were made in 1962 at CTS Studios in

London W2. Only days before he began taping in Bayswater, the Beatles were convening a couple of miles over the pass at Abbey Road. The times they were a-changin'.

The second time was in July 1990 at the London Arena, which the excellent journalist Richard Williams so memorably described as 'an aircraft hangar marooned on the Isle of Dogs'. The venue, which had opened with a gig by Duran Duran, was owned by boxing promoter Frank Warren. Nine years later, he would become Godfather to my youngest child at her baptism in St. Bride's, Fleet Street, accompanied by his bodyguard. Every girl needs a maverick in her life. Warren's dream had long been to present his idol and namesake in concert in London. It was almost as if he had built the arena for that purpose. I had no idea what the purse was, but you could bet it took more than two of them to carry it home. Four nights on Frank's 'A Summer Affair' seventy-fifth birthday tour were staged there. Tickets were a tidy £75 apiece. You could go on holiday for that in those days. Frank's son Sinatra Jnr conducted the Woody Herman Orchestra. We sang along to 'One for My Baby', 'Strangers in the Night' 'My Way' and more, and crammed into an understage corridor afterwards, to pay our respects. Oblivious of everyone around me, what I wanted to say to him was, 'That was phenomenal out there tonight, Mr. Sinatra, thank you. And you probably don't remember this, but you sang to me on stage at the Albert Hall ten years ago. I have never forgotten it.' What came out was 'fernermehneugh.' He said nothing at all in response, of course. He just looked at me as though I were an open door.

There always has to be a hook to hang a feature on. This was it: the seventy-fifth birthday, that December, of one of the best-selling recording artists of all time. Frank had neatly sidestepped interviews during the London Arena shows, but Nick was going to make him give one now. That is, Nick was going to make me make him. What my wretched boss had in common with virtually every other editor who had ever cried 'Write it!' was wanting what he could not have. The mountain wasn't coming to Muhammad. My task was to find out where he'd be blowing the candles out, and get myself invited. I lost a little sleep over this. You are not in the least surprised.

There is always a PR who owes you a favour. On this occasion, it was the big one. The Rogers and Cowan agency in Los Angeles were handling Frank's big birthday bash at the Beverly Hilton Hotel. It just so happened that I'd agreed not to expose a couple of bits of outrage which they were desperate to keep dark, in exchange for some appropriate exclusive when the time was right. And we're off.

The gala event was to be hosted by the Society of Singers, launched by one-time songstress Ginny Mancini, wife of Henry Mancini. Old man H. had won twenty Grammys and four Oscars, and was one of the greatest composers in movie history ('The Pink Panther' theme, 'Moon River' from 'Breakfast at Tiffany's', 'Victor Victoria', on and on). This was not amateur night. They were also going to give Frank a lifetime achievement award, 'the Ella'. The gong had been awarded only once before, to the First Lady of Song, Miss Fitzgerald herself, after whom the trophy was named. Ella had been nominated to present it. There was plenty of potential. I repaired to LA, walked off the plane and right onto the guest list.

In the vast, glass-paned lobby of the Beverly Hilton, guests were running the gauntlet towards the International Ballroom and getting assaulted by menacing TV hosts en route. Dressed to kill, I hung around and tried to act natural. Frank could still pull the crowds, evidently, but this lot were not as energetic as they'd once been. They shuffled. They doddered. They came on bended knee. Some hobbled, clearly in pain, and had to be assisted. Some made it on their own with the help of a walking frame. Others looked as though they might snuff it during dinner, and were never going to make it home.

Most of the guests had paid $350 a head for the privilege. Despite this, the dinner had been sold out for months. In addition, VIP tables costing $25,000, $10,000 and $3,500 had been snapped up within hours by Hollywood's biggest names. Who paid most? No one was saying. It was an expensive way to eat pasta, steak, salad and cheesecake (Mr. Sinatra's favourite, flown in specially for the occasion from Chicago). But they did throw in the odd free chocolate piano. There were also gold-wrapped gifts to take away (and how Hollywood loves a goody-bag): a Sinatra tee-shirt, a pair of his CDs, a picture postcard of him, and perfume courtesy of Revlon.

The outfits! There were more sequins, froth and unfathomable cloth than in a Tooting taffeta shop. Feathers, fringes, real fur galore. Beads, brocade, lace, embroidery, sapphires, diamonds, emeralds, rubies. Wall-to-wall pearls, every one of them real, which was more than could be said for the flesh and blood. It was a disturbing thing to behold. So much surgery, so many toupées, wigs, facelifts, prosthetic implants, nose jobs, boob lifts, synthetic teeth and false fingernails at a single sitting (and some of them boasted the lot).

I collared the grand old dame herself, as she made her entrance. Tell me, Miss Fitzgerald, why do you love Frank Sinatra?

'Oh,' she twittered, 'me and Frank, we go a long way back. He's come a long way, baby. He's the greatest. He's got a great personality, and he always tells you exactly what he thinks. He says it like it is. And he can sing to the stars.'

In trooped Cesar Romero, 'the Joker' in the original 'Batman' TV series; actress Polly Bergen, singer Helen Reddy, and Donald O'Connor: Gene Kelly's best friend and pianist Cosmo Brown in 'Singin' in the Rain' (1952), the one who sang 'Make 'em Laugh'. And in wafted Pia Zadora, whom I was excited to see. A stunning celebrity of calculable talent, Pia was the subject of the best denigration legend in Hollywood. An oft-repeated anecdote had her playing the lead in a Broadway production of 'The Diary of Anne Frank'. Her acting was said to have been so poor that, come the interval, the fans had had enough. During the first scene in the second act, Nazi soldiers rushed on stage, chucked furniture around and shouted, 'Where is she?!' Whereupon the entire audience yelled in unison, 'She's in the attic!' I relished that bad-actress story. I was looking forward to reminding her of it. It was just as well that a Rogers and Cowan representative rushed forwards to escort her to her table. Years later, I would discover that not only had Pia Zadora never had a starring role in 'The Diary of Anne Frank'; she hadn't had so much as a bit part in any production of it. Neither on or off-Broadway nor anywhere else. It was totally apocryphal. It thrills me beyond words to set the record straight.

Merv Griffin, dripping in diamond bracelets, was swanning about as though he owned the place. He did. He had one hand glued to Eva Gabor's rump. Eva was wearing a grin so fixed, you couldn't help but wonder where his other hand was. Barry Manilow whipped off his specs for a photo opportunity with singing duo Steve Lawrence and Eydie Gormé, tripping over their large feet in the process. Sean Connery and his wife Micheline alighted from a gleaming Rolls to join the bunfight. Mrs Connery's face declared a preference for the dentist's chair. In floated Jackie

Collins on the arm of husband Oscar Lerman, eyes everywhere, probably plotting a scene for her next novel. In the middle distance lurked sex thimble Dudley Moore and third wife Brogan Lane. 'Divorce? What divorce?' she cooed sweetly, when I asked her. 'She dropped the charges,' smiled Dud, as his wife mock-strangled him. They untied the knot shortly afterwards.

Carol Channing (is it a woman? Is it a man? Is it a waxwork? Is it still belting out 'Hello Dolly'?) was wearing false eyelashes with a mind of their own. Her lips had stretch marks, and her chest was heading for her shoes. She looked as though she had been exhumed for the occasion. Here was 'Police Woman' actress Angie Dickinson in turquoise sequins. There was multi-millionaire founder of Playboy Magazine, Hugh Hefner, with Kimberley, his nubile bride. He was proud to tell me, he murmured, that she was twenty-seven years old. 'My pals said to me, "You can't marry that girl, Hef, she's only fourteen!" I know, I said... but she *looks* twelve.'

Charles Bronson, Tony Bennett, Sylvester Stallone and Harry Connick Jnr dutifully trooped in. The latter being the one they were all hailing as the next Sinatra. By the look on his face, he was hoping not to have to inherit the title that night.

The privileged few with red badges were suddenly hustled into a presentation room to witness the man of the moment receiving his award. Through the milling throng, we made it just in time. No television cameras thank you very much. Yes, you can take pictures (I did). Frank, his wife Barbara and Ginny swept in. Frank looked fit, cool and up for it.

'Frank! FRANK!'

'Yeah! Whassamaddawithya! You don't need to shout, buddy, my ears are still workin'.'

'Frank! How do you feel about this award?'

'Yeah, well. I'm thrilled. I love to be given things like this. I'm delighted.'

'Frank! How do you feel about being seventy-five?'

'I'm still alive, aren't I?'

In rolled Ella. Frank moved forward to help her onto the dais. She clawed onto him for dear life, and nearly yanked him off the side in the process.

'I'm just so delighted to be anywhere with this wonderful lady, whom I've loved and adored since I was a child,' he said graciously.

'Uh-huh!' cooed Miss Fitzgerald, by way of acknowledgement, munching on her bottom lip.

'I rode in his car many years ago,' she added, for comic effect.

'Yeah,' recalled Frank, 'and she paid for the gas!'

And that was it! Meet-and-great over, no sooner than we'd arrived. The geriatrics helped each other from the stage, and the photographers were shown the door. It was now or never. There was only one thing for it as Frank prepared to leave.

'Mr Sinatra, Sir!'

'NO interviews! Mr. Sinatra does NOT give interviews! *Please!*' A couple of apes leaned in to airlift me towards the exit.

Mr. Sinatra tossed them a stare that said, 'Put her back down!', then looked directly at me. I stood hoping that he remembered we'd met before. Yeah, right.

'You're English, huh?' he said. 'Well, thank you for coming. I love your beautiful country. I wish I could be back there. I'll probably go back soon, to perform at my hall.'

He meant the Royal Albert Hall. Having been christened 'Francis Albert', he always referred to the venue as his.

'There will be no more come-backs, no more retirements, no more coming out of retirements. I'm just gonna keep going now, until I drop.'

'Until the final curtain, Sir?'

'Until the final curtain, yeah! They're gonna have to carry me off in a box. Every time I go on stage, I love it, and so does the audience. Over the years, it has become a love affair between me and them. An affair that's so special, I just can't end it. You know, I could go on stage and make pizza, they'd still come to see me! So I'm not going anywhere. I'd be insane to give it all up now.'

'I saw you perform with Liza Minnelli and Sammy Davis Jnr at the Royal Albert Hall last year,' I blurted. 'I wept all the way through' (which I did).xiv

'So did I!' chuckled Frank. 'I couldn't remember the words! Sammy and Liza had to busk it. They were the real pros, not me. I was devastated when Sammy died (shortly after that tour concluded). He knew he was dying back then, and so did we. But you never expect it to come to that. We all think we'll live forever. That world tour was so much fun, we never wanted it to end. We wanted Dean Martin to come out with us too, so we could be the old Rat Pack again. We called him all the time from the road, begging him to join us, but he never would. The sadness is now we'll never do it. Sammy's gone.'

The guy from Rogers and Cowan looked set to give birth. We were as yet some years ahead of such medical miracles. But Frank seemed relaxed, and happy to keep talking. I wasn't giving up now. Did he have any remaining ambitions, I wondered, or had he really done it all? He looked pensive for a moment. He caressed his famous silver hairpiece, then rubbed his chin.

'I'd like to make one more film,' he said seriously. 'And I'd love to have an exhibition of my paintings. What do I paint? Let's see ...desert scenes. In oils. Sounds boring, doesn't it? But the colours of the desert fascinate me. It's not all just so much sand. Not at all. I never sell the pictures, no. I just give them away to friends and charities. I live out in Palm Springs, and I have my own studio. I love views, vistas. I've been to so many places in the world, and I carry these views in my head wherever I go. I'm a creature of habit. I always go back to all the same hotels, so that I can see how the skyline has changed in my absence.'

Then he smiled, gave a theatrical half-bow and was on his way – ushered by his mob of publicists and security guys through maybe a dozen back-route sets of doors into the ballroom for his party. It was a gay old time. Frank appeared to drink more than most, from a full bottle of Jack Daniels' placed before him. Why break the habit of a lifetime? It hadn't killed him yet.

It is not every day that Ol' Blue eyes tells a kid he is going to be the biggest star in the world. So when he made that prediction about Harry Connick Jnr, you had to sit up and listen. Which we did.

'Would you believe it: somebody said that about me, once,' Frank said to me. 'To name names, if you're askin', it was Bing Crosby. He'd look at me, and wink as he said, 'a talent like that comes along once in a lifetime. Why the hell in my lifetime?'

So in awe of his idol was Harry that when he took to the stage to sing 'More Than the Greatest Love', his tribute to the birthday boy, panic took hold and he forgot the words.

'That was the best, and the worst, night of my entire life,' a cringing Connick would tell me in Atlantic City the following May, when I interviewed him during his sell-out world tour ahead of his dates at the Royal Albert Hall.

Frank's face during the finale said it all. Up there on stage with the line-up, giving it the works, clapping, swinging, rocking and rolling, wiping tears, kissing and getting kissed by all who could reach him. There was lipstick all over his cheeks, a lump the size of a golf ball in his throat, and a twinkle to eclipse the best in his faded, fantastic blue eyes. He took the mic.

'On behalf of everyone here, just ... thanks for coming,' he choked. 'And if you have the tendency not to want to go home, there's a bar outside. I'll see you there.'

Sinatra hadn't revealed anything to rock the world. But he had given the chick from YOU magazine the time of day. He had talked to me. We had our exclusive interview. Nick was a dog with two dicks. He ran the feature across four full-colour pages, as two double-page spreads. A single spread was the Holy Grail for any Mail hack, the rainbow's crock, the thing we all aspired to but rarely reached. Half a dozen of us celebrated the sensational coup over a posh dinner at Holland Park's Halcyon Hotel. The following week, he sacked me.

Ella Fitzgerald, Frank Sinatra, Ginny Mancini, Beverly Hilton Hotel, Los Angeles, 3 December 1990. Frank & Ella later sang 'The Lady is a Tramp' together.

15. THEY TRIED TO MAKE ME GO TO REHAB

The editor was confused. My contract with YOU, which had been dictated and signed by him personally, guaranteed me a minimum of twenty feature commissions a year and prevented me from contributing to their closest rivals: the colour supplements of the Sunday Express and the Sunday Times. I was not allowed to write for the Daily Mail, but there would be the occasional cross-over into the Mail on Sunday – if, for example, a feature turned out to have a hot news angle that wouldn't wait. In those days, colour sups were planned and commissioned-for up to six weeks in advance. Most non-industry folk appear to believe that the Daily Mail and its Sunday sister are one and the same; that they share executives, advertising and editorial staff, offices and printing facilities, and that they are completely interchangeable. They are not. Both titles belong to the same proprietor: in our day Vere Harmsworth, third Viscount Rothermere and last of the great English press barons, who was joined at the hip to Sir David English. Today, it is his son Jonathan, the fourth Viscount. The 'firm', in those days, was known as Associated Newspapers. It went on to be called DMG. The papers do indeed share offices and printing facilities. But they were then, as they are today, autonomous in virtually every other way. Not only that, but they compete viciously with each other for the best splashes, the greatest news exclusives, the most knockout, eff-off features. It is a rare, distinguished writer who gets away with working for both simultaneously. The lesser spotted scribe has been known to get through the net too.

My contract contained no clause to preclude me from contributing to the 'red-tops', the ''bloids' or so-called 'downmarket tabloids', including the Sun, the Daily Star, the Daily Mirror, the Sunday Mirror, the Sunday People and the News of the World. With this in mind, if an interview threw up something a little too racy for the pages of YOU Magazine, but which was likely to 'make' elsewhere, it was common, accepted and perfectly legitimate practice for contracted freelance writers to cart the cutting-room sweepings along the metonymical Street.[xv] A blind eye was turned to the fact that Associated had coughed for the travel, accommodation and subsistence expenses in the first place. This does seem a bit of a cheek, now that I come to write about it. But it was the way that everyone operated at the time. Believe me, there was far worse going on. A friend of mine on a national Sunday was regularly disgruntled by the failure of his best exclusives to make the pages of the organ for which he wrote, only to see the very same stories pop up in one of its biggest and most bitter rivals the following week. He could only conclude that his own editor was flogging said exclusives and cheating his star reporter for personal gain. As in, a sizeable cash backhander. The reporter never took this to Management. He could never have proved it anyway. But it did indeed turn out to be the case. How did he know? The buyer himself let slip to the reporter personally, after he and the underhand editor agreed on a terminal falling-out.

Mr. Gordon was delighted with my copy on Stevie Nicks. The interview with the Fleetwood Mac superstar, detailing riveting aspects of her hitherto private life, was conducted in her surreal suite at London's May Fair hotel. It concerned itself primarily with her deliverance from drug-addiction, thanks to a last-ditch stay at the Betty Ford Center in Rancho Mirage, California. The clinic was founded by the former American First Lady, wife of thirty-eighth US President Gerald Ford, in October 1982, when she decided to do something about her own diazepam addiction and alcohol dependence. If in doubt, open a clinic, stick your name on it, do good for one and all in similar boats.

The editor's delight soon dissolved into dismay when he happened upon a story in that week's News of the World, under the banner headline:

'I HAD 4 ABORTIONS SAYS FLEETWOOD MAC BEAUTY'

He called me.

'Why didn't we get this?'

'Get what?'

'Steamy Nicks's abortions.'

'I did get it. The abortions were outside the brief. You wanted a piece about how the Betty Ford clinic saved her. The rest was going spare.'

'Hang on a minute: *you* took it to the Screws? Am I hearing this?'

'You are. I did.'

'It's got somebody else's byline on it.'

'Mick Hamilton's, yes. The usual.'

'You're fired.'

'You can't fire me, I'm on a contract!'

'Cancelled!'

There ensued a stand-off, for about six weeks. Nick found himself unwittingly in a quandary. He had dispensed with my services, but he wanted to run the Stevie Nicks interview. Angry, unrepentant and never in the mood to apologise, he wrote me a letter, which came in the post. I could 'come back', he said, if I'd agree to go to the Betty Ford Center and write about the experience as an insider. How on earth was I supposed to do that? While I enjoyed a drink as much as the next hack, I had always been something of a lightweight. I'd given up completely during my pregnancy, and never resumed my original (this is milking it) capacity. I had never taken drugs, nor had I smoked so much as a single fag. Ever. I could not have pulled it off as a bona fide addict. The entry-level blood tests would have exposed me. Less Betty Ford, more Betty Fraud. I'd be ejected in a heartbeat, and perhaps even arrested for impersonating the genuine article.

To his credit, Nick could see the point. We sat opposite each other munching Rich Teas all over his desk with a cup of tea each, brewed by his long-suffering PA Jackie Holland.

'What if you spend the next fortnight drinking as much as you can, around the clock, get yourself into a suitably wrecked state, keep yourself topped-up on the plane and stumble in there as worse for wear as possible?' he suggested.

For real?

I kept a straight face, and told him I suspected I'd be rumbled.

'You'll have to go back there with Stevie Nicks, then,' he said firmly.

'That's not gonna happen.'

'Why not?'

'Nick. One of the most popular rock stars of all time, co-creator of 'Rumours', millions of copies sold, does not down tools over the courgettes in Arizona or quit a world tour and leg it back to California because some faceless British hack fancies a Sensurround experience of an addiction clinic. Why should she? Besides, these people want to leave that stuff behind.'

In the end, we make amends. Nick abandoned all thought of the kind of killer Fleet Street stunt that he still relished (old habits die hard) and ran with what we had.

I had long been fascinated by this five-foot-one-inch china doll, a combination of brazen woman and timid child, world-famous for her six-inch platform boots, her shawls and chiffon dresses, her endless on-stage costume changes, her mic-stands dripping with necklaces, ribbons and tambourines. Not to mention her 'Orson-Wells-on-helium' husky contralto voice, which took some impersonating. Along with millions, I'd loved and practically prayed to that voice in my time. What I'd adored even more were her songs, which had spoken to me at a time in my life when I lacked confidence, was unsure of myself, when I leaned naturally towards the ethereal and the mystical but felt self-conscious about this perceived pathetic tendency, given that things airy-fairy were a theme that many loved to mock. I was on the edge of seventeen and writing poetry never destined to be read by anyone else when I discovered Fleetwood Mac. Stevie was nothing if not Mick Fleetwood's pint-sized poet. I looked up to her, but I would never be her. I still have the notebooks to prove it. Mine was ludicrous, wince-inducing stuff. There was nothing remotely lyrical about it. Unlike the writing of the taffeta'd temptress, which wove irresistible fantasies about gypsies, angels and fireflies, about beauties, beasts and dreamers, about Belladonnas, Rhiannons, Saras and paper dolls, about sisters of the moon and secret loves and all that. She was a winsome alter-ego to so many of us. You only had to attend one of their concerts, survey the audience, and lose count of the shawls.

It was in 1986 that Stevie entered the Betty Ford Center, resolving to rid herself once and for all of her addiction to cocaine. The place had done it for Liza Minnelli, Elizabeth Taylor and many other distinguished people. Could it do it for Stevie? She admitted to me for YOU Magazine that part of her therapy inside was doing her share of the housework. This past-time was as alien a concept to her as uttering the phrase 'do you want salt and vinegar on them?' from behind an Aldgate fish counter on a Friday night. She would loop her faded blonde hair behind her ears, she said; sling her trailing shawl over one shoulder, and thank God that she'd remembered to pack her suede platform boots, because at least she wouldn't get her feet wet; and she'd make off down the corridor at 7.30am with her plastic bucket and string mop in one hand. There was a time when rock stars never went to bed before sunrise, I mused. 'I remember them,' she said wistfully. 'The good old days.'

Back in the spartan cubicle she shared with a fifty-five-year-old alcoholic woman who slept a lot, and who snored, she would pose before the mirror with her make-up purse and fill in the gaps. Pretty soon, eyes smouldering, lips pouting, cheeks gleaming, the blonde curls teased to candyfloss, she would hook her wasted body into a tasselled, tinselled costume, lob on another shawl, and head for her morning constitutional round the duck pond. Later, much later, when the vacuuming and dusting were done, the lectures listened to, a vast lunch devoured, Stevie would take tea with her friends, three Texan tycoons in their sixties (she was thirty-eight at the time). The tycoons would help her distribute the many cacti, plants and flower arrangements delivered to Stevie each day by the vanload.

She had been hooked on cocaine for twelve years. She went to the Betty Ford to kick the habit and save her life. Three years later, she toured America and Europe on her only solo tour. She would tell me that she had no memory whatsoever of that tour, thanks to the Klonapin she became dependent on at Betty Ford. Her psychiatrist continued to prescribe her that drug in horrifying, ever-escalating amounts. Until 1994. It is normally not prescribed for more than nine weeks max. I think of Michael Jackson and Conrad Murray, and reflect on how it's a wonder that Stevie survived.

The notion of helping an addict off one drug by assisting them into addiction to another has long struck me as suspect. So-called 'benzos', the habit-forming benzodiazepines of which Klonopin, Valium and Xanax are the best-known, are more lethal than the conditions they treat. Stevie was given all three at the Betty Ford. She would later say that they turned her into a 'zombie' in there, and that she felt like 'somebody opened up a door and pushed me into hell.' But at the time of our interview, she could not speak more highly of the clinic. She raved about it as though her life depended on it. Which it did. It was almost as though she'd bought shares in the place, and was a signature away from patronage.

The damage? $6,000 and twenty-eight days of her life. 'Find the money,' she said. 'Beg, borrow it, scrape it together. It's worth every cent. I knew that if I didn't go soon, I would be dead. I was existing on false hopes and fake substances. Drink, drugs … much more than the drinking, it was the drugs. I could, and have, stopped drinking many times. But the cocaine got the better of me. I needed that energy to keep up the pace. I'd get up in the morning and panic. 'How can I possibly make it to a photo session and three rehearsals?' and I'd be reaching for the coke. I was obsessive, addicted.' Rumours were rife that Stevie ingested the drug in un-imaginable ways, including up her bottom through a straw.

Oh please. No butts. Gere we go again. In a 1999 biography, 'Stevie Nicks: Visions, Dreams and Rumours', by Zoe Howe, it was revealed that the singer's cocaine abuse had grown so severe that it had burned a hole the size of a dime through her nasal septum. Unable to snort it conventionally anymore, she had allegedly resorted to the scenic route. The idea of her assistants administering it anally was a practice straight out of Studio 54, the celebrated New York nightclub where, whether gay, straight or keeping their options open, cocaine was one of the more 'normal' items to be presented to paying punters via the back door. Besides, what choice did she have? Freebasing, in which the drug is burned in solvent and the fumes inhaled, or painful intravenous injections, were infinitely more precarious options. Dissolving it and having it dripped directly into the eyeballs is never a good look. A 'booty bump' might well have seemed desirable, compared. True or false, the rumours have clung like bad smells. All she can do is a Richard Gere, and ignore them.

She must have been one of the more bizarre inmates the Betty Ford had ever welcomed.

'I was one chain-smoking, coffee-swilling mess while I was there,' she said. 'and I ate like a pig. They feed you way too much to make up for the other stuff you are suddenly missing. And I cried a lot. You don't have treatment as such, but meetings: with your counsellor, and with everyone together. You cry and you cry, and you tell all your secret stories. In three days you are out of pain and crying for a purpose. You are hopeful, but never really happy.'

Her Klonopin addiction continued until 1994. It's a wonder it didn't kill her. After touring America and Europe from August until November 1989, she said that she had no memory of it whatsoever, thanks to the drug. The only thing that could be said in its favour was that it prevented her from resuming her killer cocaine habit. She then went back to work with Fleetwood Mac on their 'Behind the Mask' album, which did ok in the States and reached Number One in the UK. The world tour to promote it saw her reunite with her former lover Lindsey Buckingham to perform the unbearably painfu-to-listen-to 'Landslide'. Stevie then fell out spectacularly with Mick Fleetwood, after he refused her request to include their 1977 track 'Silver Springs' on her 'Best-Of' album, 'Timespace'. In September 1991, on the tenth anniversary of her solo debut, Stevie released that album. A year later, the band followed suit with their own 'Best-Of', '25 Years – The Chain'. It included, of course, 'Silver Springs'.

Hurtling towards her eighth decade, she will never be one to grow old gracefully. She will be wearing her fanciful gowns, petticoats and silken shawls until she drops. She hopes with all her heart that they will wind up in antique dress shops on the King's Road after she does.

'In my life,' she told me, 'I have had two or three great loves.' Lindsey Buckingham? Mick Fleetwood? Don Henley? Tom Petty? Jimmy Iovine? Joe Walsh? Take your pick, she had them all and more.

'You name 'em, I've slept with 'em. There were many, many liaisons,' she admitted. 'The list would make your hair curl. I'll name them all when I'm ninety and when I write the book of my life. They'll all be dead by then, so it won't hurt anyone. If my behaviour hurt anyone at all, it hurt me. I'm the one who ended up alone. Every relationship ended because of my lifestyle. I'd meet a man, we'd start to settle into this wonderful affair, and then I'd be off across the world with Fleetwood Mac again. No one can keep up with that. I have made a lot of sacrifices in my life for Fleetwood Mac, and perhaps it is now that I am paying the price.'

Her greatest regret was that she never had children.

'I would never have had a baby out of wedlock. That would have hurt my parents too much. Anyway, my children would have to have a mother and a father. I used to think about it and despair of ever finding the answer. The fact that I am old enough to be the mother of grown-up children, and even grandchildren, and could have them all around me now but in reality am all alone, really kills me. That was my ultimate sacrifice for the band. And when you sacrifice yourself in such a way, you don't just up and leave a band or let it fall apart around your ears.

'That is why Fleetwood Mac won't ever die. We all gave up so much. I think if it died now, then so would we.'

Stevie gave me two presents. One was a gorgeous print of an oil she had painted in first class on the flight to London, of a beautiful blonde in a flowing gown. No prizes. The other was an enormous white tee shirt from the Betty Ford clinic, its logo imprinted on the front in bottle-green ink. On my next trip to LA, I arranged to hook up with my longtime friend Malcolm Payne, who was in those days living in San Francisco, but who happened to be in town. I picked him up in my rented red Ford Mustang convertible and drove him down Sunset through all the pretty neighbourhoods to Malibu, where we lunched on Bloody Marys and seafood at Gladstone's. The iconic beachside seafood restaurant on the Pacific Coast Highway was quite a haunt. Malcolm and I pulled our sunhats over our eyes and settled in for the long haul. For a laugh, I was wearing the Betty Ford shirt.

A dozen Bloody Marys in, our wannabe movie star waiter, who was called Jaime and who had seen it all before, delivered the next round with a wink and a 'This one's on me.' Whereupon he knelt beside me, drew his lips in line with my right ear, and whispered, 'Want some coffee? It's a two-and-a-half-hour drive back there. What time have they told you to be in?'[xvi]

16. YOU KNOW WE'RE GOING TO FUCK, DON'T YOU: MARCO PIERRE WHITE

The twenty-eight-year-old chef-patron of Harvey's diner was a rising star in the world of haute cuisine. In spite of its Wandsworth Common location, i.e., not exactly Mayfair, the tastefully titivated over-the-river restaurant was crammed nightly with the well-known and the well-off, the blue- and the almost-blue-blooded. Not only did it boast two Michelin stars, one of only four restaurants in the UK at the time to do so, but Marco Pierre White was already a regular on television: on Channel 4's 'Take Six Cooks' and on ITV's 'Marco'. He was also a darling of the gossip columns, infamous for insulting customers, bullying staff, and pricing his food extortionately. But he had punters queueing around the block, eating (almost literally) out of his hand. How did he do it?

October 1990 would see the publication of his cookery-book debut, 'White Heat' (Pyramid Books). I use the term 'cookery book' loosely. The autobiographical volume boasted more pictures of Marco than of things to eat: forty-nine mugshots and thirty-five dishes, to be precise. Significantly, the images of his culinary creations were in glorious Technicolor, while those of himself were in mean and moody monochrome. The book was the hook.

The editor's inspired idea was that I would work in the kitchen of Harvey's for a week and get the measure of the animal in its natural habitat. The initial approach had been made by our people. Marco's people seemed up for it. What he wanted to know was what the writer was like. He wasn't about to let any old riff-raff into the inner sanctum of his kitchen, he warned. He demanded to assess me himself, to see whether I was fit for purpose. He would interview the interviewer, before allowing her to interview him. I had never before encountered this scenario, but apparently it was not unheard-of. A date was duly arranged: 3:30pm on a Tuesday, after the Harvey's lunchtime shift. I collected my three-year-old daughter Mia from nursery, and we made our way there. We then hung about in the vestibule for what seemed like hours, barely daring to speak. We were like Belle, when she voyages from her village through the wolf-infested forest into the enchanted castle, only to find the place deserted. Of the Beast, there was neither hide nor hair ...

At last, Marco appeared. He made no apology for the wait. He was tossing his Medusa mane and wiping his hands on his apron. It occurred to me that he would look more at home frying onions in a hotdog truck outside Wembley Stadium, or shifting amplifiers for pop groups. Dangle a guitar from his neck and he might even pass for a rock star. Or at least, on a good day, for Bob Geldof. In any event, there was not much about the man that said celebrity chef par excellence.

He bid us good afternoon.

'Who's this?' he demanded, peering at Mia. She looked terrified. I explained.

'She's not welcome in my kitchen,' he said, 'just in case you were thinking of bringing her. Would you like a drink?' he roared at her. Mia nodded.

'What?'

'What do you mean, 'what'?' I interjected.

'What does the troll want to drink?'

'She'll have some water, please,' I said quietly, not wishing to upset any carts. I was on trial here. One comment out of place and the mercurial cook was likely to kick me out, refuse to have me anywhere near his kitchen, the feature would be lost and Nick would probably 'sack' me again. I munched on my tongue and kept cool.

'Jean-Christophe!' he yelled at his maître d', 'Une bouteille d'eau, s'il vous plait. Et un verre.'

J-C jumped to it, and returned with a litre-sized glass bottle of mineral water and a wine glass. He handed the glass to Mia, and the bottle to Marco. Mia said nothing. Marco began to pour.

'Say when,' he instructed.

Mia stared at him, and said nothing.

She never said 'when'. She was clearly shocked into silence by our tormentor, who seemed determined to have a bit of sport at a child's expense. He continued to pour, emptying the entire bottle into the glass. The water naturally cascaded over the sides, splashed down her yellow sun frock and ran the length of her bare little legs, finally pooling in her lace-frilled socks and brand-new white leather sandals. Why didn't I do anything? Say anything? Why didn't I whack the ogre over the head with the bottle, grab Mia and run for the door, cursing him over my shoulder as I went for traumatising my precious firstborn? Well, for the aforementioned. Marco was testing me, clearly. He was known for abusive behaviour, both in and out of the kitchen. Could I take it? Would I crumble at the first four-letter word? I had to prove that I could stand the heat, and sacrifice my own baby in the process. I have lost sleep over this for many years, believe me. Mia appears to have survived unscathed. One never knows, though.

The late afternoon sun was blazing down on the common opposite. Marco suggested a walk over the ponds to let Mia dry off. I suppressed the urge to boot him in the balls. So off we set for a nice little stroll. What a sight we must have made, the bloodied giant chef, the small, seething woman and the dripping child. Write me five hundred words on that one. As we ambled towards the ducks, Mia gambolling ahead to meet them with the plastic bag of crusts that Marco had yanked from his bulging pocket, he stopped dead, turned to face me, placed his paws on my shoulders and said, apparently in earnest, 'You know we're going to fuck, don't you?'

Cocky dick.

Whatever the perfect repudiation, and there always is one, it eluded me in the moment. I subsequently pondered but could never quite coin it. At the time, I simply stood there, open-mouthed. A few years later, while in the back of a limo with Marco's former kitchenhand turned gnashing arch rival, Gordon Ramsay, I recounted the story to Gordon's guffawing mirth. He eventually composed himself and wiped his leaking eyes. He was, he told me, in no doubt as to what my riposte should have been:

'"We're going to fucking fuck? Fuck that! You're going to fucking hell, more like, you ugly fucking c**t!!"'

A classic mot de l'escalier, it remains unused ...

Marco was, as the world appeared to know, the former teenage protégé of the distinguished Albert Roux of Le Gavroche fame, who sautéed his way out of the ranks, took the ultimate risk and lobbed all his oeufs into one panier called Harvey's. The place was formerly an inexpensive Wandsworth wine bar. Marco retained the name. It was here he was to prove that the enfant terrible could cook as well as behave badly. He has been hailed as 'the godfather of modern cooking' and as 'the first celebrity chef' ever since. Really? What about the founders of the prawn cocktail, Major Johnnie and Mrs. Cradock ('may all your doughnuts turn out like Fanny's'), and the globally-sensational Galloping Gourmet, Graham Kerr, one of whose more repeatable catchphrases was 'Madam, you could go outside and get run over by a bus, and just think what you would have missed!' Credit where due.

People will always eat. But with restaurants inclined to open and close the length and breadth of the capital at a frightening rate, it is clear that most people will not often eat very grandly. The majority of failures fall into the middle-price bracket, which is their downfall, thanks to a brutal economy which spells home cooking and takeaways most of the time for the masses. No, Marco was not silly. His was the kind of joint frequented by those with money to burn. At Harvey's, dinner for two would cost £150, all in. In 1990. I shudder to think what the outing would set you back now.

As you might expect, and he'd be most disappointed if we thought otherwise, this Italian Yorkshireman has a hugely inflated ego through which, like fine percolated coffee, every question and consideration must be filtered. Dogmatic and uncompromising in the extreme, Marco knows best and always has. Humility is not his bag. Delegation is anathema. And he sees no reason why he should explain himself. He has never liked the press. He does not believe in interviews as a rule, and has been known to refuse to meet journalists he didn't fancy the sound of on the phone. Likewise, potential customers. Twice I heard him give a fictitious address for his restaurant to telephone callers, with a snort roughly translated as, 'We don't want his/her sort around here.' 'Let's face it,' reasoned Marco, chewing the inside of his cheek, 'there is one reason and one reason only why a man takes a woman out for dinner. But let's try and be a little refined about it.'

So there I found myself, backstage at Harvey's with a pinny on. Eight o'clock and the temperature was rising. It was hardly surprising. Eyes down for a full house, fifty covers, the same story every night of the week. I wouldn't have called the kitchen tiny, but the head chef, cooks and bottle-washers were all hunchbacks. I was already starting to melt. Recognising my plight, a pastry chef helpfully emptied a bottle of mineral water down my front. A pattern was emerging here. While the dowsing should have been welcome in such confined circumstances, its application had roughly the same effect as a ladleful of pine juice over a bucket of hot sauna coals. Henceforth, it was all downhill.

Marco had reached sublimation point within half an hour. Pacing the kitchen's slippery tiles like a ravenous caged animal, his black eyes were ablaze, and his white chef's jacket was glued to his body with fresh sweat. 'Feel my back! Feel my back1' he cried. 'I am soaking!' He tossed the mane and wiped his mouth with his hand. He looked like an unkempt bear disturbed in mid-hibernation. Ruffled and unshaven, his face was half-mooned in two days' worth of whiskers. He clearly couldn't give a monkey's about his appearance.

'Hey: berk!' he erupted, in the direction of a meek commis chef. 'Did you give me this plate? You're not exactly intelligent, are you?' 'Berk' shrank back against the nearest available wall, but the ceramics refused to yield.

'Oi: ugly!' he rounded on an unfortunate waiter who bore a striking resemblance to the Prince of Wales. 'Yes, you, big ears! Where you from? France? Do you want to see France again? No? Well, carry on the way you are and you won't, ever, know what I mean? You: Irishman! Is that the best you can do?'

'Yes, Marco.'

'Idiot! What are you?'

'An idiot, Marco.'

'Who's nicked my sodding clingfilm? I'd like it back! Whoever's taken it, give it back now!'

I did so.

'Also ugly! What are you?'

'Also ugly, Chef,' I replied.

And so on. We were soon a bunch of quivering wrecks. And we knew what we could do if we didn't like it.

It was all systems go as the orders flooded in by the table-load: salt cod, pig's trotter, pigeon. Much frantic chopping of herbs (me), massacring of tomatoes (also me), and slicing of fish. Every dish originated (impressively) from scratch, no microwaves here, with Marco at the helm yelling orders like a surgeon:

'Plate, William! Olive oil, William! Pan, please, Bertrand! Caviar! Lemon juice! I said chiiiives!'

It was not so much hands-on cookery as hands-in. Marco tested not with his fingertips, but with his entire fists. Every spoon he used while preparing the food went straight into his mouth. Several of them, since I happened to be hovering beside him, also went into mine, before heading back directly into the mixture.

'If people worried less about germs and more about the taste and texture of the food, the world would be a far healthier place,' he barked. He deployed these same unorthodox methods on television, and received endless complaints. One gentleman who phoned was stoutly advised for his trouble to do something unusually athletic with his wife.

Through the sizzling garlic haze, the kitchen began to feel like a cross between a torture chamber and Dotheboys Hall. Wackford Squeers, alias Marco, was mercilessly whipping his boys with insults like there was no tomorrow, and everyone present appeared to be enjoying every minute of it. Except me.

Out of the boss's earshot, another cook explained. 'If he's not shouting, he doesn't care,' he said. 'We're here to learn, and he wants to teach us. He gives two hundred per cent, often more, and he wants that much back. Don't let him fool you. He's as soft as butter really.'

Someone with a reservation for six turned up with seven guests. Disaster! 'OK, now I'm stressed, leave me alone!' shrieked Marco, so red in the face that he looked like a balloon about to burst. 'And tell him to fuck off!' he roared, as an afterthought. In flitted Jean-Christophe with a menu and a Biro in his hands. Somebody wanted an autograph. 'That's six quid on the bill,' Marco reminded him.

Another order for seafood starters and Marco was once more poring over a cold plate, dollop of sauce here, fat prawn there, seasoned bass furled into a column in between. The sweat was dripping off the tips of his ringlets into the dish as his chipolata fingers flew. He plopped a prawn onto his tongue, licked his palms and carried on creating. Satisfied with the finished product, he took a corner of his splattered blue apron and twirled it around the edge of the plate to wipe the drips. It was a good thing his loyal customers couldn't care less.

'Service!' he cried. 'Table quinze, envoyez! Alors, vite, move it! Let's go, dumbos, quickly!'

They don't come much more dedicated to the job than Marco. Yet he insisted, as we talked at the end of the night, that first night, that cookery had never been his main ambition in life.

'It was just a job, to start with,' he said, in his eyrie of an office above the shop. The same eyrie in which, he later confessed, he once had sex with a customer while her husband was downstairs inhaling his main course. For the first time in six hours he began to relax, and he looked terrible. He had that pale gaze and churlish manner of someone who sleeps rough and rests little. He took pills for stress, he confessed, smoked sixty Marlboro a day, and existed on a diet of coffee and Mars Bars. His blood pressure was shot, and he had already been hospitalised for nervous exhaustion. He knew he ought to take the hint and slow down a little, before the lifestyle, if you could call it that, got the better of him.

Why cook for a living, when this is what it does to you?

'Because I was thick at school,' he said. 'A doughnut. My brain didn't start working until I was sixteen. I left without any qualifications, and I fell into cooking by accident.'

He sieved stockpots in Harrogate, and discovered a taste for fine food on Ilkley Moor. He came to London, walked the streets with seven quid in his pocket, and one morning called in on the off-chance at Le Gavroche. Albert Roux signed him on the spot. Whitey, as he'd been known at school, was on his way.

'I owe Albert everything,' he told me, pronouncing it the French way, 'Albear', as we made our way to West Sussex at the crack of dawn the following Sunday. We had been invited for a day's fishing on Monsieur Roux's country estate. Two hours, a dozen wrong turns and a tank of petrol later, Albert's childhood sweetheart Monique,[xvii] whom he had married at seventeen, was serving us coffee and home-made fruit cake and clucking round Marco like a mother hen. Having lost his own mother at the age of six, Marco regarded Monique and Albert as surrogate parents. Albert referred to Marco as 'my little bunny', and 'the little genius'. Marco lapped up their affection, and looked for more.

The Roux country estate was the stuff of dreams. Especially Marco's. There was an aspirant streak in him, all right. The same one that gave a working-class kid public-school vowels and aristocratic preferences in everything from women to wine and song. 'I'm a heathen,' he admitted. 'But I get on with people who are better than me. I soak it all up. It seems to come naturally to me. I regard it as a gift.'

After several hours of fishing on a private lake stocked with eels, perch, carp and tench, we went in out of the cold for lunch. 'This,' said Marco of the spread that Albert had prepared, 'is absolutely my favourite meal. The best kind of food.' We were treated to sautéed aubergine and courgette in garlic, a majestic coq au vin and the sweetest summer pudding. The meal was accompanied by a 1977 Chablis, Cuvée Albert Roux, no less. He had trodden the grapes with his own bare heels. I tried not to imagine the hard skin. A jeroboam of Chateauneuf-du-Pape 1970, followed by a bottle of vintage Bollinger, and the crew was well away. All this was served on a bed of Madame Roux's best handmade lace, and garnished with fine English bone china, lead crystal and solid silver. No expense spared. And it was all lost on Marco. By mid-main course, he was literally snoring over his coq. He had to be led upstairs to lie down.

Monsieur Roux was unruffled. 'Ah, well,' he sighed, looking fondly after Marco as his surrogate son stumbled off to bed. 'It is the price you pay. You know, the life of a chef is wild. You see life, you live and love life, and then you pay for it. Loving food is a full-time occupation. The preparation of it is emotionally as well as physically exhausting. You have got to adore food to be good at this. Enjoying cooking is saying to people, "I love you." You've got to be good at giving to be good at cooking. There isn't a good chef alive who is also mean.'

I met Marco again in September 1993. Piers Morgan sent me to interview him for the News of the World, just before he became chef-patron of the Restaurant Marco Pierre White at the old Hyde Park Hotel. This new thirty-something Marco was better-dressed and more imperious. He also seemed more mellow, more philosophical. I found him seated on an ornate armchair in the middle of an otherwise virtually empty and darkened room. As instructed, I pulled up a perch. Now that I was level with his knees, he could look down on me. His sense of humour appeared to have run dry. I tried all the usual, and attempted to jog his memory. But he'd forgotten about the Mia-drenching, and about my having worked in his kitchen. And what happened in Wandsworth stayed on the Common. Moving on.

The restaurant closed in 1997. Marco moved to the Oak Room at Le Méridien Piccadilly Hotel. Two years later, he caused a sensation by retiring as a chef, and handed back his three Michelin stars. Fame, recognition and money were not fulfilling, he said. He wanted something more meaningful in his life. He wanted his children – Letty, Marco Jnr, Luciano and Mirabelle – to know who he really was.

He has been up to his neck in business ventures and television series ever since, which have established Marco Pierre White as the inevitable global brand. He rented out his 'drunk dinner-lady' face to the makers of Knorr stock cube and stockpots. He launched further books, pubs, restaurants and hotels. He collaborated with P&O Cruises. He went through three wives, and may or may not still be in a relationship with actress Emilia Fox. They're good friends, at least. And he survived the scandal heaped on the family by his son Marco Jnr, who was filmed in flagrante on a reality TV show, and who boasted that he had spent half a million dollars of his dad's money on drink, drugs and hookers. The rest, like George Best, he just squandered.

Marco bought an exquisite house opposite Love Lane, Salisbury in 2013. I've stood outside it a few times – not that I'm a weirdo, one of my two best friends from school lives a few doors away – and wished that I lived in it. Especially as Marco never really moved in, and soon enough sold the place. He lives reclusively these days in the Wiltshire countryside at his idyllic retreat, Home Farm, near Chippenham. He once longed for a rural paradise to match that of his mentor, Albert Roux. Lucky bastard? The harder he worked, the luckier he got. It's all it takes.

17. THIS WOMAN WAS BORN ONE MILLION YEARS BC: RAQUEL WELCH

We met on Mustique in a rickety beach bar, where she sat eating tuna tartare with her tiny fingers while sipping a long Rum Punch. I barely recognised her. Her cherry nail polish was chipped, her tawny hair hung in rats' tails, and her perfect doll's feet were bare. The famous breasts were suspended like huge hams in a Lycra top, and her skin glistened with oil. Up close, she smelled like a Bounty bar. Not a single punter bothered her, most of the diners being stars themselves. Tossing a cap-toothed smile at Mick Jagger and Jerry Hall, she leapt to embrace Basil, the bar's flamboyant owner, and undulated a little to some lilting steel band tunes. Out across moonlit Britannia Bay, billionaires were turning in for the night on twinkling yachts.

Perhaps the fantasy world of a private island had worked its magic on Raquel Welch, softening this tough movie broad into the sassy woman who charmed us all so effortlessly that night. Back in LA, the Hollywood Raquel I got to know during an extended stay while preparing several stories at once for YOU magazine bore little resemblance to her Caribbe-an incarnation. I should have known. But what young, opportunistic journalist eschews the chance of friendship, however fleeting, with a gro-tesquely glamorous motion picture icon like Raquel Welch?

She was a fabled but faded drama queen old enough to be my moth-er. I was an upstart nobody, young enough to be totally in awe – which was the rub. Hollywood friendships are always symbiotic but rarely equal. Never devoid of ulterior motive, they are inevitably short-lived. It is not the fond beginnings of former friendships that we tend to recall, whenever we dwell on them, but the sorrow provoked by their inexorable demise. The thin line that divides love from hatred, fantasy from reality, has never existed in Hollywood. All the edges are blurred. Anything goes. Arguably the only town in the world in which a personality disorder is an asset, everyone you meet is from somewhere else, and everybody is Going Places. Even the guy serving your coffee and bagel at breakfast has a script-meeting later. It can take minutes, months or a lifetime to com-prehend its hidden shallows. Even then, too many fail to take heed. It is all but impossible to plant roots there. Some newcomers will last only a week, while others become trapped for an entire lifetime. When I left, it was because I had to. That place would have swallowed me whole. Looking back on heady days spent with Raquel Welch and others like her, I still believe what I suspected then: that Tinseltown is nothing but its own façade. It is certainly no place for the sane.

A chance encounter with Raquel's manager in Atlantic City had led to her granting me an audience to promote her new fitness video: a really big deal for Raquel, a workout and meditation fiend, as she was about to turn fifty that year. I was looking forward to meeting her again when I arrived at her elegant home in Evelyn Place on the Trousdale Estates, a posh, gated community within the City of Beverly Hills. An 'enclave for mid-century modern chic', most of its des reses had been designed by name architects. The most basic of them changed hands for more than $10 million. With lush landscaping affording perfect privacy, and armed guards patrolling around the clock, the Trousdale Estates attract the most high-profile of residents.

She may not have remembered our Basil's Bar encounter, but Raquel wasted no time in playing to the camera. Even though there wasn't one. Perched on the edge of a mustard leather sofa in her creamy drawing room, I found myself dealing with a real-life Norma Desmond: the over-the-hill silent screen idol played by Gloria Swanson in cult classic 'Sunset Boulevard', who is determined to make a comeback against all odds. Self-absorbed to the point of obsession, oblivious of the fact that the world had moved on from inflatable dolls in chamois swimwear, it occurred to me that Raquel would be the perfect choice for a remake.

Everywhere I looked, pictures of Raquel gazed down at me. Two huge Warhol-style portraits sat one either side of her fireplace. A vast Revlon advertising print dominated her weirdly formal dining room. Her home was part museum, part shrine, paying homage to her then quarter-century as a superstar. Not that she had worked much in movies since her Sixties/early Seventies heyday, having been denounced by the industry as too high-maintenance. A brief spell on the set of 'Cannery Row' had led to her sacking by MGM Studios, who replaced her with Debra Winger. Raquel sued so comprehensively that she banked $15 million and would never have to work again. She did, though. 'Body and Mind' videos, cosmetic endorsements, TV shows, stage work, a hair-raisingly successful line in wigs, you name it. For the maintenance of her image and profile, you understand, rather than for remuneration: the usual thing that keeps a superstar at it. If fame is a drug, the addiction knows no cure. Raquel and her ilk would sooner be dead than has-beens.

She had a peculiarly masculine energy. All-woman, scarily sex-on-legs, her smooth, tanned complexion looked more Latin than in her photographs. But her personality revealed a perplexing Alpha Male-ness. Her language was ripe, her laugh straight out of a locker room. She spoke loudly and clearly, her pronunciation at times almost English. Her maid looked long-suffering as she pottered about, fetching 'Squirt' grapefruit soda and black coffee, and serving a chicken lunch. Raquel called me 'sweetheart', 'darling', and 'Baby'. I'd heard vague bisexual rumours, and had a fictitious boyfriend up my sleeve, just in case.

'White girls are just so tightly-wrapped sexually,' she remarked through ravenous mouthfuls.

'Hmmm,' I thought. 'How does she know?'

It seemed a good time to ask why she'd never done topless or nude work.

'Dark Latin nipples, Baby,' she shrugged. 'Wanna see?'

Reader, I declined. It didn't stop her talking about her sex life. I was taken aback, as I hadn't even asked. She confided that she had a 'very European' attitude towards sex, which most American men 'found intimidating'. Munching away on her chicken and rice cakes, she'd clutch her fingers together and jab at me to emphasise a point. Her hand was like a snake's head, preparing to strike. I was mesmerised. While I found her compelling, I was terrified. She even confessed to a penchant for copulation in cars, a habit acquired during her misspent San Diego youth. Embarrassed now, I clicked off the tape and legged it to the bathroom. On my way back, a stash of racy videos caught my eye.

Hours later, when I made to leave, Raquel insisted on driving me back to the Sunset Marquis in her new Japanese car. She sang along unselfconsciously to Beatles tapes, getting the lyrics wrong – very Raquel – played Peter Gabriel full-blast, and raved about the singer Jody Watley, formerly of R&B group Shalamar. On pulling up outside my hotel, she promptly invited me out to dinner. As I sat watching her tuck in to Caesar salad and tomato soup and knocking back Martinis in the famous Musso and Frank Grill, a classic New York-style bar-restaurant on Hollywood Boulevard, the urge to phone home and squeal 'guess where I am, and who with!' was irresistible.

For what felt like years but was in fact only about three months, we seemed inseparable. At Hamburger Hamlet on Sunset and Doheny, we'd bump into Raquel's celebrity pals Carrie Fisher, Nancy Sinatra and Dean Martin. The Jack in the Box drive-through was another fast-food favourite, as was The Apple Pan diner on Pico. She adored being seen at Le Petit Four on Sunset, and at Le Dome: co-founded by Elton John in 1977 and a favourite haunt of Hollywood agents, producers and industry insiders the likes of David Geffen and Berry Gordy. During the day, with nothing better to do, we'd get together for lunch in the Polo Lounge at the Beverly Hills Hotel, then hang by the pool until dinner. When we weren't indulging in 'mani-pedis' in the hotel beauty salon, I'd sit chatting with her while she had her mane coloured and sculpted at Umberto's.

'She has to look like Sixties Raquel,' she'd say, often referring to herself unnervingly in the third person. 'This girl has to stay the same with her looks. That's the way people expect her to look. That's the only way they know Raquel Welch.'

But how on earth did she still look as fabulous as twenty-five years earlier in her only memorable movie, 'One Million Years BC' (for who can recall any other?) without ever having resorted to plastic surgery?

'That's the point!' she'd squeal, delighted that 'the work' was undetectable. 'The secret, Baby, is to start having it before you actually need it! Raquel started getting things done back in the Sixties. All it's taken is a tuck and tweak here and there ever since. You're sitting inches away from her face, you can't even notice? Result! But look at Nancy (Sinatra): richer than Croesus and one of the worst face jobs on the globe – and with *her* millions! That's because she came to it too late. Take it from Raquel, Baby, go now before they notice you need it!' At which point she reached out to shove my sagging jowl into my ear.

'By the time you really do need it, you'll be ahead of the game,' she banged on. 'Mother Nature figures she has us licked with this ageing business. But Baby, Baby, take it from Rocky: it doesn't have to be that way.'

I never did take Rocky's advice. Nor have I ever regretted it. I am just too squeamish. I couldn't help but admire her, though, for having the guts to admit to what so many in her shoes were flatly denying back then, long before cosmetic surgery became respectable. Almost.

Our regular 'Girls' Nights Out' took us from the Rainbow Bar and Grill to le Mondrian Hotel on Sunset Strip, Raquel often raunchily attired in naughty black stockings and mini skirts. Even at fifty, she got away with it. At her beloved Trader Vic's, she'd drink Mai Tai and Pino Pepe cocktails, served up in a real pineapple shell. Otherwise health-obsessed, she would usually plump for apple cider or just plain water. While her behaviour in front of me was never that wild, she certainly knew how to have a good time. Her enjoyment hinged not a little on being recognised. She'd cluck about like a mother hen among tried and trusted pals, introducing me as her 'new best friend'.

I never did work out why the most legendary sex symbol since Marilyn Monroe wanted to hang with me, an utter nobody. Was it for my plainness, which accentuated her beauty? My Englishness, my innocence, my 'minion' status? Every Leading Lady needs her lackeys, after all. Reluctant to rock a boat that may or may not be going places, I never asked. If it sounds trite to say that she taught me plenty – about love, about men in general and about husbands in particular (she'd had three by then, and there was later a fourth, restauranteur Richard Palmer; she'd dated Steve McQueen, Warren Beatty and Dudley Moore, so she knew a bit); single motherhood (which we had in common – Raquel being a mother of two); about the Hollywood piranha pool, about the importance of self-belief, about guts, determination and never giving up – I can make no apology. Her control freakery was forgivable while the ride was too exhilarating for words.

Raquel, born Jo Raquel Tejada in September 1940, could talk for Bolivia, her native land. She was under no illusions, either. It was reflection rather than talent which got her hired.

'What's wrong with keeping a hold of my image while I still have it?' she'd reason. 'It's more constructive than wailing, 'They never treated me right because I was so pretty.' Women have to be so many things, because men can't be. That doesn't mean we can't enjoy them all. I'm very grateful for my image,' she declared, 'and I will maintain it for as long as I am able. I made my choice a long time ago, and now I have to live up to it. Other people can let themselves go in middle age, and that's fine too. I cannot afford that luxury.'

And then, just as swiftly as our friendship had ignited, it faded. That's show business. I'd begun to irritate her, she said. She would tell me that my outfit was 'tacky', while she was wearing leg-warmers ... She lost her rag with me once too often, screaming and screaming before crying her eyes out, expecting me to forgive and forget, as I hitherto had. For my part, her constant compliment-fishing, which spoke volumes about her deep-rooted insecurity, was beginning to get on my nerves.

'Baby, aren't you going to tell me I look pretty today? Do I look sexy, c'mon, Baby, a girl's gotta know ...'

Worse, she had a terminal falling-out with her manager. Because he was the one who had introduced us in the first place, I found myself tarred with the same brush. It proved the perfect get-out.

Regrets? I had few. As a journalist, I'd had nothing but a walk-on part in Raquel Welch's epic and ongoing drama. I doubt she's even thought about me since. I never heard from her again after I left LA to make my permanent home back in the UK, so that Mia could attend a nice little English school. There was never so much as a Christmas card from Raquel. Even fewer happy returns, despite the fact that our September birthdays fell only a few days apart.

I was not what you could call the typical Tinseltown victim, not by any stretch. But I'd had more than my fill of that place. The tragedy was that I think Raquel had, too. Anonymity is always preferable, in the greater scheme. We bit-part players get to walk away relatively unscathed. We get to call time on the madness. More than a quarter of a century on, still caught in the trap, Raquel Welch, now (incredibly) pushing eighty, is still doing Eyes and Teeth whether she wants to or not, for a camera which is only sometimes there.

18. THERE'S ONLY ONE FUCKING STAR IN THIS FAMILY: PAUL & LINDA McCARTNEY

Like the blissfully ignorant wife who is always the last to know, Nick Gordon hadn't a clue what was about to hit him. One minute he was filling in the flatplan while giggling with staff about our randy proprietor's new golfing partner, and the rumours doing the rounds that they were plotting a jaunt to Uganda's nineteenth hole. The next, he was on the phone to Christopher's restaurant, Covent Garden, where senior commissioning editor Lulu Appleton and I were washing down squid ink spaghetti and Maryland crab cakes with an exquisite Chassagne-Montrachet, to tell us he'd been fired and that 'Barbie has got my effing job.' We made our excuses and left.[xviii]

We rushed in to find poor Nick emptying his desk drawers into cardboard boxes, considering whether to take a wall's worth of bound copies of the many YOUs he had edited (he left them behind in the end, shrugging 'It's over'), and cracking bad jokes to soothe his P.A.'s tears. Two decades of round-the-clock commitment to Associated Newspapers was ending not with a bang, but with a whimper.[xix] It was scandalous. We were all outraged and upset. Nick, unlike so many of the Mail's lacklustre lackeys, wasn't any old hack. A distinguished graduate of the University of St. Andrew's, he had abandoned a planned career in Law for journalism. He'd joined the Daily Mail as a features sub in 1973, and had risen to become a deputy editor with his eye on the big chair before his contempt for a 'teacher's pet' rival got him sidelined. Nick would have made so much more interesting an editor of the Daily Mail than grim-faced Paul Dacre. Graceless, humourless, lumbering Paul, a mere news deputy in my day (he didn't scare me), had it in for Nick, and Nick for him. Sir David English wound up sacrificing his own editorship in favour of the man he'd hand-picked as his successor. Nick, meanwhile, despite the awards his magazine had garnered, had been overthrown in favour of an ambitious woman. That the magazine became more popular than ever under the more enlightened and elegant Sue Peart was no thanks to her predecessor. Since then, Sue too has been replaced.

Nick, now liberated, took Swahili lessons, passed language exams, and flew off to reinvent himself as a newspaper consultant in Kenya and Tanzania, Egypt, Nigeria, Zambia and South Africa, importing obsolete printing presses and scrap-heap typewriters which he then had reconditioned to help his eager, poverty-stricken students launch brand-new newspapers. It was just the job. Nick had been passionate about the Dark Continent since his VSO[xx] days. He had first set foot on African soil the same day that Neil Armstrong walked on the moon. He'd met his beloved wife Theresa there. His two books – 'Ivory Knights', about elephant poaching and the illegal ivory trade in Tanzania, and 'Murders in the Mist', which revisited the killing of gorilla expert Dian Fossey in Rwanda – gave him a taste for the pace of long prose. He settled down to work, at home in Blackheath and in his native Pembrokeshire, on a string of novels and screenplays.

Back at the ranch, the writing on the wall was in blood. New brooms sweep clean. The new editor's thorny brush was no exception. A few of us still had rolling contracts which needed to roll back round to the month in which they'd commenced before they could be renegotiated. Which of course they wouldn't be. But I still had a handful of commissions to go, including a perplexing interlude with Mel Gibson at the beyond luxurious Hotel du Cap Eden-Roc on the Côte d'Azur. After that, I'd be out on my ear again.

Together with Garry Jenkins, Martyn Palmer and Roger Tavener, colleagues from the Mail, Today and the Express respectively, I had launched the features syndication agency Media Business International. We operated out of swanky offices in Chelsea Harbour with a P.A. called Hannibal, and threw a lavish launch at Viscount Linley's and Lord Lichfield's harbourside diner, Deals. It was attended, as the party snaps proved, by everyone who was anyone on Fleet Street. To begin with, we did a roaring trade. The first piece I sold to the News of the World, an interview with Madonna's comedienne pal Sandra Bernhard, went for £15,000. Which was Malteser money in those days. We four partners co-authored and co-published (with Omnibus Press) a large-format-paperback biography of Kylie Minogue, 'The Superstar Next-Door', which we wrote together around the clock in under a week. It did so well that there were plans to produce further such books, whenever we could find the time. But so committed to the cause and so focused on global expansion were we that we must have taken our eye off the ball one afternoon. That was the day the call came in from a Los Angeles-based former associate who was down on his luck, and who practically begged us to set him up as 'our man on the West Coast.' In return for a retainer, rent, a car, a landline and 'reasonable expenses' (we blithely agreed that he would never rip his friends off: words, last, famous), he would feed all his Hollywood exclusives through MBI, and we would then disseminate them throughout the industry as appropriate. Why the hell hadn't we seen the bastard coming? Several months dragged by before we discovered that he was doing the dirty on us, billing titles direct for pieces which had appeared under his byline when official invoices were supposed to be submitted by the company. A number of newspapers were incensed to find that they had been paying double for a single piece of copy, settling bills from the writer himself as well as from our agency. The mess took an almighty unravelling. By the end of this punishing episode, there was more than a little dissent among the ranks. The partners started gorging on each other. The agency was deemed no longer viable. We pulled the plug. Tavener took to the road, and was last seen selling his own landscape photography out of Sydney. Palmer immersed himself in movies, and had some sort of co-production role in the film 'Made in Dagenham' which, when I bumped into him at the Cannes film festival in 2009 and attended the press conference with the picture's producer Stephen Woolley and its star Sally Hawkins, was called 'We Want Sex'. I wonder why they changed it. Garry Jenkins carried on freelancing, took up ghost-writing, and worked on dozens of titles before the big prize fell in his lap. Working with recovering drug-addict busker James Bowen, who got his life back after teaming up with a soggy moggie, Garry wrote 'A Street Cat Named Bob', which was adapted as a screenplay and became a popular motion picture in 2016.

Meanwhile, it was time to re-trawl the contacts book, start showing my face at launches, lunches and showbiz bashes every night again, and to sweet-talk celebrities into giving me exclusive interviews. I was back on the chain gang.

I'd met Linda McCartney before. The first time was in 1987, during the eighth month of my first pregnancy, at Great Ormond Street Children's Hospital, for the opening of new facilities following the hospital's successful Wishing Well Appeal. Linda was a patron, hence her presence. I was covering the event for the Daily Mail, hence mine. I was standing behind a barrier at the front of a throng of journalists when she arrived, dressed in a floaty silk blue and green summer dress and low-heeled court shoes. Spotting my huge bump, she made a beeline for me, and introduced herself. Then, perceiving my anxiety at the thought of meeting so many poorly children, she announced, 'You're coming with me!' Hand in hand, we walked the wards together, sharing the only sodden tissue either of us had left.

What was this about? As a rule, Linda had no time for the press. A fierce protector of her family's privacy, she always put her husband and children first. As we made our way from ward to ward, she asked me lots of questions about my pregnancy, my plans for the birth and other people's babies, enquired as to whether I knew so-and-so, and insisted that I really must meet this acquaintance or that friend. Her stance was Ultimate Earth Mother. She fascinated me.

Linda had no reason to bother keeping in touch with me. Yet she did so. I was invited a few times after that to interview her at home and in her office, and we always had a good laugh. She never forgot to include me on guest lists for openings and launches, and always welcomed me personally with open arms. When her first vegetarian recipe book 'Home Cooking' was published, she sent me an inscribed copy in the post: 'To Lesley-Ann and lovely Mia, stay veggie! Love Linda'. The dots of all her 'i's were drawn as hearts. It was her trademark. For a woman who'd had a privileged start in life – her New York upbringing had been distinctly upper-crust compared to Paul's humble beginnings in Liverpool – I sometimes wondered what had rendered her so ordinary. She was as down-to-earth as a root vegetable. Organic, of course. Not that she looked it. While not conventionally glamorous, her face exuded a distant beauty and serenity which somehow managed to elude the camera.

I bumped into her unexpectedly in LA in November 1989, while I was staying with Raquel Welch. Paul and Linda were at the Four Seasons Hotel, and were in the middle of the McCartney World Tour, his first gigs since the murder of John Lennon in Manhattan eight years earlier. These were also Paul's first shows in America for thirteen years. You can imagine the buzz. Linda and I almost fell over each other in the hotel lobby, where I'd arranged to pick up tickets from Geoff Baker. An old Fleet Street rival from the Daily Star, Geoff was working at that time as Macca's tour publicist. He would go on to become Paul's right-hand man for nearly thirty years, until they suffered a terminal falling-out.

Linda was wearing tatty cut-offs and a stained white tee-shirt. Her calves were unshaven, her face was bare, and a shampoo and set seemed overdue. Among the chintzy 'Hotel Barbies' in the swanky five-star place, at least she stood out.

'How's Mia?' she cried, smacking me a big kiss. 'Why didn't you bring her! What are you doing for the rest of the day?' I had nothing planned.

'Why don't you go up to the pool and hang out?' she suggested. 'Spend the day, order anything you like, charge it to Paul – here, this is the room number. We won't tell him! Just put whatever you like down to him.' She took delight in the mischief.

So there was I, on the pool terrace of one of the best hotels in Hollywood, ordering champagne and all-day lunch on Paul McCartney's room and calling my friends in London on the pre-mobile plug-in phone the pool attendant had fetched me, squealing, 'Guess where I am…'

Gutsy Linda had a cheeky side. It contradicted her media image, which I loved. She was the first to admit that she ruled the Macca roost; that she was the strong one in the marriage; that Paul was often in awe of her; and that she never held back when she felt he could do with a ticking-off. That same year, I remember sitting with Linda, her friend the writer Carla Lane, Carla's mother, Paul's brother Mike and the photographer Terry O'Neill at rehearsals in Liverpool for Paul's debut classical work, 'The Liverpool Oratorio'. Linda was reminiscing about the Beatles' break-up. She revealed that she alone had nursed Paul through the incendiary bust-up with John Lennon. It had nearly caused Paul a nervous breakdown, the pair having been joined at the hip since their mid-teens.

'I calmed him down after all the Beatle madness,' she told us. 'He used to thank me all the time for "putting the sense" back into his life. He still does. All we really want now is to grow old together. We look forward to it, actually. We'll stay in bed all day, eat dinner and make love.'

Linda knew it was she who gave Paul confidence and repaired his self-esteem, though she didn't demand credit for it. It was just the way it was. She said she couldn't imagine her husband with any other woman, if, God forbid, anything happened to her. She was terribly matter-of-fact about this. She wasn't saying that Paul shouldn't marry again, simply that she couldn't imagine him doing so. She told me she'd got Paul to live a simple home life, to get back to basics, to respect family traditions like birthdays, anniversaries and Christmas, and to live by proper values. She had even taught him to bake, she said. There was always a birthday cake around, and bread was his speciality. Yet she had to concede that Paul usually got his way about 'the big stuff'.

A couple of years on, Linda and I were having a natter in a back room at Paul's MPL offices on Soho Square, melting HobNobs into our Lapsang Souchong, when she asked out of the blue whether I thought I'd ever get married. She knew that Mia's father had left me before my baby was born, and that there hadn't been anyone since.

'Or has there'?

'What's that supposed to mean!'

'A little birdie told me about you and John Waite,' she teased.

Well, yeah.

There was that.

There was him.

In pop culture parlance, I was never a 'starfucker'. But I did fall in love with a rock star. Once. Maybe you have to experience it once, to know it's not real.

But John was real. A Byronic strawberry blond with a unique voice and a fragile mien. A grown man, but only a child. Breakable. Skinny. Chiselled. Passionate. All too human. Immensely self-critical. He loved Aretha, Etta, Otis. He was a blues singer. An instinctive writer, he could pen a whole song in minutes, a stream of consciousness fashioned into verse, bridge and chorus in a blink. I was in awe of his talent. He carried a notebook everywhere, was constantly sketching the next line. I was Cathy Earnshaw to his Heathcliff, he'd say. He'd been an art student, a painter, and loved literature. He adored Proust and William Blake. He bought me a copy of 'One Thousand and One Nights', the Middle Eastern folk tales in translation. I read them all, eager to please. Did he speak of love made in hell to all the girls? What do you think. But he was more myself than I was, to borrow from Emily Brontë's tragic heroine. We just fitted. We did. Whatever our souls are made of, John's and mine were the same.[xxi] He made me believe in love, while showing me pointlessness.

We'd met in the butterfly days of Chrysalis Records. Fresh out of the Babys (how the pedant in me hated that incorrect plural), John had signed to the label with his debut solo album, 'Ignition'. But it was his 1984 follow-up that made his name, thanks to 'Missing You', a Number One in America and a Top Ten hit in the UK that would eclipse pretty much everything he'd record beyond. That track must have been played on the radio ten million times. Then came the 'Mask of Smiles' album in 1985. Two years later, the year Mia was born, it was 'Rover's Return.'

I was a mere art department minion when we first started hanging out. As a journalist, I interviewed him several times. We became good pals, in the way that writers and artists could and did in those days. Then John relocated to New York City, where he lived in a dolls'-house apartment on 72nd Street across from the Dakota building, where John Lennon was killed, before moving upstate to a 'house with a white picket fence.'xxii In 1988, he joined the supergroup Bad English (which perhaps referred back to the name of his first band). But that was all a bit corporate-rock for John. He went solo again in 1991. Whenever I was in New York on a story and he wasn't away on tour, we'd hook up. And he'd come home every Christmas to his home town in the North. The 'Hanging Town', they called it, on account of the famous Pendle Witch Trials of 1612. Once or twice, I took Mia up there from Euston. The first time, John met us off the train with fresh flowers, the 'Red Roses of Lancaster'. John really loved Mia. He bought her dolls and books which I still have. We'd hang with his mum and dad, Colin and Veronica, and leave her with them after tea while we muffled off down King Street and round the Market Square in search of ale, and take selfies together in freezing photo booths for a laugh, before selfies (or mobiles) were a thing. We'd overlap when I was working in LA. John would hold court at the Mondrian on Sunset, where burnished sylphs with names like Tatum O'Neal and Brooke Shields would cling to him like wet skirts. What chance did a geek from London have? That'd be none. But he wrote me letters and postcards all the time, from wherever he was, and which I still have. Because I'm only a girl. Only a fool. The kind who can never bring herself to let go of a dream.

'We'd seen a lifetime since we met,
Through good and bad, and things we won't forget...'xxiii

Could there be more than filaments that connected us to each other, that kept on twining us back to the beginning and would not allow us to let each other go? A miniscule battery in me powered a tiny torch for him. There was something in John that was really only for me, too. I could feel it. Neither of us showed it. We would have cancelled each other out. I couldn't bear to lose him. A game-changing kiss might have doused the spark that never illuminated reality, but only gave glow to doomed fantasy. Why risk it? We stayed a heartbeat away.

But hey, no fat lady.

Linda didn't like the idea of me struggling as a single parent with a full-time job, she said. She had been there herself, with her eldest daughter Heather, who was six years old when her mother met Paul. She remembered being spat at and called filthy names by Paul's fans on the steps of Marylebone Register office in March 1969, on their wedding day. A few of them later broke into the McCartneys' home in St. John's Wood, and stole photographs that Linda had taken herself. She hadn't let it rile her, she said.

'I got used to all the slagging off years ago. It doesn't bother me in the slightest. If they're crucifying me, they're leaving someone else alone, right? What's new? You become immune to it, you know? In the early days, I was so blindly in love with Paul that I missed most of it anyway. Or else I just shrugged it off. I've always rubbed people up the wrong way. Even teachers at school used to get on my case. I assumed it was my face. I've always had this long, stern look.' She didn't, particularly.

She told me that she still loved Paul just as dearly as when they first met:

'... if not more than ever. We have never stopped fancying each other. Not in all these years. Paul says that's the key to our marriage, that it's what makes us tick. I hope so. I rather like the idea of being a sexy old lady! I'm older and wiser now, and my eyes are more open to the world. I can understand why stuff has been levelled at me down the years. But Paul and I and the people who count, we know what's what. That's more than good enough for me.'

When I joined her in June 1991 for lunch at the Hard Rock Café in London's Piccadilly, her trim figure and luminous skin spoke volumes about her 'clean' lifestyle. There was nothing about her to suggest 'Rock Wife': no Spandex pants, peroxide hair or vertiginous heels. The plain preppy who'd married the world's most eligible bachelor looked anything but threatening. When I visited her at home, she wore a chunky-knit sweater thrown over a tired cotton dress. She confessed that she liked to hang onto her clothes 'forever'. And Paul, she laughed, was a worse hoarder than she was. He still had 'practically every garment he's ever worn, including his Sergeant Pepper outfit,' she said. When she went out, she usually dressed in frayed waistcoats and ancient denim. If she wore leather cowboy boots, compromising her no-cruelty-to-animals principles, they were 'at least a hundred years old, and at least second-hand'.

In her cluttered, flag-stoned kitchen at Woodlands in Peasmarsh, East Sussex, the boar-infested estate far from the glare of fame which Paul had owned since the 1960s, we sat nursing more mugs of tea. I forget which kind: maybe green. The McCartneys lived a bohemian life there, carting their stuff to jumble sales, showing their faces at village fêtes, sending their children to local schools, bombing about in old Land Rovers and Volvo estates, tending to their menagerie of dogs, cats and chickens, and a 'conservation pond'. Paul would work in his recording studio in a converted windmill. Linda would exercise her ponies in their under-heated paddock. Among the oddments of falling-apart furniture, there was a wonderful abundance of guitars and mud. In one of the small, cosy side rooms with a smoking wood fire, there was a Van Gogh.

Clearing a space among the heaps of baskets, bottles, pottery and home-made loaves on the kitchen table, we sat and discussed Linda's autobiography, which she wanted me to ghost-write. I'd suggested a title which she adored: 'Mac the Wife'. We scribbled an outline and condensed ideas for about thirty chapters, which trawled her childhood and teenage years, waded through the Beatles and Wings eras, and reviewed her roles as wife and mother, while exploring her philosophy on feeding a family as an act of love. My literary agent at the time, Giles Gordon, had three appropriate publishers up his sleeve. He was looking forward to pitching them against one other and earning Linda a record-breaking advance that she clearly did not need and which she would probably have given to charity, as well as himself a healthy fifteen per cent. As a writer for hire, I'd be getting a flat fee for my time and trouble. No royalties. Every time we spoke on the phone during that brief period, Giles would breeze, in his soft Scottish accent, 'Let battle commence!'

But Linda had made clear that her husband would have the last word. And have the last word he did. She sounded tearful when she called to impart the bad news, that Paul 'wasn't going to let her do the book' after all. She never told me why, and we never got round to discussing it. We each vanished back into our frantic schedules, and that was that.

Paul was knighted in 1997. Linda became Lady McCartney. She then became very ill, and was diagnosed with breast cancer. Her secondary was liver. As everyone who knew her expected, she put up a fight. She travelled relentlessly to and from New York for ground-breaking treatment, and eventually to the McCartney ranch in California, where she died: on 17th April 1998, the anniversary of the deaths of my maternal grandfather Charlie Watkins and my paternal grandmother, Nancy Jones. Paul and Linda had been married for almost thirty years.

Come June 2002, there was a new Lady McCartney on the horizon, more than twenty years his junior, in the shapely form of ex-model Heather Mills. The marriage didn't make four years, but it gave them a daughter, Beatrice. Paul would cut a crushed figure as he picked her up from her mother and later delivered her back home. He looked as though he was hanging by a thread. His heart nearly broke, Geoff Baker said. When I bumped into my old Fleet Street mucker after Paul and Linda had sacked him, I discovered at last why 'Mac the Wife: The Autobiography of Linda McCartney' had been dumped.

'It was Paul, bless him, being a control freak,' said Geoff. 'You know what he's like. There's too much going on in his head. He gets a bit confused sometimes, and loses sight of what counts. When Linda told him that she wanted to do it, he lost his rag.' It was along the lines of, "There's only one fucking star in this family."

When I heard that Paul had started divorce proceedings, I couldn't help but think of Linda. I wondered, with heaving sadness, what she might have made of her replacement and the mess they were now in. I thought of her awkward smiles, the squiggly hearts she drew over everything, her tideless warmth. I considered what Baker had told me: that Paul had cried in his arms every day for two years after Linda died. Paul adored 'Lin' to the end of her days, with every shred of himself. After her death, I wrote to him to express my deep sorrow and condolences. He wrote back, saying that it had given him great comfort to be reminded that I had been Linda's friend. He must have written those words more times than he could count.[xxiv]

What I wanted to say to Paul McCartney was what I didn't write. I have kicked myself over it ever since: that he should have let us do that bloody book. That the story Linda had to tell, as the wife of a member of the world's greatest-ever group and therefore forever at odds with legions of fans all over the planet who loathed her guts, would have been moving and enthralling. It would have been dynamite. We could have learned so much about the former Beatle through the eyes and words of his wife. Perhaps that was what he feared: her frankness, her fearlessness, her insistence on calling it a spade. Linda McCartney had long endured the ferocity of a compassionless press, in whose eyes she could do no right. They bored for England about it, even after her death. He 'should have married that nice Jane Asher,' they'd say. But he didn't. Jane happened not to be The One. He fell in love with Linda. Get over it.

We don't know what we've got until it's gone. No one but her could tell Linda's story. So it will never be told. Maybe that's what Paul wanted. But if he truly believed there was only one star in his family, he was wrong.

With John Waite, Lancaster, England, 1992

With John Waite, Camden, London, 2010

19. TO FORGIVE DIVINE

No one saw this coming. One minute I was travelling the world from a cluttered pied-a-terre in edgy Islington a quick cab ride from bright-lights-big-city action, which had been our base for the past five years. The next, I was exchanging on a large double-balconied apartment in Seven-oaks overlooking communal gardens rolling down to the Eurostar line, with a housebound next-door neighbour in the habit of lowering her dog in a basket on a rope for it to have a toilet break. My friends thought I'd lost the plot. What did this leafy backwater some twenty miles south-east of Charing Cross have to offer that N1 did not? Apart from Knole House, the fifteenth-century pile set in a thousand-acre deer park where the Beatles had filmed shorts for 'Penny Lane' and 'Strawberry Fields Forev-er', how did a comatose Kentish settlement lure a latter-day rock chick?

It had a school.

Not just any old school. I'd lusted after Sevenoaks School for years. Since the age of fifteen, in fact, when a few of the gang we trolled around with in Bromley and Beckenham were Sevenoaks boys. A plain red-brick schoolgirl, I had long been a sucker for ancient stone chapels and sedate seats of learning, conjuring ghosts of Michaelmas, Lent and Trinity terms Past from their thrumming time-worn walls. Sevenoaks is the second-oldest non-denominational school in Britain. It was founded by William Sevenoke, a Mayor of London and close associate of King Henry V. It had produced a number of distinguished pupils. But it wasn't about that. I simply wanted Mia to have something I hadn't, while not wanting to send her away to boarding school. I was laying the foundations for her en-trance as a public school day pupil. It was this aspect of my decision to relocate that confounded a few of our gang. We knew each other's princi-ples and ideals, were mostly on the same page when it came to politics and privilege, and tended not to take such things too seriously. But here I was, about to boot 'principles' aside in the interests of a full private edu-cational experience for the precious firstborn. What planet, you ask?

Bitter arguments ensued, over gallons of Pinot Grigio and sacks of Kettle chips. Did I not consider it my duty to support the local schools? Well, yes I did. In an ideal world, absolutely. I believed in state education – just as I believed, and still do, in paying tax to support the welfare state. I deplored, and still do, those at both ends of the scale who cheat the system to get out of paying their dues, while spending the cash contributed by the working rest of us on profligate non-essentials such as cosmetic surgery and stress-relieving Shetland ponies. I had benefited from a state education. I championed, and still do, a fair society. I worked hard, and tried to give something back. I'd grown up listening to my eccentric Welsh family extolling the virtues of James Keir Hardie and Aneurin Bevan. If I went the private route, I'd be betraying the clan, wouldn't I? Would I really. I knew folk on the dole who replaced their luxury cars every August and took five holidays a year. I'd driven the same Jeep for ten years, and had a penchant for British seaside resorts, especially Margate. Who were they to tell me what I could spend my hard-earned on?

But what about so-called equality? Looking back over my life to date, I've had my share of it. I once enjoyed cheap Housing Association rent in inner London. I'd had a free college education, and was used to affordable transport and domestic utilities, as well as excellent free care on the National Health. I was never without a job. Even Saturday jobs, during my teens. When I got bored with one, I simply went and got another. All my friends had jobs. None of us was ever unemployed. Didn't we have Thatcher to blame for the rise of inequality? For the off-loading of public assets for private gain? Hadn't the damned investment bankers exacerbated imbalance, and all that?

I wouldn't exactly describe myself as a 'leftie'. I'm just an ordinary working person who, like most, is committed to supporting the kind of society which works for the majority. So what possessed me to send Mia to a private school?

It was a no-brainer, really. Even though the decision compromised my core beliefs, I just wanted the best that I could afford for my own child. If that meant forfeiting the lush holidays, the annual vehicle upgrade, an actual house and myriad other material advantages, it was a choice I had the right to make. I was prepared to pay for Mia to get a better education. 'Better' how? A wider choice of curricular subjects, with an emphasis on modern languages. Greater emphasis on extra-curricular pursuits, such as music and performing arts. Fewer pupils to a class. No distracting disruptive element. Superior libraries, sports facilities, pavilions, swimming pools, music blocks. Official transport for away fixtures, concerts and drama tours. Plus the unquantifiable things, not exactly taught, more absorbed through observation and osmosis: manners, social skills, respect, self-confidence. Yep, the stuff that is supposed to be acquired at home.

Of course every child deserves an equal start in life. Of course it's not fair. Life isn't. But we do have the right to choose to pay for education. We who do so liberate a state school place for which we are already paying via our taxes. We pay twice. We are giving back. End of argument.

It was looking, at one point, as though I wasn't going to have to pay at all; as though Mia was about to earn her own way through childhood, and that I'd soon be reclining beside a private pool with a champagne flute in one hand and a manicurist in the other.

I still pause to sigh, on a slow day, about the day that almost changed our lives. All was easy on my mind that cloudless blue day. There was a floral scent on the breeze, a little hope in the air, a watermelon smile on my face. I had A-listers for company. I was hanging by the pool of the swanky Sunset Marquis hotel on Alta Loma Road, LA, waiting on an interview with John Travolta. While I annotated my notes, Mia was larking in the water a few feet away, playing sharks with the lead singer of the band 10,000 Maniacs. Bruce Springsteen was eating lunch across the terrace with his wife and child. U2's Bono was doing what he was best at, schmoozing and kissing people's babies. Grace Jones was preening on a nearby sun lounger. Just another boring, beam-me-up day in Hollywood.

A dozen or so men in tailored summer suits sat together at a lunch table, locked in earnest conversation. Suddenly one of them, a top studio casting agent as it transpired, got up and walked across the terrace towards me. Without bothering to introduce himself, he waded straight in. He did not mince his words.

'Take my advice, baby,' he barked. 'Drop your typewriter in the John. You are sitting on a million dollars. That,' he said, gesturing towards Mia, 'is as cute as cute gets. A walking piece of candy. We are talking Macaulay Culkin's little English cousin in 'Home Alone 3'. We are talking adorable sidekick in Billy Connolly's new series. There are pictures in the pipe that she'd absolutely walk away with. 'Mrs Doubtfire'. 'Miracle on 34th Street'. 'Matilda'. We have been watching her, and she is *it*. C'mon, kid. Three months and you'll be living in a hacienda-style home with a pool in Beverly Hills, and driving a brand-new Merc. Here's my card. Call me. We wanna get her in to do a screen test.'

That night, as I sat stroking Mia's head until she fell asleep, I admit that I considered it. Every mother thinks she has produced the most beautiful, talented specimen ever born. I was no exception. Mia Clementine was a real-life Disney Snow White, all coal-black hair, ice-cream skin and Bambi eyes. I allowed myself to dream about what life could be like as a pumped-up Jackie Stallone or a Teri Shields. Honestly, I did think about it. But then I woke up. I was a gritty showbiz journalist who had gone beyond the footlights and had seen what lurked in the shadows. I knew the risks. The thought of exploiting my own child for personal gain, the idea of dolls with Mia's face at F.A.O. Schwartz and Hamley's, of glittery pink hairdryers and make-up sets with her name on in Duane Reade, Boots and Superdrug, and the knowledge that it would be my signature on the contract – all this and more made me shudder. I thought fleetingly of 'Colonel' Tom Parker legging it to New York in August 1977 to strike mega-bucks deals on Elvis Presley merchandise instead of to Memphis for his charge's funeral. I was probably a little tired and emotional at this point.

I thought of Drew Barrymore, who starred in 'ET' as a seven-year-old in 1982, and who was smoking and drinking by the age of nine.[xxv]

Of Tatum O'Neal, the youngest actress ever to win an Oscar – in 1974, at ten, for 'Paper Moon', in which she appeared opposite her father, Ryan O'Neal. She dated Michael Jackson, became addicted to cocaine, and married tennis ace John McEnroe in 1986.[xxvi]

Of River Phoenix, who shared Mia's birthday. He'd appeared in Hollywood films by the age of thirteen, and lost his life to a heroin and cocaine overdose just ten years later, on 31st October 1993.

To that list, I would today add Britney Spears. Forget the multi-million record sales, the Grammys, the movie roles, the signature scents. Forget her superstar status as the best-selling teen artist of all time. She too lost custody of her own children as a direct result of her inability to stay sober and drug-free. She was once forced into an ambulance live on television, and hospitalised for psychiatric evaluation. The world was quick to condemn poor Britney. But the villain of the piece was surely her star-struck mother, Lynne. Desperate for her child to succeed, she enrolled her at dance school in their home town of Kentwood, Louisiana, when she was only two years old. By the age of eight, Britney was at the New York Professional Performing Arts School, and two years later had landed a part in Disney's Mickey Mouse Club TV show, alongside Christina Aguilera, Ryan Gosling and Justin Timberlake. When that was cancelled a couple of years down the line, Lynne kept on pushing, seeking her child's next big break. By the time Britney was sixteen, she was celebrating her first international hit, 'Baby One More Time', dressed in a midriff-baring school uniform. Her childhood had been stolen. She'd had neither time nor guidance to form genuine friendships or learn real life skills. She'd grown up in a parallel universe where image, ego and money are all that count. Where she was nothing but a cash cow to those along for the ride. We didn't yet have Kris Jenner, Dina Lohan or Tish Cyrus, those mothers responsible for the enrichment of the lexicon by the portmanteau 'momager': the mother of a celebrity who controls and/or directs her own child's career.

When Hollywood came knocking for Mia, we could have done with the money. I was a single mother. I was grafting around the clock between London, New York and Los Angeles, living on the hoof out of a carry-on with a child under one arm, or dropping her round at her grandparents' en route to a last-minute flight. It wasn't always easy to make ends meet. As a 'freelance', one is technically unemployed. It's a boom-bust, feast-or-famine existence. Precarious to say the least. Disconcertingly, Mia had already acquired a taste for celebrity, having travelled with me on assignments more or less since she was born. Jackie Collins once bottle-fed her in her suite at the Ritz in London's Piccadilly. Ozzy Osbourne and Alice Cooper took her out for tea. She had been entertained in Miami by Gloria and Emilio Estefan, and had attended a church service with Charlton Heston. Billy Idol had her over to play with his little son Wilhem. Mia had taken all that and more in her stride. But agreeing for her to star in a major Hollywood picture would be crossing a line. With an aching heart, I called the casting director and told him I wasn't interested.

Even I couldn't believe his response.

'Big deal! You screw up the kid's life, you'll have the money to pay for the therapists.'

He wouldn't leave me alone. He begged me to let him bring a crew to us, if I wasn't prepared to take Mia down to the studio. In the end, to get him off my back, I agreed.

Mia was her usual Disney Princess self. She chose a long calico dress, helped herself to my lipgloss, and slipped effortlessly into 'Peter Pan' Wendy mode. She floated across the lawn, danced among the bluebells and skipped the light fandango through the trees, right on cue. She sang 'Blue Eyes' and 'You Are My Sunshine' straight to camera, word-perfect, and floored the director with silly jokes in the 'my dog's got no nose' vein. He swooned. I swear I could see dollar signs revolving in his eyes. The next day, as I had anticipated, he was back on the phone.

'The proof is on its way over to you,' he squawked. 'See how she reacts to the camera! It loves her! She's a natural! Take a look at the footage, I implore you, and then let's talk.'

We never did. When I sat down to watch Mia's screentest, an alternative reality swam into view. A backlot life of 4am make-up calls, twelve-hour shooting schedules, script clinics, wardrobe fittings, publicity meetings, advertising campaigns. I could well imagine the endless trips to TV and radio studios, the photo shoots, the public appearances. The anything but normal childhood. I looked at Mia, sleeping peacefully like the baby she still was, and I knew that all I wanted for her was what I'd had myself: a secure and loving childhood, a regular upbringing, a proper English school where she would know what was expected of her, and nice little friends her own age.

I sent a note explaining my decision, and hung onto the video for posterity. My two younger children still watch it from time to time. They are fascinated by the other life their sister almost had.

Once Mia was old enough to understand what I'd turned down, she was furious, of course, and not inclined, for a while, to forgive. Her life became a relentless quest to get it back. A memorable Lady Macbeth at the age of eleven, as well as a credible singer and pianist, she wound up studying Theatre at the BRIT School in South London alongside Kate Nash, where she mixed with Music students Katie Melua, Amy Winehouse, Jessie J. and Adele before progressing to Exeter University to read Drama. That got it out of her system. She's in the music business now, God help me. She still laments, perhaps (I hope) in jest, that her own mother denied her the big break. Everybody agrees with her. They would, wouldn't they.

Piers Morgan's invitation to write a weekly column for the News of the World, 'The Lesley-Ann Jones Big Interview', was a bolt out of the blue and a ticket to tabloid heaven. A contract! Regular pay cheques! I had long adored the world's best-selling Sunday paper and fell on it gleefully each week, especially when I had a freelance piece in. There was a saying at the time, that if you took the 'Screws', the Mail on Sunday and the Sunday Times, you had the whole world in your hand. We were still in the pre-multi-media, pre-rolling news age, when the free press was still an enormous force to be reckoned with. The predominant form of mass communication, newspapers were vital in the forming of public opinion. They acted as mouthpieces for national and international leaders. They crusaded, exposed and debated contentious issues and scandals. They were the collective voice of dissent, and kept the democratic tradition alive. Allegedly. And nobody did it better than the News of the World. It was the paper that everybody loved to loathe. The same 'everybody' who was buying it.

I knew too well that this keen, charismatic, not yet thirty-year-old new editor would demand his pound of flesh. Michael Winner and Jonathan Ross knew it too. The three of us were appointed and announced on the same day. Starched former movie director Winner would write an opinion column, while gobby (in a good way) film buff Wossy would review the new releases. It was all right for them. All they had to do to comply with their contracts each week was have a few thoughts, glance at a few flicks, then sit down with an eyebrow pencil and a sickbag and write it. My own responsibilities involved rather more placing of neck on line in foreign climes – never more so than when Piers ordered me to LA in June 1995, to interview the world's hottest heartthrob.

Hugh John Mungo Grant had rocketed to fame the previous year as gauche toff Charles in Richard Curtis's rom-com 'Four Weddings and a Funeral'. Out of nowhere, it became the highest-grossing picture in British cinematic history, banking more than $245 million. Oscar-nominated in the Best Picture and Best Original Screenplay categories, it earned Grant a Golden Globe as Best Actor, and the BAFTA for Best Actor in a Leading Role.[xxvii] And it established its leading man as the quintessential upper-crust, commitment-phobe rogue.

Most journalists naturally loathed everything about the man. His 'acting', his mannerisms, that awful faux-dazed-and-confused British public schoolboy stance, all the hapless, self-deprecating mincing-about that masked an ego the size of Manchuria. Many of us assumed that Grant, a tidily turned-out, well-spoken Oxford graduate with a degree in English (he got a 2:1) who had 'fallen into acting by accident', was simply playing himself. His love scenes in 'Four Weddings' were tender enough. Presumably he was drawing on real life, his relationship with Elizabeth Hurley upping his ante. The model and would-be actress became a household name the night of the 'Four Weddings' Hollywood premiere, when she turned up in 'THAT dress': a borrowed, punk-inspired, black silk-and-Lycra Versace creation that all but revealed what she'd had for breakfast. Her modesty was contained only by a handful of giant gold safety pins. Hurley was a red-carpet sensation. It wasn't even her premiere.

'Nine Months' was designed to capitalise on Grant's success in 'Four Weddings' and consolidate his superstar status. An American remake of the French film 'Neuf Mois', it was directed by 'Mrs. Doubtfire's Chris Columbus, boasted a score by my friend Hans Zimmer, and co-starred Julianne Moore and Robin Williams. The film's distributor was 20th Century Fox: the legendary Hollywood film studio founded in 1935, which Rupert Murdoch had acquired in 1985. Mr. Murdoch, notez bien, also owned the News of the World. It was thanks to this fortuitous connection that we landed the world-exclusive.

On Sunday 25th June, I flew to Los Angeles, picked up the Mustang convertible at LAX, drove to Alta Loma Road, checked in at the Sunset Marquis, and turned in for some shut-eye. Late the next afternoon, I meandered over to the 20th Century Fox lot, cleared Security, did the requisite meet-and-greet, and took my seat at the private screening. The film was so-so. Grant is his usual floppy-hair-flicking, bumbling self in it, reluctant to commit, his pennies (two Ns) dropping only when it's almost too late. He wins back the pregnant girlfriend about an hour and a half after we see it coming. Conspicuous lack of big twist. Absence of agonising cliffhanger. Major yawn factor. The usual. The handful of us in attendance were then ushered into a side room for a few sherbets, after which Hugh and I were scheduled for dinner and chat.

It was about three glasses of champagne in that it dawned. No Hugh. Who knew? No one, apparently. The apoplectic publicist was frantically doing her pelvic-floors (you can tell by the eyebrows). How many days would I be in town? I'd stick around for as long as it took, of course, but we were on a deadline here. This was Monday night. The features editor Rebekah Wade wanted copy by Wednesday night, Thursday morning at a stretch, to run on Sunday 2nd July. The film was due for release on 14th July. It was already Tuesday morning in London when news leaked out on the Associated Press wire that Grant had been arrested by the LAPD off Sunset Boulevard, for 'receiving oral sex in a public place' from a prostitute called Divine Brown. Show time! The world's media zoomed into panic-stricken overdrive. By the time I got through to Stuart White, the paper's American Editor who was based in LA, he'd already had Piers on the phone, screaming these immortal words:

'Stuart: I don't care what you fucking do, or how much you fucking spend, I want you to get that woman!'

'Stand by your bed, kid,' Stuart advised me. 'I'm going to need you on this. I'll be in touch.'

Together with smooth operator David Shumacher, Stuart tracked down Brown to an address in Oakland near San Francisco (while the flood of incoming Brit hacks headed hopelessly for Oakland LA). They paid an off-duty police officer to visit the address, which turned out to be the home of Miss Brown's milkman uncle and his punctilious wife. Divine, real name Estella Marie Thompson, had been charged with lewd conduct, bailed and released. The next thing Stuart knew, he was signing away his Amex to rent a Lear jet for the family, despatching a limo to convey them to the plane, and gunning it a hundred and twenty miles in his car to meet them in the desert, at the luxurious Hyatt Palm Springs. There, watched over by her boyfriend and pimp 'Gangsta' Brown, who had sniffed sizeable wads of wonga on the breeze and got himself into position sharpish, they struck a deal for Divine's exclusive story to the tune of $100,000. The first $20,000 was being wired from London overnight. The balance would be paid once they'd nailed the story.

'Don't talk to anyone!' Stuart warned them all. 'Don't answer the door, don't pick up the phone, don't reply to notes. And whatever you do, do not under any circumstances leave the building!'

The story that unfolded beggared belief. Divine told it as only a happy hooker could. She'd been minding her own business, plying her trade on the street as per usual when up rocked this English dude in his BMW. Did she recognise him? Not at all! She'd never seen the schmuck before in her life. She quoted him $100 to go to her hotel room. Grant had only $60 on him, the cheapskate. So she agreed, against her better judgement, to get in his car.

'He had a very strange accent, just like you,' she told White. For which, read 'nothing at all like White.' She clambered in, dispensed with the undergarments and braced herself for a Cape Canaveral-style lift-off. At which point Grant proposed a diversion that turned her stomach and made her want to run for her life.

'"No, I am definitely not doing that," I told him. 'I've had a lot of Johns in my time, but this guy was scary. Fucking weird. I knew it from the moment he opened his mouth. When I got in the car, I checked all the door handles, to make sure I could escape if I needed to.'

It begged all the questions. This was not some fifteen-year-old innocent who'd just ventured out on the game. This was a seasoned pro who knew how to take care of herself. When Divine alluded to the 'sickos out there', it was clear that she included Grant. 'You don't know,' she elaborated, 'when you go with a guy, whether he's going to just get what he came for and say 'so long', or turn around and murder you. You let him do what he has to, you think about something else, you take the money and that's it. If you're lucky. Bye bye loser, and on to the next trick.'

It still stumps me. You are a massive movie star, you're in Hollywood to launch your latest flick, and you're getting paid millions of dollars. Why not just get the studio to fix you up with a discreet, high-class call girl (oxymoron alert), about whom no one will ever be the wiser? They do this kind of thing all the time. But not for Hugh. He evidently craved rough trade. He reneged on our dinner date, slipped away to cruise the Strip, picked up a black prostitute, conveyed her to a side street and demanded the kind of in-car entertainment he could never have swung off Her Indoors. And he got caught how? According to Brown, a cop was alerted by the BMW's brake lights flashing, which they did automatically every time Grant toed the brake pedal. Which he kept doing, for some reason, over and over again. Almost as though he was asking for it.

Late that night, Stuart filed more than three thousand words of sweltering copy. Piers was ecstatic. They now had photos of Divine as a little girl, in high school, as a mother of newborns, the complete picture. Plus the icing on the cake: images of the most wanted woman in the world wearing a red-hot replica of Liz Hurley's black Versace safety-pin gown, run up specially and couriered from London. These shots were captured on an Instamatic in her hotel room. I still have them.

It was now Thursday. All Stuart had to do was get her through to Saturday without a syllable to the outside world, and the exclusive was assured. It was as much as he could do to contain Divine, not least when a cousin of hers was killed in a gangland shoot-out and she insisted on attending the funeral. Stuart talked her out of it by reminding her of the fortune she'd lose.

Back in London, Piers gleefully laid out nine spreads of dynamite. An editor likes nothing better than to slaughter the competition. What he had for that Sunday was going to kill the world. He rubbed his hands together at the thought of a congratulatory communication from his proprietor. Perhaps even a nice fat bonus. It was all looking very good indeed. But then Rupert called.

'What are you splashing on, Piers?' the boss enquired. 'I hope it's not that prostitute in LA...'

Excluded thus far from the real action, but gagging to get stuck in, I almost fainted with relief when a shattered Stuart called to tell me that he needed me. Not that the guy on the phone sounded like him. Little wonder, given what he'd been going through. The overwrought wreck was existing on just two or three hours' sleep a night, he said. He was responsible around the clock for Divine and her entourage. As Piers Morgan recalled in his 2005 memoir 'The Insider', Stuart was 'prowling the corridors of the hotel through the night with the demented attentiveness of an Israeli secret service agent', a description that White confirms as accurate. I can still picture him scanning the arid landscape and hillsides with binoculars, and jumping over rattlesnakes and at his own shadow. Now, finally, he was calling to give me my chance. I was on: the next British Airways flight out of LAX, that was, in First Class, seat 1B ... beside Grant himself, who was booked in 2B. Or not 2B. That was the question. How in Yorick's name did he manage to swing that?

'Easy,' chuckled White. 'I fixed it through a contact at BA. He put me through to the head honcho, I pretended to be Grant's personal assistant, insisted that I had to book 'her', an anonymous bird, into the seat beside him, and that under no circumstances must the press be informed. I was matter-of-fact and non-specific. I didn't even have to give your name. The plan is, you board the plane, doze off, sit tight, make a mental note of everything Grant eats and drinks, time him when he goes to the toilet, keep an eye and ear on what he reads, watches, mutters in his sleep, and hawk-eye his every move around the stewardesses. Come the eleventh hour, you surface from your slumber, feign surprise that it's him, offer your condolences over what happened in LA, but you say never mind, eh, we're all grown-ups, and how do you think poor long-suffering Liz'll take it? It'll make five more pages in the paper, with pictures!' Little did Stuart know that Piers had already reduced the allocated page count to just four, with or without the interview every paper on the planet would have killed for.

It was the longest shot. What can go wrong, will go wrong. Picture Grant boarding the aircraft, bunging his bag in the overhead locker, sitting down, buckling up, glancing to his left, and almost regurgitating his tonsils. You have never in your life seen anyone move so fast. He is outta there before you can say 'blow job'. I'd blown it, all right.

To make matters worse, Mr Murdoch was experiencing hemoptysis. He'd just signed on the dotted line to commit 20th Century Fox to three pictures with Hugh Grant. Now here was his own newspaper, stitching up the very actor who had cost him a boggling fortune. His own employees were exposing his new best friend as a felon, to the tune of around £50,000 on top of the hundred grand that Divine had already been paid. Could it get much worse? Of course it could. The excrement hit the air-con big-time. In splash-headline-speak,

'HUGH TOLD ME I WAS HIS SEX FANTASY'

I might as well have checked into Battersea Dogs' Home. I'd just wasted several grands' worth of News of the World budget on a total non-story. I crawled home to lick my wounds. Collected Mia on my way back from Heathrow, retreated to Sevenoaks, marvelled at the trust of the Yorkie going over the side in the basket on a rope, which I now regarded as the perfect metaphor for my dilemma, and kept watching the Divine/Grant horror story unfold. Not even the better broadsheets could resist having a go. But no other newspaper came close to eclipsing the News of the World's, or should I say Stuart White's, spectacular triumph. It was the scoop of his life. The Divine Brown story scored the Screws an all-time record for an unpublicised edition, adding a quarter of a million sales to its circulation. White and Shumacher were bunged a five hundred quid bonus each for their trouble. It was an insult. Hugh and Liz held inconclusive crisis summits over the Pimms in their English country garden. Then Hugh was back in America, appearing on 'The Tonight Show' with Jay Leno, who asked the inevitable and less than inspired 'What the hell were you thinking?'

'I think you know in life what's a good thing to do and what's a bad thing,' quoth the quintessential upper-crust, commitment-phobe rogue. 'And I did a bad thing. And there you have it.'

Grant was fined $1,180, given two years' summary probation, and ordered to complete an AIDS education programme. Divine was commanded to attend AIDS classes, perform five days' community service, fined $1,150 and sentenced to a hundred and eighty days in jail. Grant went on to make 'Notting Hill' with Julia Roberts in 1999; created Daniel Cleaver for 'Bridget Jones's Diary' in 2001, gave his saucy Prime Minister in 'Love Actually' in 2003, and reprised his cad in 'Bridget Jones: The Edge of Reason' in 2004. More recently (2016), he partnered Meryl Streep in 'Florence Foster Jenkins', and won plaudits for his portrayal of former Liberal leader/closet gay Jeremy Thorpe in 'A Very English Scandal' (2018). Divine flaunted her stuff, dived dauntlessly into the porn industry, became a TV presenter, made commercials, and played herself in an X-rated docu-drama based on the incident, called (great title) 'Sunset and Divine'. She was the subject of the biopic 'Million Dollar Hooker' in 2006, and appeared on 'Hollywood Lives' for ITV in 2007. Grant's films are estimated to have raked in more than $2.4 billion. Divine is reckoned to have earned around $1.6 million. She did something with the money she'd never dreamed she would ever afford. She sent her daughters to private school.

It has confounded me all these years that Grant has never stopped going on about it. He'd never bothered to conceal the fact that he loathed the cult of celebrity and despised all journalists on principle. But it wasn't us who wrecked his life that fateful night. He did that by himself. He was a user of prostitutes. He'd gone and got caught. It was the police who arrested him, not the media. He should have buttoned his lip, taken it on the chin, banked the cheques and got on with his life. Oh no. Not Hugh. At every turn, given the flimsiest excuse to blame it on the press, he was in like Flynn. To this day, he appears bitter about 'being exposed by tabloid newspapers'. But a man of his 'class' would not, by definition, be well-disposed towards tabloids in the first place. The red-tops are not compiled for the likes of him.

There are millions of people around the world who would never have heard of Hugh's extra-curricular activity with a harlot, but for his ad infinitum banging on about 'press intrusion'. It was Grant himself who blew his own strumpet, continuing to draw attention to himself and the story. He even seized upon the Leveson Enquiry as an opportunity to present himself as the wounded party.[xxviii] It seems to have escaped him that the world has moved on. In an age in which every variation on the theme of carnal collaboration is discussed and illustrated graphically on television, no one gives a toss that some screen actor once played a few rounds of front-seat poker with a woman not his betrothed, and subsequently spent a night in the cells. Been there. Done that. The laddie doth protest too much.

Divine Brown, Hyatt Hotel Palm Springs, California, June/July 1995

20. YOU ARE MY SON SHINE

Few were surprised when Piers accepted an offer from the Mirror, and jumped ship in September 1995. His goal had long been to edit a daily newspaper. Such posts arise rarely, and the opportunity was too great for him to refuse. His successor at the News of the World, Phil Hall, was bound to reconfigure the paper and put his own personal stamp on it. My interviews began migrating onto the pages of the paper's colour supplement, Sunday magazine, the piece on Frank Bruno at a Lanzarote training camp on the eve of a comeback fight being the first. A cover story, fair dos, but perhaps it deserved better. I looked about for the broom. Here it was, sweeping clean again. In a tense meeting at the Tower Hotel with Managing Editor Stuart Kuttner and features editor Rebekah Wade, having already sought legal advice, I held them to account over our contract. A week later, I walked away with twenty grand. I was planning a Bucket-List expedition to Machu Picchu when I got waylaid.

I had a bone to pick with love.
What had it done for me lately?
Not a lot.
Not that I'd had time to notice the absence of it.
The long-term plan had been to carry on writing books. I had authored or co-authored five, to date, and now had the taste for it. Fitting the work in was the problem. My time was never my own. Now that I was freelancing for two mass-audience American tabloid news and celebrity TV shows, 'Hard Copy' and 'E! Entertainment', writing features for various publications in the UK, the US and Australia, and raising Mia by myself, there were few unspoken-for hours on the calendar to devote to publishing commitments. Nor was there a minute left for 'going out' with anyone. Which is what we called it back then. We didn't yet have 'dating', not at any speed, let alone partner-hunting websites or apps. As for 'tinder', it was anything used for lighting fires (come on, baby), or came in a box used by Hans Christian Andersen's soldier boy to summon dogs to do his bidding. Which, when you think about it ...
Phil Lynott's widow Caroline Crowther was making a mint running a sensibly-shod 'introductions' agency, primarily for respectable Home

Counties types with lacquered hair and abundant bank accounts. This was unequivocally not for me.

Did my solo status matter? What if it did? Something had to give, and there wasn't exactly much choice. I'd had my share of take-it-leave-it romance, of flirtatious irritants and abrasive potential mothers-in-law. Who needed it? So I'd written it off. Que sera. But my mum had always maintained that these things tend to happen when you least expect them. As usual, she was right.

October 1995. Richard Hughes and I had just finished shooting a strand in the middle of Dean Street for 'Hard Copy', about the hidden assets of actor Tom Cruise. 'That's a wrap,' yelped the director, and it was suddenly time for lunch. Rich and I took a jog through the Soho mists over Shaftsbury Avenue, down Cranbourn Street and up the bottom of Long Acre, and arrived at Le Palais du Jardin gasping for a Campari and grapefruit just as they were locking up for the afternoon. They let us in anyway. The restaurant, since closed, had a dichotomous reputation: smart premises, decent food, shame about the staff. Their seafood platter may have been the finest this side of Kivukoni, but the maitre d' was rudeness personified. Although he did seem quite partial to 'telly people'. Only one other table in the place was occupied, by a pair of executive-looking types deep in conversation. We planted ourselves at the bar, and said yes to whatever the kitchen was about to bin.

I saw him in the mirror behind the optics. He and his companion were striding towards the exit when he stopped, did the double, and caught my eye in the glass.

'Lesley-Ann?' he said.

He was very tall and dark-haired. A fetching stranger in a sharp tailored suit and bright tie. There was a deep red stain on his lower lip. He'd had a good lunch, clearly.

He repeated my name, and I nodded, stumped. I had never before set eyes on this man. I knew that I was going to marry him.

All that about the so-called coup de foudre: humbug. My beloved mother has long been fond of old black-and-white romances, in which the concept of love at first sight is frequently the theme. 'There's someone for everyone' was a mantra she muttered mechanically. But how were you supposed to know which one was The One? You just know, she said. I couldn't imagine it. Given that there are about six billion people on the planet, the notion that every single one was pre-destined to be found by the only living soul who was right for them was as far-fetched as horoscopes, or as the idea of a princess on a pile of mattresses being kept up all night by a pea. Get a grip. Love, I was sure, was just an illusion. A Hollywood invention. 'What about Shakespeare?' said my mother. 'You love Shakespeare. What about "Romeo & Juliet" and "A Midsummer Night's Dream?" Almost all the plays say something about love. What about sonnets? Would we still care about Shakespeare four hundred years down the line, had he got it so wrong?'

What was my mother trying to say: that Shakespeare invented love? Where were Eros and Aphrodite when you needed them? Shakespeare invented modern English, cornered the market in creative consciousness, and captured the essence of how humans view the world and experience life, in plausible poetry. He made emotions matter universally. He embellished and dignified lust. He repackaged romance. Thanks to Shakespeare, we find ourselves' 'unable to live without' the object of our desire, rather than without 'love'. Because of the bloody Bard, we are all too often pathetically in love with love itself. I know: speak for myself, yeah?

So I was lusting after complete strangers now? Desperate or what? Could this be the ticking clock thing I'd read about, or was I losing the plot? The next thing I knew, I was exchanging cards with the tall, dark stranger in the Palais du Jardin. At least I now knew his name and what he was: a management consultant. Far removed, in mien, from any male over whom I had hitherto swooned.

Mia and I departed for the Caribbean shortly afterwards, where we stayed in David Bowie's home, Britannia Bay House, on Mustique. I wrote the initial draft of my first biography of Freddie Mercury. Between conversations with my new soul mate. Which was weird. There was definitely 'something there that wasn't there before.' The phone bill was astronomical. I'm probably still paying for it.

He proposed in Cape Town on New Year's Day 1996, two months after the apparent coup de foudre. We were married six weeks later at Caxton Hall on London's Marylebone Road, and had a small, beautiful reception at the Halcyon Hotel on Holland Park. The emerald and diamond engagement ring he'd had made for me was designed, he said, to reflect the colour of my eyes. Which prompted my future sister-in-law to demand of my brother a chunk of ruby to match hers. We honeymooned in Prague, on the News of the World's timely pay-off. Five years later, while on holiday in Tobago, a masked assailant rammed a gun up my nose outside the restaurant we'd just dined in, and attempted to tear the ring off. It was my big, unarmed husband who saved my life. What a guy. What a great fit. Other than my parents' and grandparents' marriages, I couldn't imagine anything better. It was my downfall.

I miscarried our first baby. I was in Munich at the time, interviewing Barbara Valentin, an Austrian-born actress known as 'the German Jayne Mansfield' who had been the lover of Freddie Mercury and had shared a flat with him there. At the end of an afternoon spent trawling Queen and Freddie haunts and downing Happy Hour cocktails in one of the band's favourite bars, I left Barbara at the door of her apartment and walked to the corner to find a taxi to take me to drinks with a friend. I was about three months pregnant, fit and well. We'd only just made the announcement to our families. One minute I was scanning the early evening traffic for a vacant cab. The next, I was on my knees in the gutter, the pain in my belly so intense that I thought I'd been knifed. My head was a block of ice, and was throbbing unbearably. Clutching my bag, I tried to get up. People rushed past on their way home from work. No one stopped. Perhaps I looked drugged or drunk.

A taxi pulled over eventually. The deluge held off until I got back to Barbara's. As she unlocked the door, I heard myself whimpering like a wounded animal. She took one look at me, and screamed. I knew what was coming. A torrent of red against stark bathroom tiles. Tidal waves of cramps and contractions. My heart seemed to unfurl and suck in on itself, like someone folding a pair of socks together, over and over. But no worse than a bad period, my new husband reasoned on the phone. No. It wasn't remotely like that. Black thoughts and swirling spaces. Barbara stood helplessly in the hallway. It didn't occur to either of us to call a doctor. Nor to my husband to come to Munich and get me. Which was all I wanted. I wanted him. I mopped the mess myself with my hostess's pristine towels, then lay down in my room, grimly awake, until it was time to leave. A few hours later, alone on the plane, I was engulfed in grief. I went straight to hospital instead of home, where they whisked me to the front of the ultrasound queue. I could see right through the shape on the screen. There is no heartbeat, they said. I could have told them that.

I hardly dared believe the thin blue line. If truly pregnant again, several months on, how would I bear it? What if it let go, like the last one? Sarah Creighton was our consultant at the Portland Hospital. Our baby boy was born there. Name? His father, who loved Egyptology, favoured Ramses. I'm not joking. Only when I pointed out that they'd call him 'Rambo' in the school playground, which might lead him into all kinds of trouble, did common sense kick in. Henry had been the given name of his paternal great-grandfather, 'Grandpa Bill' Bunker, a celebrated microbiologist who worked with scientist Alfred Lucas during the 1920s on materials gathered from the tomb of Tutankhamun. It was Lucas who famously demonstrated that when the inner chamber of the tomb was opened for the first time in 1924, there were no bacteria present. The tomb could not, therefore, have been broken into and plundered prior to the official opening, as had previously been believed. Henry Bunker's swab analysis of the walls, floors and furniture of the tomb confirmed this. His tests altered the understanding of everything that had happened during and after the tomb's discovery. Little did I know at the time how all this would return to haunt me.

Henry it was, then. His middle names would be Edmund, an old Shine family name, and Emlyn, after my paternal grandfather. He had been longed-for. He was 'our son Shine'.

Nine days later, on Sunday 31st August at around 4am, the lights went out again. I was back at home with my newborn and sitting up in bed, feeding him. The television brought dawn news, an unthinkable flash to stun the world. At twenty-five past midnight, Henri Paul, deputy head of security at the Paris Ritz, had apparently driven Diana Princess of Wales and her beau Dodi Al Fayed away from the hotel, pursued by lupine snappers and hacks on motorcycles. Moments later, Paul had lost control of the car in the Pont de l'Alma tunnel, killing himself and Al Fayed outright. Diana and her bodyguard Trevor Rees-Jones, both seriously injured, were rushed to the Pitié Salpêtrière hospital. Only the bodyguard survived. The curdling sounds from my lungs made my baby cry and woke my husband beside me. 'They've killed her!' I sobbed, 'they've killed Diana. Her babies... her babies...' She was thirty-six. She will be that age forever.

We took baby Henry to Kensington Palace, and placed him in his Rocka-tot on the sea of flowers. We photographed him there. What a thing to do. But what else do you do? The nation was helpless. We watched the awful Westminster Abbey funeral on television. Even my scornful husband wept. Nineteen million succumbed to grief as Earl Spencer damned the Royals.

'William and Harry,' he said, in his seething conclusion, 'we all cared desperately for you today. We are all chewed up with the sadness at the loss of a woman who was not even our mother. How great your suffering is, we cannot even imagine. I would like to end by thanking God for the small mercies he has shown us at this dreadful time. For taking Diana at her most beautiful and radiant and when she had joy in her private life. Above all we give thanks for the life of a woman I am so proud to be able to call my sister, the unique, the complex, the extraordinary and irre-placeable Diana whose beauty, both internal and external, will never be extinguished from our minds.'

'Grief is the price we pay for love,' said Her Majesty the Queen in 2001, in a message from Balmoral, read out at a New York service of remem-brance for two hundred and fifty British citizens still missing a week after 9/11.

'Every one can master a grief but he that has it,' wrote Shakespeare in 'Much Ado About Nothing.'

Both statements are true. Neither helps. There is no way round it. The only thing to do is go through.

I found it difficult at the time to process my immense grief over Di-ana. Why did I feel it? I had no right. She was a complete stranger to me. She had not been in my life, nor I in hers. She was neither my sister nor my friend. She was not even a casual acquaintance. She was a photo-graph, a news bulletin, a remote do-gooder, her face as familiar to me as my own. I copied her make-up, though I resisted the clothes and hair. She was everywhere and nowhere, simultaneously right there and inac-cessible.

Maybe I understand it better now. To those of us who were not so far removed from her in age, her death was our own death. It marked the loss of our youth, of our optimism, of our wildest dreams. It was time to grow up now. To draw a line under reckless fun and games, and under our yesterdays.

Marital bliss began to crumble the night the men in blue turned up. I had retired early to feed my newborn, and had left his father downstairs watching television. Henry was sound asleep in his rocking crib beside our bed, and I was dozing over a book, when my husband's head appeared round the door.

'The police are downstairs,' he said coldly. 'They want to see you. Would you mind telling me what the fuck you have done?'

Trust was shattered in that moment. I felt the direct hit, and reeled from the snap in my soul. Although we would 'move on', make the best of things, assume the communal brave face, have another much-wanted child together and soldier on as a family, I knew that night that 'love', whatever 'love' is, or was, had been destroyed. My husband's default setting had been to believe the worst of me. It did not occur to him to give me the benefit of doubt. That night was the first time he cruelly abused me with the insult 'lowlife'. 'The Ugly Sister' had described me thus, deeming me to be nowhere near good enough for her brother. Not only was I 'lowlife', but my entire glorious, eccentric family were too. Demolished, post-partum hormonal and unsteady to say the least, I said nothing. I bottled it. This was shock that was to revisit when I needed it least.

The Leader is behind bars. Neither the image nor the performance fooled anybody this time. The crocodile tears and last-gasp protests of innocence left the jurors at Southwark Crown Court unmoved. No one felt sorry for the sad fur-coated old man with tufted clown hair, white goatee and coloured-in eyebrows. They saw only the gaunt, defiant face of a paedophile – a habitual sexual predator who had wrecked the lives and stolen the innocence of young girls.

Gary Glitter was eventually brought to justice in 2015 for attempted rape, indecent assault and sexual intercourse with children. His youngest victim was under ten years old. The others were not much older. The then seventy year-old father of three born Paul Francis Gadd in Banbury, Oxfordshire, the faded glam rock star who spent much of his childhood in care, who topped the charts in the early Seventies with the hits I danced to as a child – 'I'm the Leader of the Gang (I Am)', 'I Love You Love Me Love', 'Do You Wanna Touch Me (Oh Yeah)' – and whose 1984 recording 'Another Rock & Roll Christmas' remains one of the most popular Yuletide hits of all time, was sentenced to imprisonment for sixteen years. Many were angered by the leniency of his sentence, believing that, given the severity of the crimes, he should have been jailed for life. The Judge agreed, but was confined to the passing of sentence commensurate with the law at the time the crimes were committed.

I stayed up all night after the Guilty verdict was passed, restless with revulsion and relief. I dug out a photo and forced myself to look at it, of Gary with an innocent young fan. But not just any young fan. For more than a year, during the Eighties, because this vile pervert was at the time my bosom pal, because I hung out with him, cooked for him, drank with him, shared secrets with him, and because I was oblivious of his intent, I allowed him to groom my sister.

How it sickens me now to think of partying with him for almost a year of my life, deluding myself that we were best friends. In New York, Gary took me to legendary hot-spot Elaine's on Second Avenue, the restaurant in Woody Allen's 'Manhattan', which heaved with famous authors and movie stars. Sylvester Stallone sat on the adjacent table, and bought us a drink. In Los Angeles, we dined with Michael Jackson and Frank DiLeo, who played gangster Tuddy Cicero in Martin Scorsese's 'Goodfellas.' Michael, fresh from 'Thriller' success, had just signed Frank as his personal manager. In London, our favourite watering hole was Frederick's in Camden Passage, Islington, conveniently close to my little flat, which had both a private conservatory and hidden garden. In Brighton, where we often spent what he called 'The Long Lost Weekends' – including the horrific Friday in October 1984 when the IRA bombed the Grand Hotel in an attempt on the life of Prime Minister Margaret Thatcher as she hosted the Conservative Party conference – I stayed on his boat, a twenty-two-foot sloop moored in the marina, which he said he would one day sail around the world. 'Gaz' fancied himself as a nautical man, and played the part to the hilt. Yanking on waterproofs, he'd pace the teak in his deck shoes, the wind terrifying his candyfloss bouffant. He eulogised life on the ocean wave, declaring it to be 'the perfect antidote' to his self-declared 'shipwreck of an existence.' It never occurred to me to ask what he meant by that. I perceive now that sailing was perhaps his way of escaping the monster within; the reptilian Gary he must have known he was.

I was young, impressionable, wincingly unworldly, and beyond flattered, I suppose, that a globally-revered rock star with a surfeit of celebrity pals had chosen me as his special confidante. More fool me. There was only one reason why Gary Glitter wanted to know me.

We first met at Ewart Television studios, Wandsworth, where my co-presenters Gary Crowley, Nicky Horne and I filmed, each Friday, the live elements of our weekly rock show 'Ear Say' for Channel 4. I'd been a huge Glitter fan in the early 1970s, and was thrilled to meet the artist in person. His impact and influence on pop culture had been supreme. He defined glam rock as one big send-up. He had careened off into self-parody almost the minute after he'd had his first hit. That initial rush of fame was followed by obscurity. But now he was making a comeback as a solo artist and father-figure to post-punk acts. His image was 'safe-sexy'. How ridiculous, those ankle-threatening silver platform boots. How absurd, the loose middle-age paunch packed tightly into sequinned pants. He might have looked more at home on a circus-tent tour, which indeed he attempted. Backed by no less a ringmaster than Gerry Cottle, who lived to rue the day.

Stars are never as you imagine or want them to be. They are not, as they might hope, rendered invincible by fame and fortune. Most are a tangle of insecurities. They tend not to own the room, as bystanders expect them to. They skulk around the edge, treading gingerly, as if wearing two left shoes. Despite his obvious unease, which he put down to an inhumanly early start (telly is always an early start), Gary managed to outshine us all. Bewigged and made-up – come to think of it, I never saw him without the hairpiece or paintwork – he was hovering over the trays of bacon butties when I went into the Green Room to introduce myself. Studio Fridays were frantic and full-on. The place was teeming with glam guests, journalists and prize-winners. One of my visitors was my youngest sister, then aged twelve. Gary took an immediate shine to her, which pleased me. She was painfully shy. A congenital medical condition had forced her to endure regular surgery. Spending the day with me in a TV studio and meeting the stars was a huge treat.

Gary was charming. He paid assiduous attention to Sam. He was affectionate, gentle, and made a great show of kissing her hand. She admired his gold bracelet, which was dripping with apparently real rubies the size of boiled sweets. He promised it to her – 'later' – along with 'a ride in my Rolls Royce'. He plucked a red rose from a vase on the buffet table, which he presented to her. Sam blushed furiously. She was loving it.

'I was star-struck, but he was just like a big kid,' she said, years later. Which reminds me of something Gary once said. 'I love young people. They bring out the kid in me.' It was obvious that he interacted better with youngsters than with adults.

We repaired to the studio. Gary charmed the floor manager, took his seat and was mic'd up. He was up-beat and animated. He effervesced with saucy tales. We drank champagne in his dressing room afterwards, and I invited him to join me and the gang that night. Sam came too.

That was it. Gary and I were new best friends. We were joined at the hip. He called me 'the Queen'. He was all over me, spoiling me and complimenting me. I was travelling regularly for work, and we'd often find ourselves in far-flung cities at the same time. In London, whenever we arranged to meet for brunch or lunch, dinner or tea, or another of our 'Long Lost Weekends', he would invariably ask 'can Sam come too?' Sometimes he'd write me quirky little notes, reminding me to bring her. He made a huge fuss of her whenever he saw her. He'd consume her in bear hugs, kiss her forehead and hands, tickle, wrestle with and tease her. I put this down to him being childishly over-friendly. He was like a big puppy. He'd sit next to her at dinner, pour her water, order her meal. He'd offer her wine, giggling like a little boy. He'd play with his food, pull faces, impersonate the waiters. He was funny, and never bored me. I found him neither devious nor manipulative. I didn't suspect a thing. He gained our trust, and he reeled us in. I understand now that such pathological behaviour is about finding sexual relationships these people can control. Paedophiles select their victims carefully. They invest time and effort, grooming vulnerable and easy-to-manipulate children into submission, often right under the noses of unsuspecting adults. Don't they just. Reader, it happened. To me, Gary was simply kind and avuncular. As safe as Boy George in a dress declaring a preference for a cup of tea to sex. We all fell for that one. It wasn't true. The only thing that assuages my guilt today is that Gary never molested my sister. He didn't get the chance to. I never once left them alone.

I'll say this, because people ask: there was never any suggestion of romance between us. He never made a pass. I never wanted him to. We did not discuss sex. I had no idea that he watched child pornography, and would have run a mile had I known. His behaviour was child-like most of the time, which I found endearing. I assumed he was a closet homosexual. In Brighton, he would disappear by himself for hours. We knew not to ask. He was fond of the town's jazz scene, the buskers, its quaint pubs and edgy bars. He loved poking around alone along North Laine.

I questioned my assumption the night he told me about his girlfriend, Alison Brown, a 'leggy blonde' whom he said he'd met through her Glitter-fan parents. We'd been out one night, the news was brimming with Bob Geldof's announcement of the Live Aid concert, and we were back at my flat. Gary hadn't been asked to take part, and seemed disappointed. He drank a lot, and admitted a bit too much. In a raspy voice eroded by Budweisers, vodka shots, clammy cocktails and German wine, and with a face that hinted at trouble, he opened up about his first marriage, at the age of nineteen, and about having had children 'way too young.' And he told me that he'd cultivated Alison's parents at their West Country pub, in order to get close to their daughter. He 'really loved' her, he said, but admitted that it was 'difficult' because she'd been only fourteen when they 'started'. So, he said, he'd had to 'find a way.' I wondered fleetingly why he'd never mentioned her before.

Then instinct kicked in, and I froze. We were both the worse for wear, and it was time to throw him out. Gary unravelled himself from his chair and wandered off into the early hours. The next time I saw him was on the stage at Wembley Stadium – not for Live Aid, but for Wham!'s The Final concert in June 1986. Incongruously, he was one of the support acts. Five years later he contacted me out of the blue, and I interviewed him about his yet-another-comeback for the Sunday People. The piece was published on 5th May 1991.

Fast-forward six years. A computer-repair technician found four thousand child pornography images on Gary's personal computer, and reported him to the police. Alison Brown exposed their illegal relationship, and charges were brought against him for having had sex with a minor. But her case was dismissed after it emerged that she'd struck a lucrative deal with a newspaper. Gary went to prison for possession of child porn. Subsequent abuse of Asian children led to a jail term in Vietnam, after which he was deported.

My sister, meanwhile, had grown into a withdrawn young adult. Lacking the confidence to leave home for university, her twenties were a reclusive wilderness. At thirty she found the courage to enrol at college, graduated with Honours, and landed her ideal job, in a primary school. She married, and is now the blissful mother of twins. The impact of having known Gary Glitter hit home only years later, after he was exposed as a sex offender. She realises how close she came to being his victim.

'I felt uncomfortable when I thought about what he might have done to me, given half the chance,' she says. 'I used to think he was lovely, always so kind to me, always over the top and playing practical jokes. He'd walk into a room and every head would turn. Now, I just think of him as a very sad, sick old man.'

'They' say that it's difficult to recognise a paedophile. It's not. It's impossible. Anyone could be one. Even your best friend.

Police investigators trawled the press cuttings, and turned up the piece I'd written for the Sunday People entitled 'Day I Fell For a 13-Year-Old' in May 1991. It was why those officers came to our London house that night: to find out what else I knew. How odd that they should call round so late: to make sure that we'd be at home, I suppose. That my husband assumed the worst when they asked for me by my maiden name was perhaps, in one way, understandable. Then again, not. He should not have leapt to conclusions. He should have hastened to defend me. Which is what I would have done for him. Which is what you do when you love someone.

They're still asking me why it went wrong.

With Gary Glitter, Camden Passage, London, 1984

Bobby Bluebell (Robert Hodgens), Sam & Gary Glitter, 1984

21. SWW

There was a sinking of self in the aftermath. A realisation that something was missing. Time passed. We had married in haste, and would repent forever, if not at leisure. Why had we rushed into it? I'd have to say that it was because he wouldn't take no for an answer. If we'd waited, he explained, we would come up with all the reasons why not to do it. It was better to plunge in, then sink or swim together. I embraced the wife-and-mother role with all I could give. But there was no denying the boredom generated by the daily grind. Why did I feel, most of the time, as though I were acting a part? Going through motions? Conforming for the sake of it? Marriage, I had assumed, would afford us mutual security, stability, companionship. A firm foundation on which to build a family. There were fleeting moments when I felt confident about our future together. It later felt as though I'd been under a spell, and the spell was now broken. I had relinquished my former life to give my husband the life he thought he wanted. But there was no indication that he was willing to do the same. He eventually accepted a Monday-to-Friday post in Poland, returning home to be a cursory father and husband at weekends. My consolation prize was an au pair.

Our youngest was on the way when we relocated to Tooting, for a bigger house and easy access to the schools we liked. Bridie Rose Joy arrived in April 1999. Her father had argued throughout the pregnancy that she should be named Hatshepsut. Not again. As 'the first great woman in history of whom we are informed', and the first to wear charred frankincense resin as kohl eyeliner (for which Cleopatra always got the credit), the Egyptian pharaoh was a worthy enough role model. But try saying 'Hatshepsut Shine' after a few wines. Besides, it would only be shortened in the playground to 'Hattie', rendering elaboration and affectation absurd.

We were still arguing about what to call her when we were driving to St. Bride's one Sunday about eight weeks before the birth, having watched an episode of the original television adaptation of 'Brideshead Revisited' the night before. During an animated discussion about the Earl of Brideshead in Waugh's great novel, who is never named but is both addressed and referred to as 'Bridey', its similarity to the name of our destination that morning caused a few scales to fall. Bridie our new baby would be.

But the more deeply immersed in family life that I became, the more I missed my old job. Having moved to an extremely neighbourly street, it was no accident that the friend I came to depend on the most, mother-of-four Jane Wroe-Wright, had once been a colleague of mine at the Sun. The success of the Freddie Mercury biography convinced me I should write more books. But what about? I was hardly exposed to anything worth writing about anymore. Then I remembered Desmond Elliot, my first agent and publisher, whose ideal novel was, he said, 'a cross between a treasure hunt and a race', and whose claims to fame included introducing Tim Rice to Andrew Lloyd Webber and discovering Penny Vincenzi and Jilly Cooper. 'It's easy,' he assured me, 'you just have to write about what you know.' It's what they all say. I penned a handful of novels that never saw the light of day. In Desmond's honour, I began a tongue-in-cheek book called 'SWW: A South-West Woman's Guide to Everything That's Anything in Life.' About the Neighbours. Perhaps because I would never be like them.

You could smell their scent as you drove around the tree-lined streets on Saturday mornings, squinting at curtain linings and tasselled ecru blinds which concealed magazine lifestyles of mythical proportions. Stop for a cappuccino on Bellevue Road, having taken almost an hour to park the car, and you might spot Ian Hislop strolling with a child in each hand, or 'Birds of a Feather' actress Lesley Joseph tottering on designer spindles towards what used to be Marco's place, or Jack Dee in the pharmacy, queueing for cough linctus. But none of them would impress you more than SWW.

South West Woman, I decided, was the 21st century's answer to the Sloane Ranger, with designer knobs on. She lived South of the River, in neighbourhoods such as Balham, Tooting and Streatham, where property prices had recently soared, and where affluent families had more children than they could want or need, just to fill the many bedrooms. The difference between SWW and Sloane was very simple: Much, Much More Disposable Income. A Sloane may have sworn by her third-generation pearls, but SWW sported brand-new diamonds (better new than heirloom any day). A Sloane always had access to Somewhere in the Country. SWWs had boltholes in Norfolk or Cornwall. Some owned, others rented.

If the latter, they always took the same house every year, so that other people would think the place was theirs.

Everything in SWW's charmed life was justified because it Made Sense. They always spoke like that, in Capital Letters. She'd dragged her darling husband over the Thames from Fulham because you got Much More for Your Money on the other side. You could accommodate the staff and the step-children. Oh yes, plenty of SWWs had those. They added extortionate rear extensions to their late 19th-century redbrick terraced houses with unbelievably vast kitchens and gigantic family rooms. Hence, elaborate interior design, exaggerated soft furnishings and genuine paintings (never framed prints). It was a look that yelled To the Manor Born. These were homes that looked Christmassy all year round. But SWW, eminently creative, blended her red gingham, chintz and mints with modern and ethnic pieces: a stainless-steel table top, a distressed teak bowl brimming with chunks of amethyst, her heady Diptyque candles. She drove a spotless four-wheel drive, which she manoeuvred around the neighbourhood like a tank. The only time the thing ever went off-road was into the Fulham Sainsbury's car park. Where SWW still shopped, because (a) it was next to the Harbour Club, so she could kill two birds with one stone, and (b), she was more likely to bump into a soul mate there than in the somewhat scruffier Balham branch. For this reason, SWW always put her make-up on to go shopping. Likewise ahead of the school run. And what other kind of school but a School with Rules? One Head I heard about circulated a letter asking parents not to wear denim when they came to pick up their kids.

SWW was called Belinda or Lucinda or Alexandra. She'd grown up in Kensington, Hampshire or Gloucestershire. She had married quite young. Her husband was Old Etonian, and In the City. Their children were Archies or Freddies, Lucias, Sophias or Georgias. They were all born at the Portland, or at Queen Charlotte's.

Most SWWs were not in paid employment. They might, eventually, decide to do Something Part-Time, but were putting off the dreaded moment. Meanwhile, they chatted animatedly about fundraising for the Hospice and their donations to designer charity sales. In their hermetically-sealed environment – their soles rarely touched the High Road – SWWs had frantic, sometimes brilliant, social lives. Their au pairs were expected to babysit at least three times a week. Au pairs were referred to as 'Your Girl', as in 'does Your Girl do extra ironing?' Some au pairs learned to retaliate by becoming kleptomaniacs, nymphomaniacs or both. The primary preoccupation was dinner parties and kitchen suppers (which SWW couldn't lay on for less than two hundred quid), with like-minded types who lived a few doors away. And no one ever brought wine: didn't everyone have cellars nowadays? And if ever anyone did turn up with an embarrassment of Soave or Frascati, you'd simply leave it out for Your Girl. Champagne, on the other hand, was welcome. Mr SWW would do a business dinner each week, they'd do a function together each week, and she'd have a girlie night out once a fortnight, during which she moaned for England about Mr SWW's business dinners, his rapidly dwindling sex drive, and his habit of wedging half-eaten apples between the mattress and the bed frame. They almost never went Up West any-more. Which SWWs really did say, just like on 'East Enders', but possibly as a send-up. I could never tell. SWWs never did theatre or opera. They might quite like to, but they never did seem to get round to it.

They talked non-stop about the Most Important Things: holidays: at least five a year, and at least one of those without the children. There had to be some compensation to living in Tooting, after all. Schools. What the house was worth that week. Schools. The au pair. Schools. Which gym they had joined, and whether it was Value for Money. They moaned about their husbands spending every bloody Saturday watching Chelsea or Wimbledon play football while they were left minding the bloody chil-dren. And if he wasn't doing that, of course, he was off playing tennis at the Harbour Club. At least, he said he was.

To be fair, SWW conversation did get serious from time to time. Di-ets. Botox. Collagen implants. The latest youth preservation technique short of a five-gear facelift, which of course they would only put them-selves through for their beloved husbands. Which was a sixty-four thou-sand-dollar lie. It was for their friends.

So no, I didn't fit in there. And I never did finish that book, either. Within a year or two, we were on the move again, to Dulwich, where we made lots of SEW 'friends' instead. Most of whom ran a mile after our marriage ended. Invite a single mother to your dinner party? Even one you've been skiing with, to a villa in the south of France with, left your children overnight with, shared your dingiest, darkest secrets with? You're having a laugh. Yes, people can be that shallow. I'll never forget the mother who crossed the road outside school one morning when she saw me walking towards her, to avoid conversation. I thought I was being over-sensitive and must have imagined this, until a divorcing GP I was chatting with days later happened to mention that the same thing had happened to her.

'What did you do?' she asked.

'Nothing?'

'Why?'

'What was I supposed to do?'

'Exactly what I did. I chased her to her car and demanded to know why she'd just blanked me.'

'Crikey. What did she say?'

'"I wasn't aware"'.

'Well they're not, are they. They barely know what day of the week it is half the time, and the other half they're hungover. God help them when it happens to them.'

'Which is the rub. They think it's contagious. That it's leprosy. Remember Bella, telling Claire to stay away from you because staying friends with you would be bad for her own relationship?'

'Yeah. And we've all seen the gargoyle she's married to. I'm fed-up, not hard-up.'

'Resting my case.'

Did I fret too much about the pointless things, and not worry enough about what mattered? Yes. Did I squander time on my appearance, on the house, on colour-coordinating my children's outfits, on holiday destinations I wasn't really interested in but could later boast about having been to, on Christmas Lists, on menus for all those ridiculous kitchen suppers? I confess. Was I so silly that I'd let a lost mascara ruin my day? You know that I was. I can't explain the woman I became during the married years, because she is alien to me. I don't recognise her. She crept up and moved in, like a parasite. She scoffed my food, guzzled my booze, abused me and absorbed me. And, the most infuriating thing of all, she never stuck up for herself. She accepted scenes and situations (where did he get to without explanation for three weeks at a time, with his phone switched off?) that I would have refused to put up with. Why did he think it ok to smash up the entire kitchen in a rage, twice (two different houses), and leave me to sweep smashed glass, wipe up wine and olive oil, and whitewash walls through the night before the kids got up for breakfast and school? She let herself become a punchbag. She couldn't stand her ground. She never fought back. She allowed a toxic relationship to eradicate her identity, and eventually relinquished her personality for its preservation. In the end, it was all for nothing. It wasn't worth preserving. She was the last to know.

There are moments that will always torment. They return when we least expect them. Perhaps their purpose is to remind us that we don't ever 'get over it'. All we do is learn to live with 'it'. We get used to 'it'. Whatever 'it' is. We adapt and mould ourselves to what they call 'the new normal'. Sadness never subsides. It simmers beneath the surface. It is only ever a sob away.

The startling sight, in 2007, of a colossal gold statue of a jackal-headed Egyptian god sailing under Tower Bridge, heralding the return to London of Tut-Mania, sent shivers down my spine for all the wrong reasons. The Boy King's glittering tomb treasures would soon arrive from America for a major exhibition. More than three hundred thousand advance tickets were sold. That eight-metre high Anubis, ancient god of the dead, evoked disturbing memories. As a schoolgirl in 1972, I was one of almost two million people who braved interminable queues at the British Museum to view Tutankhamun's burial artefacts. But the statue also reminded me of another astonishing discovery made in 1999, the year of Bridie's birth.

I am a rational person, and no aficionado of the paranormal. But there were times when I questioned my sanity following the break-up of my marriage. And I still wonder, against better judgement and in darker moments, whether there really was such a thing as a pharaoh's curse.

In the cold light of day, I agree, it sounds ridiculous. Yet the 'Curse of Tutankhamun' is said to have claimed the lives, fortunes and happiness of scores of people who were involved in the discovery of his tomb in 1922. I still shake sometimes when I remember the string of disasters which occurred after I handled a clutch of obscure objects which had been buried with him. How did I come into contact with them? It went like this.

After some forty years of marriage, my beloved former parents-in-law decided to separate. While they were packing up their home and dividing their belongings, a pair of battered Cognac boxes emerged from the back of a spare bedroom wardrobe.

'Just the family jewels,' my late father-in-law joked. 'I'd forgotten they were there.'

Inside lay a collection of dusty glass petri dishes, some of them taped together, containing cloth and bandage fragments, seeds, palm nuts, food scraps and other samples. When I asked what they were, I was told that they had been gleaned from Tutankhamun's burial chamber. They had lain undisturbed in their boxes for half a century. How on earth did they find their way onto the top shelf of a wardrobe in Surrey? My former mother-in-law then recounted the story of a friendship between two remarkable men who, despite their considerable scientific achievements, are barely referred to in any history book.

The afore-mentioned Henry James Bunker, my ex-husband's maternal grandfather, was the microbiologist who carried out tests on objects gathered from Tutankhamun's tomb after he had become acquainted with chemist Alfred Lucas. The boxes containing these artefacts were brought back to Britain by Bunker. They passed eventually into the possession of his daughter. Alfred Lucas had been the right-hand man of Howard Carter, the Egyptologist who discovered the tomb in 1922. It was Lucas who famously demonstrated that when the inner chamber of the tomb was opened for the first time, there were no bacteria present. The tomb could not, therefore, have been broken into and plundered prior to the official opening, as had hitherto been believed. Henry Bunker's swab analysis of the walls, floors and furniture of the tomb confirmed this. His tests altered the understanding of everything that had happened during and after the tomb's discovery. And here, in a humble housing estate bedroom, were displayed before me a selection of ancient samples that had been excavated from the tomb. They came directly from the lifetime of a Boy King born more than three thousand years earlier. His life and death remain shrouded in mystery blurred by elusive fact, erratic data, supposition, invention and fantasy. Every scrap taken from his tomb is, therefore, an object of fascination. What was once secreted in the earth beneath the Valley of the Kings was about to take up residence in our Tooting drawing room. Tooting-khamun, you might say. I was enthralled.

Those boxes sat on our coffee table for months. I imagined them inhabited by genies, like Aladdin's lamps, with incredible tales to tell. I took to visiting them late at night; I'd lift out the yellowed glass dishes and stare at their unfathomable contents. They were the most ancient things I had ever held. I was terrified of spilling them, of destroying what little was left. It occurred to me eventually to research and write a book about the lives of the two men directly responsible for the relics which had found their way into our home. I spent months ploughing through paperwork at the British Library. Meanwhile, we took the samples to the British Museum, where they were verified by thrilled experts. Jeffrey Spencer, assistant keeper of Egyptology, declared them 'the most important collection ever to have been brought to us from the tomb of Tutankhamun by a private individual.' We were even warned to be wary of aggressive Elgin Marbles-style headlines in Egyptian newspapers. They also advised us to present the samples for academic valuation. We soon learned that private collectors were prepared to pay around £1million for them. Although there was no inclination to sell, they proved impossible to insure.

Shortly after signing a publishing deal through my new literary agent, Giles Gordon, for a book about Henry Bunker's exploits in Egypt, the first incident in a string of tragedies and disasters occurred. As the temporary custodian of some of Tutankhamun's possessions, was I now falling prey to the curse carved out in hieroglyphics on the walls of his tomb? Surely this was nonsense, but it was asked.

Having at last tracked down the private papers of Alfred Lucas to the Griffith Institute in Oxford, the entire archive suddenly became inaccessible due to a two-year rebuilding programme. After that, the papers were mysteriously 'lost'. So near, yet so far. The story was shelved, and the publishing opportunity was cancelled.

Then Giles, my agent, suffered an appalling freak accident. He tripped at the top of the stairs in his Edinburgh home, fell from top to bottom, and was killed. His death rocked the publishing world, and left a gorgeous young family fatherless. As I stood at his memorial service at St Martin-in-the-Fields overlooking Trafalgar Square, among authors who had Giles to thank for their great careers – Vikram Seth, Fay Weldon, Sue Townsend, Joseph Connolly – I felt suddenly unwell. I couldn't be responsible for this tragedy, could I? Restaurant critic Giles Coren, standing beside me, saw the blood drain from my face and urged me to sit. All around, friends and colleagues sobbed quietly as moving eulogies were delivered. I closed my eyes to the menacing image of Tutankhamun's mask.

Bridie was born soon afterwards, following which I was forced to submit to life-saving surgery which left me bedridden for months. My friend Fiz Shapur, former musical director of 'Cats' and 'Les Misérables', visited me one afternoon, and brought a present: a large-format hardback book entitled 'Egypt: The Land of The Pharaohs'. Its cover featured a huge close-up of the famous mask. Having never previously discussed my fears with him, there was no way Fiz could have known of my obsession. It wasn't even his idea of a bad joke.

A year later I contracted meningitis, became critically ill and was hospitalised for six weeks. Sweating into the small hours in an intensive care isolation room, I began hallucinating. My visions were filled with hieroglyphs and scarab beetles. My mother later told me that, during spells of raging delirium, I had implored her 'not to put me down on the sand.'

Another year on, I looked death in the eye again when I was ambushed at gunpoint outside a restaurant on Tobago. During the attack, my masked assailant struggled to tear off my finger, complete with engagement ring. Jewels, masks ... could there be some connection? Despite my misgivings, I still refused to give in to the far-fetched notion of a 'curse'. But anyone would have been horrified by our seemingly endless run of 'bad luck'. To add insult to injury, I was diagnosed with skin cancer. But I had not sunbathed since my teens. The specialist who removed the tumour from my cheekbone was dermatologist Professor Christopher Bunker: a cousin of my then husband, and another grandson of microbiologist Henry Bunker. Did I really believe in some malevolent force reaching out across the centuries? Get a grip, I told myself, and eventually I did, while struggling to shake off my nagging fears.

The catalogue of misfortune grew.

My father became seriously ill, and was hospitalised. Finally, after all that we had survived together, my husband and I celebrated ten years of marriage with a renewal of our vows at St. Bride's, followed by a lavish party. A fortnight later, without a word to the children or me, he packed his bags and left us while I was out on the school run. I thought the devastation would kill me. Our divorce was declared absolute the following year.

There had been little but sadness, I reflected, since the day we brought those relics into our home. It would make anybody wonder.

I heard that my former mother-in-law was planning to donate the artefacts to a British college, for research purposes. Meanwhile, Henry, Bridie and I gritted our teeth and set off for Cairo, for our own expedition into the Valley of the Kings. It was the only place on Earth, reasoned my then ten-year-old son, who loved the idea of a 'curse', where we might shake it off. It was there that we began to rebuild our shattered lives. There, underground, in the silence of death, that my grief settled. In the back of my head was a sound I still hear: the sometimes deafening, usually faint, always mournful tolling of bells.

The memories still haunt me. I can be out for supper with friends having a laugh when a waft of scent or the opening bars of a song will stop me in my tracks, and drag me back to the time when pain began. Never a day spares me. Never a beat of my heart fails to hurt. I'm a survivor because I had no choice: I have three children. I remain shackled to hurt that could have ended my life. I will be happy again, perhaps. I live in hope. But I will never be free.

22. LOVERS AND GAMBLERS

Never go back. Never, ever go back. It's what they tell us. Not to lovers, school friends, college pals, colleagues, homes, holiday destinations or a job we once adored. We should resist, resist, because we will only be disappointed. Because nothing stays the same. Leave the past right there, my mother always says. Leave behind what you left behind. But my marriage was over, my heart was broken, and there were little mouths to feed. What else was I going to do?

I turned to face a strange and barely recognisable industry. The price of newsprint, a slump in advertising, receding classified ads and circulations in freefall were just some of the factors to blame for its grave decline. Burgeoning technology was obliterating jobs. The era of ruthless cutbacks had begun, in anticipation of inevitable web domination. Within the decade, some would have shut down their print operations completely, and would exist exclusively online. Cue ferocious criticism of the newspaper industry for having failed to keep pace with a rapidly changing society. They should have seen it coming, shouldn't they? They did. As if faced with an avalanche or a tsunami, what could they do but panic, then try to make the best of things? No longer did readers have to hang about with a mug of builders' and a dressing gown pocket crammed with Custard Creams, waiting for the daily rag to pop through the letterbox or to remember to grab one on their way to work. The tech revolution would deliver it directly, instantly, accessibly, in ways that demanded no more of the consumer than the tap of a finger or thumb. Newspapers had no choice but to cut overheads in a bid to keep going for as long as possible. They did so drastically. Budgets were slashed, foreign bureaux folded, journalists junked. Investigative journalism was a massive casualty. Such snooping often stretched over many months, with no guaranteed result to offset the spend, and was no longer justifiable. The younger generation was not in the habit of reading print anyway, and would soon be running their lives, keeping up (when they could be arsed) with current affairs and ordering everything from Xacuti to Xanax on their phones. Not only that, but most info on the 'net is there for the taking, free. No wonder readers would soon be reluctant to pay for subscriptions to the Times and other websites when they could access for nothing the world's biggest news, views and screws outlet, mailonline, with its iniquitous Sidebar of Shame.

There was a tangible 'Last of the Summer Wine' air about newspapers when I crept back in. It was a party on its last legs, the boxed Chianti Classico all slurped, the vol-au-vents scoffed, the egg-and-cress sand-wiches curling, the office lech slumped pissed in a corner with vomit down his shirt, and the last-stand boppers slip-sliding to Abba and Slade around a pile of dead handbags in a puddle of beer. Overseas jaunts and expense accounts were history. Exclusives that once earned 'a pound a word' now fetched a third. Eric Bailey, a deputy editor on the Mail on Sunday for whom I had worked often as a freelance, and Martin Town-send, a former fellow music writer and shot-caller at OK! Magazine turned Editor of the Sunday Express, returned my calls. It was a yes from them. They held the door for me, coughed for the cheesburgers and Bulmers, and started commissioning me again. I dusted off the contacts books, called every celebrity who owed me, and went rummaging for the rubber gloves.

Joan Collins knew a thing or two about men, I reflected, the day I board-ed a British Airways flight to Nice in June 2007 to have lunch with the Dame and fifth husband Percy. My memory was also jogged back in time to a 1987 May day when I cruised the same route, my onward journey taking me to San Remo on the Italian Riviera and its annual rock festival. That was the first time I ever met Joan. I found myself sitting next to her on the plane. She was on the aisle, I was in the window, and she had to get up to let me in.

She was miserable, she confided, having just split from fourth spouse Peter Holme – 'the Swede' – and was on her way to hang out for a few days with Rod Stewart. Expressing concern for my well-being – I looked less fetching than something the cat dragged in, she tutted – she told me she thought that I was pregnant.

'Don't think so,' I said.

'Trust me,' Joan retorted, 'I can always tell. I'm a witch about these things.' She was right, too. Joan has been my role model ever since.

She wanted to know what had happened in my life to reduce me to such a mess. I found myself pouring out the excruciating details. Joan neither flinched nor interrupted. What she had to say about absent fathers was an eye-opener.

'I've made my mistakes,' she admitted. 'The wrong men. Lots of them. But there have been the right children, and grandchildren. They are all my life. I'd be nothing without them. However, I raised all my kids without a father. I mean, they all had fathers, but they didn't stick around. Men who walk out and leave a woman with children are disgusting. It is the most despicable thing to do, and I see it everywhere, more and more. Who do these men think they are? Such lowlife. I have often wondered down the years whether I shouldn't become a lesbian.'

Down on the Côte d'Azur twenty years later, I found Joan gliding as if on roller skates towards the top table in Le Club 55, otherwise known as 'Cinquante-Cinq', the resort's most fashionable watering hole. Linen-clad waiters fell aside as she approached, like the palm trees in 'Thunderbirds' when Virgil Tracy takes off. Others leapt to puff cushions, to straighten the tablecloth, or to pat, completely pointlessly, the flower bowl. Or perhaps, it occurred to me, this was a silent, French variation on 'The Farmer's in His Den' game: ee-ay-ad-ee-oh, we all pat the fleurs.

De toute façon.

Beyond the pale sands onto which the restaurant spilled, the yachts moored in the bay were the size of department stores. Who cared. That day, all eyes were on Dynasty's Queen of Mean.

She was then seventy-four years old. She sported a floppy white canvas hat, black sunspecs, wedged sandals, and carried a white Chanel clutch. At her throat sat a diamond-encrusted heart pierced by an arrow with the initials 'P' and 'J' on the end. She wore three diamond bracelets on her right wrist, and a five-quid watch on the other. She'd forgotten her Cartier, she said. On her left hand was the wedding band which matched Percy's, and the 19th century heart-shaped, diamond-filled engagement ring it took her beloved a year to find.

'I've just cleaned it with my toothbrush and toothpaste: the best way,' said Joan. Her voice veered between Snow White and Helen Mirren, depending on the subject matter. The accent crossed West Coast with West End.

Percy, at the time forty-two, a handsome Manhattan Latin born in Lima, was effortlessly masculine despite a yellow Hawaiian shirt. He sat combing his damp black hair with his fingers. He grinned unselfconsciously, and called her 'Darling'.

'He's my Alpha male,' Joan purred. 'I love Alpha males.'

She shunted her way along the banquette until our bodies were touching. She was more bird-like and petite than I remembered her. I'm only five-foot-three and not exactly chunky, but I felt like a giant next to her. Most of her appeared to defy gravity. Her tiny face was barely made-up. The mouth, however, was drawn with Norma Desmond precision, a millimetre or two outside the lipline, and crayoned-in with a deep, metallic red. Her facial skin, chamois-pale, was at odds with that on her limbs (which was more mock-croc). Although she loved sunbathing, Joan had not exposed her face, neck or décolletage to the sun for more than fifty years. Instead, she said, she hid her 'delicate parts' under sun hats and umbrellas. I still squinted rudely. I couldn't help myself.

'Have you really never had any work?' I cross-examined.

'No knives,' she responded coolly. 'Had Botox once, years ago. Hated it. Can't bear needles. And I loathed what it did to my face. I'm an actress, I have to have expression. I'd much sooner slap stuff on at night.'

Did Joan honestly feel oblivious of the marital age gap?

'I honestly never give it a second thought,' she said. 'He's just Percy. His age is the last thing on my mind. We met while working together, became friends, and fell in love quite unexpectedly. He's my reward: as everyone knows, I kissed a lot of frogs.'

Indeed, and where do you start? Warren Beatty, Dennis Hopper, Ryan O'Neal, Terence Stamp ... did it bother Perce that his beloved had bonked so many nobs, as it were?

'You might as well ask any man what he feels about the guys who came before him,' Percy reasoned. 'That is the profession she's in, so those are the kind of people she's going to meet. I don't have a problem with that. What matters is the relationship that she and I have with each other now – and it couldn't be better. I never think about her age, it's the least interesting thing about her. The most interesting thing is that she's a fantastic mother, her kids are great, and the three grandchildren more than make up for us not having babies of our own.'

I watched Joan picking delicately at an artichoke vinaigrette, enjoying her wine, and savouring a ham and cheese omelette. She consumed only half of everything served, always practising what she preaches.

'The reason diets don't work is because they are too complicated,' she moaned. 'We don't want to stand there measuring out four milligrams of groats. The simplest diet in the world is Eat Less Food. You need half the amount of food at fifty as you ate at twenty-five. And probably half as much again at seventy-five. And I'm going to live to be a hundred. I'm determined. I tell all the women I meet, look after your skin and eat less. Don't diet. It doesn't work. If you diet too much, it's really bad for your skin. And if your skin looks on the way out, eat a ton of olive oil, like I do. Never drink tap water. I have an aversion to drinking recycled urine and hormones. If you really need to drop a few pounds to fit into something, eat boiled eggs and broccoli for three days. And if you need to snack, more broccoli. Exercise a little and you'll always look much younger than your age.'

I would survive, she assured me. She'd been through the lot, herself, and it hadn't killed her. She had endured so much, in fact, that she felt deserving of a little happiness now.

'But do you know what?' she said, 'you make your own. My parents instilled in me that life was not going to be easy and that you have to do things for yourself. And that's what I've done.'

She was not worried by death: 'It's all part of life.' But she hated the thought of life-threatening illness.

'I do know quite a lot of people right now who have cancer,' she said. 'I have noticed that several friends of mine have been diagnosed with it two or three years after they'd been through a terrible shock, or had dreadful things happen to them. My advice, for what it's worth, is GET OVER IT. Don't brood, darlings. Be resilient. Never think what might have been. Play the cards you've been dealt, and just get on with it. Any day soon could turn out to be your last.'

She seemed suddenly weary. We had been talking for almost four hours, and it was close to 5pm. She turned to me with great affection, eyes glistening. The look was at once dryly theatrical and the moist gaze of a long-lost friend. She took my hands in her (much younger-looking) hands, and kissed me with her cheeks. She smelled like toffs' chocolate.

'So lovely to see you again,' she mwahed. 'And please: let's not leave it another twenty years. Percy might be dead by then ...'

We didn't leave it quite that long. In May 2016, I was invited by Philip Norman to the chic launch of his new book 'McCartney' at the Baglioni Hotel on Hyde Park. I was just about to enter into far too serious a conversation with an ex when Songlink publisher David Stark came to the rescue. He whispered that Joan was also launching a book that night, 'The St. Tropez Lonely Hearts Club', at Harry's Bar in Mayfair. 'Let's go,' I said. 'How will we get in?' he frowned. 'Watch me.' We old hands. Even during the good old days when we had triple-A passes, backstage wristbands, VIP stickers and every permutation of laminate, real as well as fake, we were in the habit of stashing them in our back pockets and attempting to blag our way in. If all else failed, we still had the wherewithal...

On then to Mayfair, where I wedged my old Renault between two gleaming Ferraris, and where we wafted into Harry's as if we owned the place. Which is the only way to gatecrash. Dame Joan had clearly had enough for one night. Still, my magnificent role model made us welcome, and even refilled my champagne flute herself. She was about to turn eighty-three years old. We toasted her. I wished, and still do, that she could live forever.

In 2008, I was approached by a former hospitality employee who had retrained in the medical profession and was now working at a private clinic in Sydney as a nurse practitioner. While visiting relatives in West London, she made contact with me via a former agent and mutual family friend. We arranged to meet for lunch on Great Portland Street, where she divulged some extraordinary information. Not only, she said, did Michael Hutchence and Princess Diana enjoy a tryst in the Ritz Carlton Hotel[xxix] in the Double Bay suburb of Sydney, the same hotel in which Hutchence would commit suicide in November 1997; but his passion for Diana, originally kindled in Melbourne in 1985, had fuelled his affair with (and ultimately caused the disintegration of the marriage of) Bob Geldof's wife Paul Yates. Unable to have Diana, his 'impossible princess', Hutchence allegedly made a play instead for 'Indie Di': the flirtatious, racy pop TV presenter who had interviewed him twice, on Channel 4's 'The Tube', and several years later on 'The Big Breakfast'. A 'cut-price Di' and 'default royalty', who bore more than a passing resemblance to the princess in her new, improved incarnation, Paula went on to bear her lover a daughter, Heavenly Hiraani Tiger Lily. But she never succeeded in her quest to get Michael up the aisle.

Diana died in August 1997, at the age of thirty-six. Shortly after news reached him of the Paris car crash in which she and Harrods heir and playboy Dodi Fayed were killed, Hutchence collapsed. At his last-ever concert fronting INXS, on September 27, at the Star Lake Amphitheater, Pittsburgh Pennsylvania, he sounded drunk and disengaged, and sang more than a few bum notes. It was said that he never came to terms with Diana's death. Only weeks later, at the age of thirty-seven, he too was dead.

Room 524 of the Double Bay Ritz Carlton, top floor, harbour view, had previously hosted Kylie Minogue, John Travolta, Lionel Richie, and Madonna. The room, with its ivory painted wallpaper, emerald green carpet and sturdy, dark wooden furniture, was nothing to write home about, but it was there that Michael prepared for the band's twentieth anniversary tour. He had checked in under the pseudonym Mr Murray River. It was behind the room's main door that his naked, hanged body was found kneeling. His own leather belt was around his neck. There was no suicide note. A statement later made by an actress called Kym Wilson, who claimed to have spent that final night in the room with Hutchence and her boyfriend, led to one theory, less than popular among his fans, that Michael had died during an experiment in autoerotic asphyxiation which had gone tragically wrong. The contents of his stomach were a cocktail of street drugs, prescription medication and alcohol. The coroner concluded that he had taken his own life. Paula Yates never recovered from the shock. Three years later, aged forty-one, the soi-disant suicide blonde[xxx] succumbed to a heroin overdose.

The evidence offered by the Australian nurse, of which I was shown a series of snapshot photographs, was a fold of dog-eared letters handwritten on hotel stationery, purportedly penned by Diana in the approach to and during their alleged brief liaison. The notes were found hidden in a fake Coca Cola can in Hutchence's hotel suite after his body was discovered, and removed before police had sealed the scene. My contact wanted a million Australian dollars for them: in today's money, just over £600,000. I called a former colleague on a British Sunday newspaper with 'an incredible story about Princess Di', and quoted the seller's asking price. The features editor laughed me off the phone. It was then that I decided to take the tale to America.

'She's dead, and no one cares,' was the callous dismissal of the New York Times correspondent with whom I supped Stolichnaya Crushes at the bar of Soho House New York that September. I got what he meant. The clear implication of his blunt statement was that America's love affair with the British Royal Family was over. We had slaughtered our golden goose, and we had only ourselves to blame. With the People's Princess gone, and with the Royals themselves widely suspected of foul play – never proven – the United States had washed their hands of the British Monarchy, and were now focusing with renewed vigour on home-grown 'royalty': the Hollywood kind.

Then along came Catherine Middleton. The 'Kate Effect' influenced young female fashion around the world, and captured the media's imagination. But it wasn't just that. We were back where we'd started, in a Hans Christian Andersen re-run, obsessed once more with a fairytale princess. Kate's wistful on-off romance with the second in line to the throne, Diana's own firstborn, rekindled the fantasy. When William dumped Kate, we denounced him as an idiot and rooted for his ex. He got the point. Their eventual 2010 engagement was sealed on a wildlife reserve in Kenya. He pledged his troth with his late mother's sapphire and diamond ring. The wedding of the future Duke and Duchess of Cambridge, watched by an audience of three hundred and fifty million on 29th April 2011, restored the British royals to their comfort zone. It made us miss Diana even more.

Diana had originated the role. She had played it to perfection. Her own 1981 wedding had been witnessed by a global TV audience of some seven hundred and fifty million. Only a few years after, there was Live Aid.

In her frumpy pale blue spotted frock with low-slung sash belt, gobstopper pearl earrings and an outsize blonde blow-dry which doubled the size of her head, twenty-four-year-old Diana could not have looked more out of place at the feed-the-world fanfare at Wembley Stadium on 13th July 1985. To her left in the Royal Box stood her buttoned-up husband. The heir to the throne's dark hair glistened stickily in the blazing afternoon sun. You could almost smell it from the wings of the stage. To her right posed perhaps the greatest solo rock artist who ever lived. In sleek grey suit, dark shirt and silver tie, David Bowie exuded cool charm and seductive rock god-ness. Directly behind the royal couple sat Brian May and Roger Taylor of Queen. The juxtaposition, whether deliberate or accidental, was hilariously apt. Little did anyone know, that historic day, that rock stars would prove Diana's undoing. After Live Aid, everything changed.

Although she had previously expressed interest in the high-profile pop artists of the day – she would talk of listening to Duran Duran and Spandau Ballet albums on her Sony Walkman while she roller-skated for exercise around the ballrooms of Buckingham Palace – it was not until now that her lightbulb moment occurred. The friendships she went on to forge with Elton John, Bob Geldof and Paula Yates, Paul McCartney, Michael Jackson, Phil Collins, Freddie Mercury and Brian May were only the hors d'oeuvres. She would soon develop an obsession with 'Lady in Red' crooner Chris de Burgh, and a a close 'gal-pal-ship' with Cliff Richard; she would even, it is claimed by insiders, have a covert affair with Canadian artist Bryan Adams, the composer of perennial love dirge 'Everything I Do, I Do It For You.' Did it happen? Intriguingly, the former rocker turned photographer has never denied it.

The princess submitted willingly to a startling transformation during the months after Live Aid. She found her fashion feet. Discarding the curling tongs, the hairspray, the flat patent pumps and the mumsy chiffon two-pieces, she yielded to a younger and glossier magazine style. The Mario Testino portraits are the most memorable. A true beauty emerged from the chrysalis. The butterfly took flight. Although still trapped in her loveless royal marriage, she would no longer take Charles's infidelity lying down. She would wield her power to extremes. She would do the unthinkable, go all-out, and fall in love with a rock star. Why not more than one?

It was in November 1985, four months after the Wembley extravaganza that had opened her eyes to alternatives, that Diana and Charles flew to Melbourne for the massive fund-raising concert Rocking the Royals: a charity gig staged as part of Victoria's one hundred and fiftieth anniversary celebrations. The headline act that night at the Melbourne Concert Hall were hugely popular Australian rockers INXS, fronted by the stunning and charismatic Michael Kelland Hutchence. The band performed eleven songs, including 'What You Need', 'This Time', 'The One Thing' and 'Burn for You'. While Charles looked bored and jet-lagged, Diana was transfixed. Whatever passed between her and Hutchence backstage after the show is not recorded. But there remain those who believe the intense encounter led to a brief liaison between the two, which convinced Michael that Diana was the love of his life.

The books kept on coming. Andrew Morton's bestselling 'Diana: Her True Story', the quasi-authorised biography, was originally published in 1992. It was reissued during the twentieth anniversary year of her death. Morton had previously cashed in further with 'In Pursuit of Love' in 2004. Lady Colin Campbell's gushing 1992 offering 'Diana in Private: The Princess Nobody Knows' made a relative fortune. 'The Bodyguard's Story' by Trevor Rees-Jones, who survived the Paris car crash that killed Diana, did too. We've had her butler Paul Burrell's 'A Royal Duty'; the late Noel Botham's 'The Murder of Princess Diana: The Truth Behind the Assassination of the Century'; a feminist examination of her life and times by Julie Burchill; a dissection of her spiritual transformation by her therapist Stephen Twigg. We have also been treated to 'The Diana Chronicles' by her friend Tina Brown. But there has never been a book about Diana's secret, relentless obsession with showbiz celebrities, in particular with rock stars.

I did consider writing it. I adored Diana. I remember exactly where I was on her wedding day in 1981: on a balcony in the Barbican, watching the coverage on a huge old television set positioned on the floor in the middle of a gathering of cartoonist Frank Dickens's squiffy friends. In common with many, I have forgotten nothing of the tragedy of her death.

I researched, compiled and submitted to my publisher a proposal on Diana's apparent obsession with rock stars, some fifteen thousand words long. They were nervous about it. In the end, it was not commissioned. There are still times when I wish that we had gone for it. Why? Because Diana was the perfect example of what the power of celebrity can do, as well as destroy. She was perhaps the greatest celebrity of all. But could it be that not even she could resist the fame, fortune and downright danger of rock stars?

'Diana felt the need to break out of her royal cage into celebrity culture, where she found her power and used it to devastating effect,' commented Tina Brown, referring to Diana's twirl with former ballet dancer

Wayne Sleep on the stage of the Royal Opera House, Covent Garden, and to her shimmy around the parquet with John Travolta in the White House. She missed the point. Despite the fact that she herself was perhaps the most photographed woman of all time, the most famous living face, Diana fell helplessly for rock'n'roll. Even the stars have their stars.

Charles and Camilla have long been held accountable for the collapse of his marriage to Diana, and for the princess's premature death. But was it really their fault? Diana, at only twenty, had been a tragic child bride, who was forced to grow up quickly with the world's media eyeballing her every move. Hailing from the dysfunctional Spencer clan, her childhood had been blighted by her parents' divorce, abandonment by her mother, and the general recklessness and selfishness of both. She had made no secret of her mission to escape misery and penny-pinching by marrying her sister's royal former beau. Diana was too young to understand that her role was one of duty. There would be precious little passion and negligible affection. When she discovered that she could not force her husband to love her, not even by giving him William and Harry, the requisite heir and spare, because he was in love with another woman, Diana's childish instincts drove her to punish Charles and to take her revenge on the family that had 'imprisoned' her.

The rock stars kept coming. In January 2008, shortly after George Michael had agreed a publishing deal with Harper Collins to the tune of about £6 million for a no-holds-barred autobiography, the Daily Mail ran a story entitled 'DID PRINCESS DIANA TRY TO HAVE AN AFFAIR WITH GEORGE MICHAEL?'

In the fact-lite feature, 'close friends' of George were quoted as having claimed that Diana became 'obsessed' with the idea of an affair with George after her marriage disintegrated. George himself was said to have given 'serious consideration' to sleeping with her. Despite the fact that he'd already made up his mind that he was gay.

Who knows what became of the lady with the letters. I expect she touted them around, couldn't sell them for as much as she'd hoped, hid them behind the immersion heater for another go at a later date, and forgot about them.

With Dame Joan Collins, Harry's Bar, Mayfair, London, May 2016

23. A NIGHTINGALE SANG IN MARKHAM SQUARE

6th May 2008. In a chilling stroke of irony, it was my ex-husband who alerted me, in a phone call, to the death of my divorce barrister. A sick joke? I couldn't believe it.

'Put the television on,' he said, 'it's all over the news.'

I complied, only to be confronted by repeat footage of police marksmen swarming into Chelsea's desirable Markham Square, where Mark Saunders QC lived with his lawyer wife Elizabeth, and where, it was now confirmed, he had been killed. All they knew so far was that he had started firing a shotgun through closed windows at neighbouring buildings and randomly into the square. Was he deranged, or high on drink or drugs? A siege had ensued. Whatever occurred during crucial split seconds, however hysterically the situation had been miscommunicated, the police had not disabled him, arrested him, nor taken him in for questioning. They had taken his life.

I sat glued. Further details trickled frustratingly. Mark had apparently returned home from work at around 3.45pm. He hit the bottle; wrote to his wife; went for his gun. No one was hurt, but the neighbours were frantic. Homes were evacuated. Mark ignored police instructions, did not respond to their pleas to negotiate, and continued to fire the odd shot. After a five-hour stand-off, the police opened fire, hitting Mark's vital organs and the main vein of his lower body. They also attacked with stun grenades and gained entry to his apartment, to find Mark (perhaps predictably) fatally wounded. He was carried into the street, which was where he died.

A shattered marriage, financial fall-out and bitter recrimination had been the foundations of our professional relationship, which began just before Christmas 2006. Though a period upon which I still look back in unfettered anger, the fact that I survived was largely thanks to Mark. Diplomatic, judicious and profoundly compassionate, his approach to divorce was different from any I'd known. He maintained a conviction, based on countless previous cases, that all would be well 'once the machinery is oiled'.

'We'll get the finances sorted, agree a set of rules going forward and define expectations,' he promised. Rage would then subside, he assured me. Calm would resume. All concerned would emerge equipped to deal with their new normal lives. I doubted that, and said so. 'Oh, but you will,' he insisted.

There was no going back.

It was my solicitor Julian Ribet who recommended instructing Mark. They had often worked together and 'got results'. Having heard him described as 'the brightest button' and 'the sharpest of minds', I investigated Mark and was impressed. I was unprepared for the talc-fresh babyface who greeted me at our first meeting. Immaculately attired in a hand-tailored suit, his crisp cuffs silver-linked, he scrawled copious notes in ink with a Mont Blanc pen. His go-to lunch hardly fitted the image: a microwaved Cornish pastie. Despite foppish charm and Victorian manners, his ruthlessness was thinly-disguised. He was a man clearly used to getting his own way. I was on the verge of losing everything. I gave him my life.

I had come to him shredded and unprepared. Mark had seen it all before. He was unfazed by my panic attacks, tears and vomiting. 'Divorce is only ever about money, and these days nobody gets their blaming-day in court,' Julian had warned me. But while solicitors sow seeds in the soil of decaying partnerships, a fundamental aspect of a barrister's work is to cultivate hope. Mark's comprehension of the female psyche and how best to plot a route forwards seemed instinctive. He was gently business-like throughout. I would watch, mesmerised, as he turned on charm and wit in Court for our mature lady Judge, whose withering ferocity folded whenever Mark took the floor.

Tempering success and high profile with beguiling humility, he was never intimidating. At thirty-one, he remained inhabited by the fearless twenty-one-year-old Law graduate who had dreamed of making legal history. Boyishly pleased when things worked out, elegantly philosophical when they failed to, his infectious smiles could be both disapproving and victorious. Whether escorting me to the Ladies' or to stand before the Judge, Mark held my hand. That never once felt weird. Although I was small-fry compared to his billionaire clients, I was assured that Mark treated us all the same.

That he was going through his own marital trauma while unravelling mine was a fact of which I was lamentably unaware. When the pressure consumed him and his personal life imploded, the divorce lawyer supreme was incapable of helping himself. Did we contribute to his stress, we who smothered him with our misery? I'm certain of that. Trawling through ransacked marriages had taken the ultimate toll. If Mark reached for the bottle in order to unwind, to park agony and angst while he visited his own life and tried to make sense of it, it made him a man who drank, not an alcoholic. Mark Saunders wasn't one, I'm sure. I would have known.

'Chins up!' he would say at the end of each gruelling session. His death made no sense. Does anyone's?

A few of us had been saying for months that Michael Jackson's 02 concerts would never go ahead.

I think Michael knew so, too. He may have had an inkling that his days were numbered, that his fragile heart wouldn't take the pace. Was his announcement of a comeback, the frantic scramble for tickets and the consequent tidal-wave revival in global Jackomania, his way of checking out?

On May 23, 1988, under a merciless sun, I took a stroll down Rome's Spanish Steps towards the Trevi Fountain to get an ice cream, toss a couple of coins in, and gather my thoughts ahead of Jacko's big gig that night. As usual, it was a lot to take in. The sensational 'BAD' tour, which had enthralled Japan the previous September, had mind-boggled Australia and had thundered halfway across America, was set to light up the sky above Rome's Flaminio Stadium on this, the first of two remarkable shows. They were billing it as the greatest rock spectacle the Eternal City had ever seen, on a tour which would, by the time it concluded in Los Angeles the following January, have notched up a hundred and twenty-three concerts, played to 4.4 million people and grossed over £76 million: more than any other entertainer on a single tour. In the UK alone, Jackson was to shatter a world record that July, with 504,000 fans attending seven sold-out Wembley Stadium shows. More than any other artist in history, the story goes.

'MJ' was the biggest artist on Earth. No surprise, then, that the world's media had descended for the European kick-off. The city was full, my walk frustratingly slow. Hot, anxious, and running out of time, I was unprepared for what awaited me at the fountain: a shy face peeping out through the tight curls of a nylon wig, a fake moustache, the raised collar of a raincoat, its shoulders hunched and turned against the throng. He was dropping dimes into the water, and talking to himself about the Coliseum.

'What are you doing here, Michael?' I asked. 'Aren't you supposed to be over at the stadium?'

'Not for a few more hours.'

'How did you get here?'

'Walked. Ran out of the hotel, then I walked.'

'On your own?'

'I did. I did it. For once in my life. I wanted to find the Vatican and see the Pope, and I want to see the lions at the Coliseum. I've been everywhere. I've seen nowhere. I just wanted to see something for myself, on my own. Just this one time.'

'Security will be going nuts,' I said.

'Didn't even see me,' he smiled. 'But I'm lost now. Do you know where this is?'

'All roads lead to Rome', I told him.

'What does that mean?'

'Maybe it means you're where you need to be right now'.

Who writes this shit?

That stupid comment still makes me cringe. At least it made him laugh. We lingered for twenty minutes or so, not saying very much. I bought him an ice cream at a nearby gelato parlour (wild Sardinian strawberry honey flavour, in a tub, with a spoon, no cornet).

I bought Michael Jackson an ice cream: words you never imagined you'd write.

We squashed in for a few photos at the fountain, taken by Daily Express reporter Roger Tavener, who had rocked up to infiltrate our quaint interlude, before hailing a taxi and dropping Michael back to the luxurious Lord Byron Hotel near the Villa Borghese. Tavener's Canon Sureshot was left behind, on the back seat of the cab. He never got it back.

Our encounter in Rome wasn't the first time I'd met Michael. Having long been an acquaintance of his pop wannabe sister and Playboy centrefold La Toya, whom I'd met in Atlantic City and with whom I'd hung in a midtown Manhattan apartment, I was one of only a handful of journalists who could say for sure that Michael and La Toya were not the same person: a rumour that had long been doing the rounds. I'd had dinner with them both together. I had also got to know Jermaine, their libidinous brother, and cute sister Janet, who was forging her own pop career. Globally famous since the late Sixties, when he had been a child star and focal point of his family's group the Jackson Five, Michael had not yet assumed the reclusive stance which defined him at the height of his fame, and which later served to offset fascination with less palatable aspects of his personality.

In those days, Michael would talk openly about his bleak childhood. Born in Gary, Indiana, into a working-class family, his primary role models were his Jehovah's Witness mother Katherine and strict steel worker father, Joe. The seventh of nine children – five brothers, Jackie, Tito, Jermaine, Marlon and Randy, and three sisters, Maureen ('Rebbie'), La Toya and Janet – Michael admitted he'd been forced against his will to perform in the group which their frustrated musician father was determined would make the family's fortune. Thus, Michael was singing and dancing for money before he'd even started school. He never got off the treadmill. What chance of a normal life did he ever have?

'There were sad moments in my childhood,' he admitted. 'It's true for any child star. Elizabeth Taylor told me she felt the same way. When you're young and you're working, the world can seem awfully unfair. There were times when I hated my father. Times when I wanted him to die, when he beat me like a dog.'

But he always spoke fondly of his 'adorable' mother, recalling a meek materfamilias who deferred almost unquestioningly to her brute of a spouse, even turning a blind eye to his beltings of her cherished children.

Softly-spoken like his polio victim mother, whom I met only once, Michael smiled a great deal, but hardly spoke. He liked to listen, he said. He would absorb information and general knowledge like a sponge. He wasn't stupid, but he was pathetically under-educated. It was always obvious from the level of conversation, both with Michael and his siblings, that formal learning had never been a priority. Their collective intellect had barely moved beyond first grade. What Michael had, however, was gut instinct about music, the writing, recording and performing of it, which came so naturally to him that he seemed to take it for granted. He'd been doing impressions of Stevie Wonder, James Brown and Ray Charles since the age of five. He was a natural. When the original Jackson Brothers first stepped out on the mid-east American black club circuit during the late Sixties, they often found themselves the support act for strippers and other explicit entertainers. It was a rude awakening for Michael, and one that he never forgot. Having been exposed to adult sexuality at such a tender age, without anyone ever explaining it to him, sex became his obsession. It was also, he hinted, the dimension of adult relationships that he feared most.

Those who would later describe the King of Pop as 'undeniably sexy but absolutely safe' missed the point. The public fell for his sexless sensuality, even as he polished his crotch. With so many of his lyrics and gravity-flouting routines revealing a mature male, how could he be oblivious? What drove him to present it as all an act?

Few who were around in the Eighties can have forgotten Frank DiLeo: the redoubtable Pennsylvania-born record industry executive and sometime movie actor with a mobster's deflectional gaze. He was ten years Michael's senior. The star turned to Frank for personal management in 1984, after the terrifying success of 'Thriller'. It was the biggest-selling album of all time, and its impact all but drowned its creator. DiLeo's apparent genius was in interpreting the value of everything Michael wasn't, as well as maximising interest in what he was. Contradiction had long been DiLeo's game. Thus, Michael's inherent shyness was hyped to Howard Hughes levels of reclusion. His light, breathy speaking voice was deployed as proof of boyish innocence. His plaintive, cracked-ballad vocals betrayed a broken heart. But who broke it? – and so on. Nor did DiLeo deny rumours of Michael's extensive cosmetic surgery, despite MJ's eventual insistence that he'd only ever had two nose jobs. The fact that we could all see otherwise was irrelevant. By preventing the media from getting close to him, by dismissing all requests for personal interviews and never allowing him to be photographed – in the Eighties, Michael spent most of his time in the open air with a blanket over his head (it affected him so profoundly that he chose 'Blanket' as the nickname for his own third child) – DiLeo created a Wizard-of-Oz-like aura of mystery around his charge. As in the fairy tale, it was out of all proportion to reality.

How odd to sit listening to DiLeo giving Michael's press conference in Rome, when I knew, having spent a day with him earlier that year at Barry White's barbecue near Santa Ynez, that Michael could have given it himself. He should have been allowed to. The comprehensive gagging of artist by manager privately outraged his siblings La Toya and Jermaine.

They were beginning to feel, despite having hired DiLeo to manage the family's acclaimed Victory Tour, that Frank was selling their brother short. Worse, that he was turning him into a laughing stock. It certainly seemed that way when, contrary to Michael's protests that his skin was lightening due to treatment for the skin pigmentation deficiency condition Vitiligo, DiLeo led us to believe that he was deliberately having it bleached. It contradicted the line in the hit that it doesn't really matter if you're black or white, but what the hell. Then there was Bubbles, the pet chimp, who accompanied Michael on every leg of the tour and shared his hotel room; rumours that he slept in a hyperbaric oxygen chamber, to preserve his vocal cords; his landmark endorsement deal for Pepsi, during the filming of a commercial for which a pyrotechnic display set his head on fire, leading to tales of hair-weave treatments hitherto unknown.

Meanwhile, back in Encino, in the grounds of the mock-Tudor mansion he'd purchased, Peter Pan began building his personal paradise. Neverland was both fortress and amusement park, complete with zoo, movie theatre, animated model museum, ice cream parlour and toy store, filled with models of the 'friends' he'd never been allowed to cultivate as a child. He was now able to have fantasy conversations with them. Neverland upset me when I visited. The topiary cut in animal shapes. The snakes slithering around the house. The collection of hard-core pornography, of which he was creepily proud. The guy had won eight Grammys for 'Thriller'. Whatever that meant, it didn't add up. Of the actual human beings he deigned to hang with, every one of them seemed damaged, compromised or challenged, just like him. Elizabeth Taylor, Liza Minnelli, Jacqueline Kennedy Onassis, Diana Ross, Marlon Brando. All significantly older than him. Perhaps only Paul McCartney, whom he'd met through music industry executive Judd Lander, with whom he later recorded and whose Beatles publishing rights Michael purchased in 1985, was a genuinely sane and balanced friend. Needless to say, it didn't last.

When he wasn't duncing around with eccentric pals, Michael was filling his ranch with innocent children. Many of them were cancer victims, and some were terminally ill, while others were deprived and poverty-stricken. It was, he insisted, about giving them a chance at the childhood he'd never had. That Michael's heart was loving was never in doubt. Having watched him inter-act with my then five year-old daughter Mia, whom he invited with a little gang of others to sing with him on stage during his Wembley Stadium concert in July 1992 – he had a dressing room on the stage itself, his legendary hat dangling from the bulb-popping mirror – there was no doubt that he identified better with children than adults, and that he was clinging to a childhood he hadn't experienced. It was the reason he was desperate to have kids of his own, despite the fact that he was incapable of maintaining relationships with their mothers. His childless 1994 marriage to Elvis Presley's daughter Lisa Marie ended in divorce after two years. He then had two children, Prince Michael I and Paris Katherine, during a brief marriage to nurse Debbie Rowe. Former actor Mark Lester may or may not have provided the sperm. A third, Prince Michael II – who made headlines as a baby when his father dangled him from a hotel balcony – was born to a woman Michael never named.

Why did it go wrong for him? The edges became blurred. His fantasy dream world was always doomed. Michael would learn to his cost that some children are more innocent than others – often in direct proportion to the ambitions of their parents. There was no clean-break comeback from accusations of the corruption of minors, however fanciful those accusations may have been. His 2005 trial was one of the largest and most documented legal battles in history. The debate rages to this day as to whether, despite conclusive verdicts, Michael was ever guilty of child abuse. The tell-all films keep on coming. His consistent argument – that innocent kids were the only people who made him feel secure – would turn Neverland into Dangerland, a sinister realm where adult urges invaded childish innocence.

As for the money. A millionaire since the age of fourteen, he had banked fortunes during the good years. But big-spending shopaholic Michael was now monstrously broke. On the brink of bankruptcy, and owing millions in tax as well as to a string of individuals for defaulting on deals, including one with Prince Abdullah of Bahrain for two unmade albums for which he allegedly advanced the singer £3.3 million – Michael was forced to flog Neverland and to agree to a killer fifty-date O2 comeback. Without DiLeo to mastermind all this, the debts had continued to mount. As his impossible half-century loomed, he stepped out from behind his Oz-style smokescreen, confronted 21st Century reality, and vowed to reinvent himself as an adult for the sake of his kids. The trouble was, he couldn't do it. He wouldn't even allow his children to go to school. He couldn't bring himself to let them enjoy the normal childhood he'd never had. His family rallied. They ranted about the O2 commitment. They warned that Michael, who by this time was addicted to painkillers and the sedative Propofol after having allegedly broken a vertebra, was too frail to commit to such a punishing run of shows. It fell on deaf ears. Cocky promoters AEG, who were under-insured, paid the price, after Michael died from a drug overdose at the age of just fifty on 25th June 2009. His personal physician, Conrad Murray, served two years for his involuntary manslaughter, and emerged to tell his tale in 2013. Two years later, in his memoir, 'This Is It!', the doctor described the making of a scapegoat.

Flaminio Stadium, Rome, May 1988, on Michael Jackson's BAD tour:
Simon Climie, Gill Pringle, Billy Sloane, LAJ, Roger Tavener

24. ECHO BEACH

Long time no see, Andy Stephens. What a nice man. I used to bump into him often when he was managing George Michael. After that, not a glimpse for years. Then he had Geri Halliwell for five minutes. When we met again at the Utopia Village business complex in Primrose Hill, he had become the personal manager of Susan Boyle. He hadn't wanted to touch the 'Britain's Got Talent' superstar with a bargepole, he confided. Simon Cowell made him do it.

Soon afterwards, in December 2009, Spandau Ballet invited me to the Groucho Club launch party of their friends-again comeback tour DVD. I had been commissioned, that day, to write a spread on the 'Hairy Angel' for the Sunday Express. The first person I ran into at the party was her manager, Andy.

Over here! Lovely to see you! Tell me everything! Rarely does it fall in your lap. I remained sober – this is relevant – chewed some cud with Spandau's drummer John Keeble, did the rounds and made a run for it back to my car, intent on recording all that Andy had shared.

Back home, I did something I rarely do. A single parent of three, I almost never drink alone indoors. Slippery slope. Libation only liberates among close friends. Alone, I find drinking degrading. That night, however, I was on a high as well as a mission. I'd had a great night, had caught up with old friends, and was in a buoyant mood. I poured myself a goblet of Merlot, gulped it back, glugged in a bit more, kicked off my Choos at the bottom of the stairs – also relevant – and legged it up a flight to my desk.

The Susan Boyle CD had landed on the mat only a day or two earlier. Where is it? I know, it's in the car. I'll go and get it: a bit of background SuBo while I'm sketching the piece might help. Down the stairs and back out into the freezing December night. The car is right in front of the garden gate, I'll get away without shoes if I hop. I didn't bother with my coat.

I'm in my car. No ignition key, but a key-card that you insert into a slot to activate lights, sound, vision and other functions. In it goes. Glove compartment, CD, action. The digital clock catches my eye: it is almost 2am. Oh. I can hardly go blasting the family with Boyle at this hour on a school night. The kids will go nuts. I know: I'll just sit here and listen to it for a couple of tracks. Right here, in the car.

As awakenings go, it was a rude one. One minute I was dozing soundly, lulled by the dulcet tones of the dreamy Scottish songstress. The next, two uniformed officers had me up against my own front railings, reminding me that I did not have to say anything, but that anything I did say may be taken down and used in evidence. I was breathalysed, despite my protests that I'd not driven anywhere under the influence.

'Tell it to the Beak.'

'But look, I have no shoes on.'

'And?' sneered Plod.

'You won't find them in the car,' I tried to reason, 'because they're in my house, right there.'

'But you've been out for the evening?'

'Yes I have. I came home, went straight upstairs, and sat down to work.'

'What, at this time of night?'

'Yes, it's normal. I'm a writer. Then I was looking for a CD, I came out here to get it, I stuck it on to listen to it, and I must have fallen asleep.'

'Your headlights are on.'

'The keycard does that, automatically.'

'Get in the van.'

'I haven't even got a bag or coat on me. Please, how the hell would I have driven home from an event without shoes, bag or coat?'

'Just get in the van.'

'Can I just go inside and tell my kids? They've got school in the morning.'

'No. Get in the van. And mind your head.'

I spent the night in a cell at Peckham police station. Not what you'd call a high point. I remained there until well after four o'clock the next day, when my eldest daughter and a friend came to rescue me. For that entire day, my family had had no idea where I was. Even my former husband spent several hours ringing around hospitals. My children were trauma-tised, with good reason. My office lights and my computer were on. My coat and bag were on the banister. The shoes I'd gone out in were at the bottom of the stairs. The scene almost eclipsed that of the Marie Celeste.

Come the February hearing, luck looked in. I had a female Magistrate for a start. The last thing I am is sexist, but you get it. She got it. As she explained, she had no choice but to find me guilty of being 'drunk in charge of a vehicle', because I was. She had to do it by the book. The fact that I'd consumed alcohol in the privacy of my home, and had then gone outside to sit in the car, was inadmissible as mitigating. According to the law, I should have lost my licence. I kept it. Madam Magistrate was merciful. I was awarded ten points. A further mishap over the ensuing three years, and I would be banned.

I saw Spandau's lead singer Tony Hadley again a few months later, during summer 2010. I was about to interview him at Century Club on Shaftsbury Avenue, for my series 'Me & Mrs Jones' on Vintage TV.

'A funny thing happened to me on my way home from your party at the Groucho last Christmas,' I said.

'Tell me.'

I told him. His piercing eyes grew Baskerville-huge and round.

'Fuck me,' he said, as the sorry tale concluded. 'Not even Gary Kemp could make that up.'

When rock band Queen announced the biopic they were planned to make about Freddie Mercury, nineteen years after his death, I could hardly believe my luck. Thirteen years had elapsed since the publication of my original Freddie biography. The book had done well, but had been and gone. Now, Hodder & Stoughton wanted to re-publish it.

I was nervous about this, for all the reasons. I'd spent two years researching it and a year writing it, after having read every previous about Freddie and Queen that I could find. There was so much conflicting information that I knew I'd have to start from scratch. I retraced Freddie's footsteps. I went to Zanzibar, where he was born. To India, where he'd gone to school. To the States, Brazil and various European countries relevant to him, including several I'd visited with Queen during the 1980s.

Almost a decade and a half down the line, dust had settled and grief had waned. People close to Freddie who had felt too raw to be interviewed for the original book might well be inclined to talk to me now.

Just as importantly, having matured as a writer, I hoped that I could do a better job.

While my then literary agent Ivan Mulcahy was re-negotiating with the publisher, I was approached by Peter Morgan, who created the screenplays for 'The Queen', 'Frost/Nixon', 'The Other Boleyn Girl', 'The Deal', and since then, 'The Crown' for Netflix. He had been engaged to write the script for Queen's film. Sacha Baron Cohen had agreed to play their frontman. Worldwide release of the movie was scheduled for November 2011, to commemorate Freddie's anniversary. Jim Beach, Queen's manager, and guitarist Brian May apparently informed Morgan that my book was the seminal work on the subject. He wanted to meet me.

Peter flew in from his home in Vienna. We convened for posh lunch at Daphne's in Brompton Cross. I'd dressed up for it. Peter hadn't. The left sleeve of his charcoal sweater had an elbow-sized hole. The rich and famous don't need to bother about making an impression. He quizzed me about Freddie 'the private person', explained his story arc, and got quite graphic. He then asked me, over the char-grilled swordfish, to act as a script consultant. I pinched my Gevrey-Chambertin-polished cheeks the whole cab ride home.

Ivan came back with good news: Hodder were keen for me to rewrite my biography. A massive opportunity. The book was not published in the US originally: Queen's popularity there was in decline at the time of Freddie's death. Thanks to the subsequent global success of their musical 'We Will Rock You', devised by Queen and Ben Elton, and with this forthcoming film, there was huge new potential. Simon & Schuster's Touchstone imprint secured an American publication deal for 'Mercury', as the book is known there. My new biography of Freddie would soon exist in many translations.

I was then approached by Andy Hill from the digital supply company I Like Music, now known as Startle, with the idea to create both a radio documentary and a TV documentary on Freddie Mercury. The former would be produced by Phil 'The Collector' Swern, the award-winning radio producer, and accompanied by a compilation CD of rare, unreleased and cover material. The latter would be led by John Fielding, the eight-times Emmy Award-winning producer. Both properties would be made and licensed for international sale.

Everything Freddie-related would be released just ahead of the film, to take advantage of Queen's pre-launch promotion. It was even proposed that Peter Morgan should receive a share of my publishing royalties in return for allowing us to bill our revised biography 'The Book of the Film', and deploy stills from the movie as cover and content illustrations.

All of which seemed too good to be true. It was.

While the book went ahead, and sold brilliantly in every territory, the film didn't happen. Peter Morgan penned a couple of versions of the script, but Queen were not impressed. 'Everybody knows what happened to Freddie,' Morgan told me. 'I do not want to make a film about a sick gay guy who dies of AIDS. I want to celebrate the pinnacle that was Live Aid, which was perhaps Freddie's finest hour.' Queen, aka Brian May, Roger Taylor and manager Jim Beach (bassist John Deacon having retired and gone off the radar years earlier) had other ideas. They wanted a film about the whole band, not just Freddie. They were determined to capitalise on their achievement of having gone from strength to strength after Freddie's death, their music more popular than ever – not realising, or ignoring the fact that, had their frontman not died so tragically, their music would most likely have faded away. As Simon Napier-Bell often says, the best thing a rock or pop star can do to guarantee the immortality of their music is die young.

Sacha Baron Cohen was the next to pull out, blaming creative differences. In 2016, he told US radio host Howard Stern that he had hoped to star in a warts-and-all picture about Freddie that opened the floodgates on his hedonistic lifestyle, but Brian and Roger were fearful of damaging the legacy.

'A member of the band – I won't say who – said, "You know, this is such a great movie because it's got such an amazing thing that happens in the middle,"' said 'Borat'.

'And I go, "What happens in the middle?" He goes, "You know, Freddie dies ... and we see how the band carries on from strength to strength."

'There are amazing stories about Freddie Mercury. The guy was wild. There are stories of little people walking around parties with plates of cocaine on their heads!'

Every word is true.

Ben Whishaw ('Q' in 'Skyfall' and 'Spectre', 'Bright Star', 'The Danish Girl') was favourite to replace him. Daniel Radcliffe ('Harry Potter') and Dominic Cooper ('Mamma Mia') were also in the running. They wound up with Rami Malek ('Mr Robot', 'Night at the Museum', 'The Twilight Saga'), an Egyptian-American actor who does exude something of Freddie's African/Asian essence. As for directors, they went through Stephen Frears, Tom Hooper and David Fincher before settling, controversially, on Bryan Singer. He was later fired, and the film was completed by Dexter Fletcher, although Singer is still credited. Previous screenwriters include Stephen J. Rivele and Christopher Wilson. They proceeded with Justin Haythe and Anthony McCarten. Principal photography began on 8th September 2017 at Bovingdon Airfield in Hemel Hempstead. The film, 'Bohemian Rhapsody', is the joint production of Robert de Niro (TriBeCa Films), Graham King (G.K. Films) and Queen Productions. Lucy Boynton, the daughter of my friends Adriaane Pielou and Graham Boynton, plays Freddie's girlfriend turned PA, Mary Austin. The press announcement described the film as 'A chronicle of the years leading up to Queen's legendary appearance at the Live Aid concert in 1985.' 'Bohemian Rhapsody' the motion picture has grossed more than $600 million worldwide. It was the ninth highest-grossing film of 2018, and is the highest-grossing musical biopic of all time. It has also done well on the awards circuit. All this despite very mixed reviews and some glaring historical inaccuracies.

So near, yet so far. I had no part to play in this film, beyond my early consulting work for Peter Morgan. In September 2016, Ivan sold the rights to my biography of Freddie to another Hollywood production company. 'Bohemian Rhapsody' tells us little about Freddie's early life. The incredibly story of his childhood is the film I'd love to make.

Every cloud has a silver lining. If Whitney Houston's cloud was her marriage to a drug-crazed bully who dragged her to the depths of misery, whose idea of fun was spitting in her face in front of their daughter or scissoring the heads off all her photographs, and who amused himself spray-painting 'evil eyes' on walls and furnishings all over their house, then the lining was what we saw on 'The X Factor' in October 2009. Despite Whitney's shambolic, cringeworthy performance of her new single 'Million Dollar Bill' that night, in front of a live studio audience and fourteen million viewers, it was in every way one of pop's greatest comebacks. We knew, despite the cock-ups, that we were witnessing soul.

Ironic, isn't it, to think that the woman known worldwide as 'The Voice', who sold two hundred million albums and fifty million singles, who created the best-selling movie soundtrack of all time (for 'The Bodyguard') and who is credited with having broken down the colour barrier for black female artists, just as Michael Jackson had done for the boys, had to endure living hell with fellow artist Bobby Brown in order to achieve the real thing. That's art for you. Many assumed it came with the Whitney package when she started wowing audiences back in the Eighties. It didn't.

I tied myself in knots once, trying to get to the soul of Whitney, in an interview in October 1986. Reluctantly, I had to admit that it wasn't there. The smile stopped short of her dazzling eyes. The lights were on. Chandeliers, even. But there was no one home. Whitney was gorgeous. A squeaky-clean, perfectly manufactured confection. The brain-child of Arista Records mogul Clive Davis. You didn't say no to Clive. No one did. Not Janis Joplin, not Bruce Springsteen, not Pink Floyd, not Billy Joel. Not to mention Earth, Wind & Fire or Aerosmith. Having masterminded the careers of some of the world's most successful artists, multi Grammy award-winning Davis was not the kind of mogul a girl turns down. He had a vision for Whitney, and created her from scratch: Pop Barbie. I said as much in the piece I wrote in the Mail the next day. That night, at her 'Greatest Love' concert at Wembley Arena, I sat surrounded by lackeys and heavies who did their darnedest to put the frighteners on, blowing smoke in my eyes as I tried to review her show, and reminding me to look under my car when I left.

I had nothing against Clive Davis. I had met him a handful of times. We'd had lunch. He paid. They don't usually. He was clearly devoted to the job, cared passionately about every artist he'd ever signed, remained personal friends with most of them, and walked on water as far as they were concerned. I merely tried to point out that 'soul' is not something you can be born with, or be taught. You have to suffer, and do the Gloria Gaynor thing, as Whitney herself came to know.

It was not enough that Dionne Warwick was her cousin, Aretha Franklin her godmother, that she cut her teeth on Gospel in a New Jersey church and sang live to the whole of New York with her soul singer mother Cissy – although, granted, those factors made her a marketing man's dream. Whitney was going to have to get soul the hard way. No one would have wished on her the horror film that her life became. All that grief and suffering, the despair, the life-altering mistakes, the sackings, the no-shows, her addictions, her rehab, the brushes with the law – not to mention her early grave of a marriage – made it onto her album 'I Look to You'. But her voice on that record sounds remarkably unscathed.

I had to wonder. How did Whitney come to loathe herself so completely that she couldn't bring herself to leave the man who made a crack addict of her, and almost destroyed her career?

Her fame, she told Oprah Winfrey, contributed to the demise of her marriage.

'Something happens to a man when a woman has that much fame,' she said. 'I tried to play it down all the time. I used to say, 'I'm Mrs. Brown. Don't call me Houston.'

She defended Brown, and got slapped for it. She took drugs with him to make him feel better, and wound up addicted to marijuana and crack cocaine herself. She tried to share her success and money, to give them a good life together, but Brown couldn't bear the competition. He was insanely jealous of all that she had achieved. He needed to be top dog. In the end, because she was weary, Whitney stopped caring about her music.

'I had totally forgotten about that life. He was my drug,' she admitted. 'I didn't do anything without him. I wasn't getting high by myself. It was me and him together. We were partners, that's what my high was. He and I together. No matter what.'

Saving herself just in time, with intervention from her mother, Whitney divorced Brown in 2007, and retreated with her daughter Bobbi Kristina, of whom she had won custody. They relocated from Atlanta to LA and rented a small canyon home. Whitney contrived for herself a 'comfort zone' of school runs and kitchen suppers. Then Clive called.

'"It's time", he said. "Time for what?" I asked. "Time for you to come back and sing for us again." My daughter said "Mom, get up, you can do this." She encourages and inspires me. I look at her eyes and I see myself, and I go "Ok, I can do this."

'I'm still going to remain the quiet, private person I have been for the past ten years. I just want to be recognised for my music, for what it does and how it inspires people. How it makes people feel, as opposed to talking about Whitney all the time.'

She made us feel. But she couldn't feel. She was too numb to fetch herself back from the brink. Five years later, on 11th February 2012, the most awarded female artist of all time was found dead in the bath in her hotel room at the Beverly Hilton LA. Cocaine, cannabis, prescription drugs. Unthinkable. She was forty-eight.

What drove Bobbi Kristina to mirror her mother's demise? Three years later, at home in Georgia, she too was found face-down in the bath. She lingered in a coma for half a year, but never recovered. She was pronounced dead on 26th July 2015. Alcohol. Cannabis. Prescription drugs. Unthinkable. Unspeakable. She was twenty-two.

Remote death hits just as hard, sometimes, as death close to home. On August 29, 2013, we lost Cliff Morgan. The mercurial rugby international and broadcaster, my father's oldest friend, was a proper Welshman, albeit one with a CVO and an OBE. Low-level charming, quietly passionate, he was blessed with a resonant voice and disarming modesty. He'd be the loudest person in room, even without a voice.

He hailed from Trebanog in the Rhondda Valley, an ember's throw from my father's birthplace, Merthyr Tydfil. Both were the sons of coalminers. Neither forgot it. It was the memories of their childhood that united them. When life has literally been the pits, getting paid to play sport in the open air is a dream. Cliff turned down an offer to sign for Tottenham Hotspurs, and made for the rugby pitch. My father opted for football, became a marginal pro, and watched from the stand as another talented Jones, another Cliff, our Uncle, made soccer history at Spurs.

In 1951, aged nineteen, Cliff Morgan was selected for Cardiff. He was part of the Grand Slam-winning team of 1952. The following year he showed his colours against New Zealand's fearsome All Blacks. In 1955 he was the star Lion during the team's tour of South Africa, scoring a momentous try against the Springboks in Johannesburg. Their 23-22 victory before a crowd of ninety-six thousand in the Transvaal was, Cliff said, the greatest moment of his sporting life.

Retiring at twenty-eight, he took to broadcasting with BBC Wales. He became editor of 'Grandstand', and then head of outside broadcasting, revolutionising the way the Corporation covered sport. He shocked the lot of them by moving to ITV to edit current affairs show 'This Week'.

He suffered a stroke in 1972, which left him partially paralysed and unable to speak. Astonishingly, he recovered sufficiently to commentate on the legendary match between the Barbarians and the All Blacks at Cardiff Arms Park the following year. He went on to star on 'A Question of Sport' alongside his friend Henry Cooper, and to Radio 4, where he became a legend.

The cruellest blow was the terrible illness that silenced him: cancer of the vocal cords, resulting in the removal of his larynx. Even so, he insisted on giving a speech at his eightieth birthday party on the Isle of Wight. I recall every word.

Cliff Morgan CVO, OBE, aka 'Morgan the Magnificent', possessed of one of the best broadcasting voices of all time. With Ken Jones, LAJ & Hugh McIlvanney at Cliff's 80th birthday lunch, the George Hotel Yarmouth, Isle of Wight, England, 2010

25. IMAGINE

On April Fools' Day 2015, Cynthia Lennon died of cancer. She was seventy-five. I cried for her with no personal reason to. I experienced a sense of injustice on her behalf that was out of proportion to our acquaintance. In truth, I barely knew her. But our paths had crossed, we had conversed at length, and we came very close to working together. It hardly gave me the right to grieve for her. Yet I did.

Her death was quite savage. It didn't seem right. Punished for what? For being good? She had felt destroyed for most of her life, she once said, despite which she'd always refused to attack the woman who caused it. That was Cynthia. Kind and brave, an honest sort, who always did what she said she was going to do. She made a point of that. She knew that she hadn't been singled out for misery, that life's random cruelty is never personal. She was no stranger to the losses we all endure: youth, looks, love, ambition, hope. She had been forced to abandon her dreams before their time: the usual. But terminal illness was insult to injury. Perhaps there is something in Joan Collins's advice about not bottling pain, about refusing to give in, about 'just getting over things.' But some of us never get over things. We just can't. Cynthia Lennon didn't. She might have been the most wronged wife in rock history. A dutiful spouse and devoted mother whose agony was felt by the entire world, because of who her husband was.

The truth about John Lennon and his relationships with women is complex, and vastly more revealing of his true nature than the enduring myth. I know this because Cynthia told me. She said that her former husband believed the real love of his life was not Yoko Ono, but Alma Cogan, a fading singer eight years his senior. Far-fetched though it may sound, John believed Alma to be the reincarnation of his beloved mother Julia. This was despite the fact that the two co-existed, their lives overlapping by twenty-six years. It was Cogan's death, said Cynthia, and the need for a replacement mother figure, that threw him into the welcoming arms of Ono.

'John thought I didn't know anything about him and Alma, because I never let on that I did,' Cynthia confided.

'Now, with all the emotion gone out of it, I can see the attraction. Alma was years older than John, and very much the Auntie figure.'

John, she said, had a soft spot for the older woman.

'Don't forget that Yoko was also older than John, by about seven years,' she pointed out. 'Like Yoko, in so many ways, Alma was a very compelling woman. Both were driven by self-worth. You couldn't really say that either of them was beautiful, could you, not in the conventional sense. But it was as if they truly believed that they were special. If you can convince yourself of that, other people tend to think you are too. They were very alike in that sense. No, the idea of John and Alma doesn't surprise me in the least.

'When Alma died from ovarian cancer in 1966, at only thirty-four, John was inconsolable. The woman he'd perhaps earmarked to replace his beloved Aunt Mimi in his affections was now lost to him. He met Yoko when he needed to, just a fortnight into his grief. She was this obsessive fan who'd turn up and follow him around. She irritated the life out of John to begin with. But Alma died, and something odd happened to John. Things turned. Yoko must have seen her opportunity, and seized it. She wore the trousers, and would control and dominate John for the rest of his life. Yoko was John's 'new Aunt Mimi'. She worked out what John needed in a woman, right under my nose, and she re-invented herself.'

Alma Cogan, 'the girl with the laugh in her voice' and the UK's first female pop star, was the highest-paid British woman entertainer of the 1950s. She became a household name at the advent of television. Born Alma Angela Cohen to Russian-Rumanian Jews in London's Whitechapel, she was competing in talent competitions from an early age. She sang at tea dances while studying dress design, and performed in musicals and revues before becoming the resident band singer at the Cumberland Hotel. Her first release, recorded on her twentieth birthday, launched her on BBC radio. She had her first hit, 'Bell Bottom Blues', in April 1954, four years before the death of Lennon's mother.

'She was this typical East End Jewish glamour girl with a heart of gold, a beehive and these amazing frocks,' remembered Cynthia. 'Not the sort of thing I'd ever have been seen dead in myself. She was a bit passé. Her songs were all Fifties-America froth, like 'Dreamboat' and 'Sugartime'. When John and I were at college, Alma Cogan was a big star. John couldn't stand her, he used to take the mickey out of her all the time. He'd do this wicked impersonation of her. At the time, I would never in a million years have thought that he could have fallen for a woman so much older than him, whose music he couldn't bear and who he ridiculed mercilessly. Because John did have this incredibly cruel streak. He couldn't help himself.'

When the Beatles hit the big time, and shared a bill with Cogan on TV's 'Sunday Night at the London Palladium', it was inevitable that they would be invited to one of the legendary parties thrown by Alma at Stafford Court, Kensington, the opulent flat she shared with her widowed mother Fay. Alma was close to their manager Brian Epstein, who with composer Lionel Bart, the creator of the musical 'Oliver!', was one of her regular 'walkers'.

'I never got invited, I was kept under wraps,' said Cynthia.

'John was a famous pop star, and it was all about keeping the legions of female fans happy. It wasn't good for his image to have a wife and baby trailing on his coat-tails. Brian Epstein insisted, and I just had to accept it. Everyone who was anyone used to go to those parties: Princess Margaret, Noel Coward, Roger Moore, Audrey Hepburn, Michael Caine, Cary Grant. I never went,' she said, although she described the apartment in her memoir.

'I only heard years later that John and Paul used to spend a lot of time round Alma's. John's nickname for her mother was 'Ma McCogie.' It was on Alma's piano, with her sister Sandra sitting beside him, that Paul composed 'Yesterday'. Paul was supposed to be having a thing with Sandra, too, I don't know whether that's true. The working title of the song was 'Scrambled Eggs', because that was what Fay had just cooked them for tea. 'Scrambled eggs, oh my baby how I love your legs...'

Cynthia spilled all this when we met in London in 1989, shortly before the opening of her ill-fated restaurant, Lennon's, on the fringes of Theatreland. Despite the fact that she and her partners invested handsomely in the venture, and that she had even poached Peter Stockton, her Upper St. Martin's Lane neighbour Peter Stringfellow's flamboyant general manager, to run the place for her, the business soon died a death. She invited me to the restaurant one afternoon during launch week.

She had divorced twice more since John. She married second husband Roberto Bassanini, an Italian hotelier, in 1970. They managed three years. Her third husband, John Twist, was a Lancastrian engineer. They tied the knot in 1976, and divorced seven years later. She was now living with a Liverpudlian chauffeur four years her junior, called Jim Christie. They had a house in Penrith on the edge of the Lake District. She would eventually say yes a fourth and final time, in 2002, to Barbadian night-club owner Noel Charles. They made their home in Majorca, where, in 2013, Noel died.

Cynthia had reverted to John's surname by the time I caught up with her, because it was 'good for business'. She had been busy: design-ing home furnishings for the Viyella fabric company under the family name, and launching her own perfume, 'Woman', in response to the eponymous 1980 hit that John wrote for Yoko. An enthusiastic cook, she had previously owned a restaurant/bed-and-breakfast establishment called Oliver's Bistro in Ruthin, North Wales. She was candid about her money-making ventures: 'Needs must. My divorce settlement from John was very modest (£100,000 plus custody of Julian), and of course it's all gone now. I'll do whatever it takes to get by. I have to pay the bills like everyone else.'

Paul McCartney's late wife Linda was the catalyst for our encounter: Linda and I had collaborated briefly on her memoir, 'Mac the Wife', which never progressed. Paul had remained in close touch with Cynthia after her split from John, and had apparently written the hit 'Hey Jude' for Julian. Released by The Beatles in August 1968 when John's firstborn was only five years old, and still one of their best-loved hits, Paul com-posed it to comfort the child through the agony of his parents' break-up.

Cynthia and I met to discuss a new memoir that she wanted to write. She was looking for a ghost-writer, and Linda had recommended me. Cynthia's first book, 'A Twist of Lennon', published in 1978, had left a bitter taste. She had been so frustrated at not being able to communicate with John after he left her for Yoko that she wrote the book as a 'long, open letter to him, pouring it all out.' With hindsight, she admitted, she wished that she'd done it differently. Now that the dust had settled on John's death nine years earlier, she was keen to have another go; to get her side of the story down accurately, for the record. She had decided that she needed professional help. She had then become immersed in her new business venture, and the project was shelved. Years later, in 2005, she wrote and published a further memoir, much bolder and more con-fessional than its predecessor, entitled 'John'.

Sitting at a corner table that day in her monochrome eaterie, Cyn-thia chain-smoked and got through a tank of wine.

'It all began with the death of John's mother,' she said, chocolate eyes dancing behind huge gold-rimmed specs. She flicked frequently at her thick blonde fringe. Her pleasant voice had a whisper of Scouse to it. In her fiftieth year and no temptress, she was still turning heads.

John's mother Julia was knocked down and killed by an off-duty policeman outside his Aunt Mimi's house in July 1958.

'It was complicated, the way that all happened,' Cynthia said. 'The effect of his mother's death on John's psyche was profound and damaging. He was seventeen years old, and I don't believe he ever recovered from it. It disrupted his ability to have normal relationships with women.

'His mother was bohemian, an uninhibited sort, who had given John up as a little boy into the care of her childless elder sister Mimi Smith and her husband George. Julia was estranged from John's father, Alf, and was living with another man (Bobby Dykins). John went to visit Julia whenever he could. He idolised her. She'd taught him how to play various instruments, and got him his first guitar. Mimi brought John up very strictly. Julia was arty and laid-back. John identified with her. He was very much his mother's son. Although Mimi worshipped him, John was a disappointment to her. To her, he never fulfilled his potential and wasted his opportunities.

'John never amounted to much at school. He got into Liverpool Art College by the skin of his teeth, which was where we met. I'd come up from Liverpool Junior Art school. Mimi disapproved of us, of course: I'm not sure that any girl would ever have been good enough for her John. When John and the boys went to Hamburg, I rented his bedroom at their house 'Mendips' from Mimi. I have often thought since that there was something of the 'keep your friends close and your enemies closer' about the arrangement, though of course it never occurred to me at the time.'

It was inevitable that The Beatles would cross paths with Alma Cogan.

'They became part of that same showbusiness world. When I first heard about them, I didn't care, to be honest. I was deeply in love with John. I have always been in love with John. I have never stopped loving him. Once you've had a child with someone, the bond that you have never leaves you. I realised early on that I was going to have to share my husband with the entire world. But it was the so-called Swinging Sixties. Times were permissive, apparently. Everyone was doing everything with everyone. John would do as he pleased, I had always known that about him. I couldn't change him, I couldn't control him. So I accepted him as he was. All that mattered was that he came home to me, and to Julian.'

After his mother's death, his relationship with Cynthia intensified. He wrote his girlfriend passionate love letters, and could be fiercely jealous, but he never wrote songs for her. Those were reserved for his dead mother, notably 'Julia' and 'Mother'. When the couple married in a civil ceremony at Liverpool's Mount Pleasant Register Office on 23rd August, 1962, Cynthia was pregnant. Their son John Charles Julian (to be known as 'Julian' in honour of the paternal grandmother he never met) was born on 8th April the following year: seven months after the release of The Beatles' first single 'Love Me Do', and on the brink of the Beatlemania that floored the world.

Cynthia was adamant that, had Alma lived, John would never have abandoned his family for her. The affair, Cynthia believed, would have fizzled out naturally, and John would have come home with his tail between his legs, 'as he had always done.'

When Cogan's star began to fade, she resorted to recording Beatles songs, such as 'Help' and 'Eight Days a Week'. She was desperate to hang onto her audience. After her death in October 1966, John found his new 'Aunt Mimi replacement' in Yoko Ono. The real Aunt Mimi died in Dorset in December 1991, aged eighty-five. It was former BBC Radio One DJ Andy Peebles – the last British broadcaster ever to interview Lennon, just forty-eight hours before his death, in New York – who told me that John always addressed and referred to Yoko as 'Mother'.

Did Cynthia really believe that Alma Cogan was John's true love?

'We can convince ourselves of almost anything in grief,' she said quietly.

'Because she was dead, it was safe for John to convince himself of that. It didn't threaten anything else. It certainly didn't threaten us. It couldn't. As I said, he was complicated. More screwed-up than most people ever knew. I wanted more than anything for John to be happy. I don't believe he ever was, and that kills me.'

Five months later, the day after my birthday, Jackie Collins died. I was so sad. She and her sister Joan had long been my role models. I so admired Jackie's spirit and guts. Much-maligned and often ridiculed, she was in fact a magnificently clever and incredibly rich writer, who invented a genre from scratch and who wrote in the old-fashioned way: on foolscap pads, with pencils and felt-tip pens, never plotting or planning but allowing stories and characters to emerge from her imagination and to bring themselves to life. The way she connected her players and knotted her plots was almost Dickensian.

She kept her cancer to herself for six years. She didn't even share with Joan until a fortnight before the end. Only her three daughters knew. Rather than penning a woe-is-me cancer diary, she went quietly about her business until the end. It seems an infinitely more elegant way of dealing with death. Living her big life to the last – she was in the UK from LA only a week before she died, giving an interview on 'Loose Women' – Jackie refused to give her illness column inches. That's class. She was kind to me. I interviewed her several times over the years, notably at the London Ritz, with a newborn baby under my arm (I was breastfeeding). Jackie seized Mia and sat nursing her while we talked. She later wrote to me to thank me 'soooo much!!!' for bringing my baby, on cream vellum personalised notepaper with 'Jackie Collins at the Ritz' embellished top-centre in royal blue. How cool is that. I have coveted such stationery ever since.

I can take or leave Kenneth Branagh, but there was no avoiding him that November. 'The Winter's Tale' at the Garrick was his own theatre company's adaptation of this oft-overlooked Shakespearian masterpiece.

It's nothing personal. Ken may well be an ok bloke. In there, somewhere. It's his histrionics and superiority complex that I can do without. Nor do I care for him gagging, spitting and dribbling all over the stage the way he does. What if someone slipped in it? I realise that many disagree with me.

There were compensations. Dame Judi Dench in anything is a gift. I confess to a special fondness for this divine actress, who first played Ophelia in Hamlet at the Old Vic sixty years ago, and who has since won an Oscar, ten BAFTAS, a record six Laurence Olivier awards, an OBE, a DBE and a Companion of Honour. She is also a thoroughly dear, humble and compassionate human being. Of this, I have first-hand experience.

In April 2006, less than a month after my marriage collapsed and in a tremulous state, I drove Mia to the Haymarket to see Judi in Noel Coward's 'Hay Fever'. We were late, it was raining, and I couldn't find anywhere to park. In the end I threw the firstborn out of the car into the bus lane outside the theatre, hurled a ticket at her, and told her I'd join her in the interval. I hung a left, only to see a tiny yellow Porsche Spyder pulling out of a biscuit-sized space. It was mine, all mine. In I backed, too quickly and at too sharp an angle, crunching the rear near-side bumper of the Roller in front. Distracted and not quite right in the head, I confess to doing something that now horrifies me: I legged it, without leaving a note.

We returned to the scene of the crime about three hours later, only to find a gorilla sitting on the boot of the Rolls. He was Dame Judi's driver. The Rolls was hers. I explained the circumstances, and offered to pay. 'You'll be hearing from her lawyers,' he growled.

Several written exchanges later, a charming letter from Judi and a 'compromise' cheque from me – not for the damage (thousands) but for two hundred quid for 'polishing' – I was off the hook. I could barely believe it. I've worshipped the ground she rolls on ever since.

She brought dignity, gravitas and magic to 'The Winter's Tale'. The challenging play tells the story of a king who loses his grip after falling prey to the ultimate destructive force, male sexual jealousy. No longer able to distinguish between reality and delusion, he destroys the things he holds dear. Shakespeare was approaching the end of both his career and his life when he wrote it. The piece is a confounding blend of psycho-trauma and sweet nostalgia, tragedy and comedy. All's well that ends well, kinda sorta. In order to think so, one must suspend disbelief. It's something I'm good at.

Freddie Mercury adored this play. He appeared in it at St. Peter's School in Panchgani, India. An unusual choice for an all-teenage cast, n'est-ce pas, but the experience remained with him his entire life. We talked about it. I was reminded of the conversation in 1995, four years after his death, when Queen's fifteenth studio album 'Made in Heaven' was released. A Requiem to and a showcase for Freddie the diva, the album features a haunting track entitled 'A Winter's Tale'. This was Freddie's swansong, which he wrote and composed at his Montreux apartment overlooking the lake he so loved. The lyrics, describing what he could see from his window, celebrate the peace and contentment that he found there towards the end. The song's title casts him back to the play he performed in as a boy, and appears to be an homage to the old romance. A major character in the play is Polixenes, the King of Bohemia: an ancient kingdom corresponding roughly to today's Czech Republic. If, as scholars believe, the play was an allegory on the demise of Anne Boleyn, its long-lost Princess Perdita character was based on the daughter of Anne and King Henry VIII, who would grow up to become Elizabeth I, England's Queen ...

Queen's magnum opus is 'Bohemian Rhapsody'. See what he did there.

I had always felt as though I'd known Jim Diamond forever. For more than thirty years. He was the life and soul at Henry's eighteenth. He and my Dad were plotting lunch, and had started calling each other for long chats. He was putting the finishing touches to a play he'd just written. I hadn't read it yet, but I knew he was pleased. A few days after Henry's do, we convened at Carluccio in Richmond to talk about it. On 8th October, just after I returned from a lecture trip to Chicago, he died.

He was more than a brother to me. My real brother had receded, and Jim had fallen out with his, so we became each other's brother. He knew my secrets. I knew his. When my husband ran away and our lives collapsed, Jim was there.

He was a tiny Celt with a gigantic heart. He was so proud of his Glaswegian roots. He loved music more profoundly than any other musician I have known. He'd weathered his share of adversity. His voice set him free. His was a more important talent than the industry knew.

He'd lost his mum a couple of weeks earlier. Her death cracked his heart. 'I don't think I'll get over this,' he said. 'I've been crying for my Daddy for thirty-five years, and I'll cry for my Mammy forever.' He couldn't let her go.

All those years of grief and loss.

Jim was the kind of guy who taught you things. In a simple way, never ramming it. He was wise beyond. He'd remind you that death is never convenient. That it throws whatever we're doing at the time. Everything stops and yet nothing does. Not even the departed simply cease. We comfort ourselves that love is undiminished by death. That energy, once created, can't be destroyed. That the spirit lives. That we'll never forget, so our loved ones haven't gone far. They are in the next room, aren't they? How pivotal to survival such platitudes are.

It doesn't matter how many times you go down. It's the getting up. How do we do that? Jim knew. We do it by believing. We stop drowning our sorrows. We remind ourselves to breathe. We recognise the importance of the moment. We remember that there are no accidents. That every ending is a beginning. That every bad goodbye is a good and hopeful hello.

How do we live, after the lost ones? We just have to, Jim insisted. We have to. We can take their chances as well as our own. We can stop caring what other people think. We can ignore the lives and achievements of others, and just live a life that is good enough for us. We can remember that love is a verb.

There are no shortcuts. No quick fixes. There is no one else to blame for what we've done wrong. There may be no tomorrow. We'll make a few more mistakes, and we will never regret the past, because some of it matters. We'll fail forwards. We'll let go of yesterday. We will accept. We will be more patient. We will sense when the time is right. We must realise that happiness resides in our hearts right now – not 'out there', sooner or later, when we've lost some weight, got the right hair, or bought better clothes. We'll remember to smile, today, and to be the first. Jim was always the first. We'll spend more time with those who won't last long. We'll waste ourselves no further on folk who diminish us. We'll accept that blood is thicker, if only in the lab.

And we will forgive. For our own sake. To move on. Because forgiveness is not weak, nor an admission of guilt. It is the thing that sets us free.

And we'll forget about 'the journey'. How we hated hearing celebrities talk about their wretched 'journeys'. We will remember to be present, in the now. We'll stop yearning for more, and just love the less. Because it's all there is.

26. ALL THINGS MUST PASS

Time is intangible. It is an illusion, a construct, a concept. It doesn't exist. It was invented by Man, to keep track. It varies, stretches, diminishes and vanishes, depending on your point of view. You can make a day last longer than a year, if you want to. Try it. You can make it last a lifetime in your mind. That's what births, marriages, anniversaries, 'big birthdays' and deaths are all about. Time is no more than an abstract measurement, a scale by which we chart life. It is designed to give it shape and discipline. To make it easier. It is not to blame for the things we would rather had not happened. It is not an excuse for devastation we can't explain.

Try telling that to the bleaters. As far as they were concerned, it was all 2016's fault. True, it was an annus horribilis of extraordinary loss in entertainment: David Bowie, Robert Stigwood, Jefferson Airplane's Paul Kanter, Alan Rickman, Glenn Frey of the Eagles, Ed Stewart, Terry Wogan. Maurice White, of Earth, Wind and Fire. Tony Warren, the father of 'Coronation Street'. Paul Daniels, Ronnie Corbett, Keith Emerson, George Martin. Merle Haggard. Billy Paul. Prince. I wanted to strangle the many moaners all over Twitter and Facebook, to tell them to snap out of it and get real. As if a random twelve-month period controlled by none of us could be to blame. George Michael liked to say that 'timing is everything'. He proved his point by dying on Christmas Day.

The suggestion that he may have taken his own life, as many believe, was not so far-fetched. George was an extreme control freak. An obsessive planner. The significance of Christ's designated birth date was not lost on him. He wrote 'Last Christmas', one of the great modern Yuletide classics, to link his name indelibly with the day, at a time when 'the Christmas Single' still meant everything in the music industry. Every Christmas, as far into the future as we can think, we will remember and give thanks for George and his music. His arrogance, though breathtaking, is divine.

I spent time with George and Andrew Ridgeley in the Eighties. We worked together. His former manager, Simon Napier-Bell, his agent Gary Farrow and his Sony publicist Jonathan Morrish remain my friends. I have other close pals who went to school with George in North London. From time to time, I got to glimpse the real Yog. He was a tormented soul who lived a closed life for longer than he felt able to be open. He never came out to his family while his mother was alive. He hung on until she died to 'admit' that he was gay.

The self-deception of youth is often viewed as a disease, now. Self-inflicted damage of that kind is rarely repaired. George confessed to a void, created by a distance from his parents and wider family, which generated misery and deprivation. He admitted that he sought adoration from complete strangers, to try and fill that void. The harder he tried, the less he could compensate. He had no idea what 'peace' meant. He accepted that his need to become an artist was a cry for help. He agreed that he was desperately insecure, and that he was addicted to applause. He fell in love with Elton John at a very young age. Performing his Elton favourite, 'Don't Let the Sun Go Down on Me' on stage with his idol was, he said, the pinnacle of his career. The pair later fell out, made up, fell out, made up, in that intensely emotional manner that tends eventually to prove the downfall of superstars.

George pressed the self-destruct button years ago. He gave in to his desires, and even did time for them. He lost out in love, giving away his whole heart, and having it returned to him in shreds. Few can recover from that, least of all those whose every nerve ending is exposed to and raked over by millions, all dependent on his music and demanding, always demanding, answers to questions about love and the meaning of life that he was never equipped to give.

This is how I want to remember George: at Live Aid on 13th July 1985. He was twenty-two years old. In his exuberant prime. Thrilled to be part of the greatest show on earth. Lapping up every moment of it, as if he could hardly believe that he was there I watched him from the wings that day. I witnessed him getting what he needed, if only for eighteen minutes. It was enough.

'Fantasy is the poetry of sex,' intoned the man at the deep end with his feet in the pool. What was that supposed to mean? Without my glasses and in the gloom, I was squinting to see who it was. It was only when I reached the side that I recognised him.

John Hurt was dressed in a patterned shirt and rolled chinos. His thick hair was a birds' nest, and his eyes were glazed. He had a can of beer in one hand and a glass of red in the other. Swigging vigorously at both, he swiped the backs of his fingers across his thin moustache.

'Have you ever thought what it must be like to have a baby?' he slurred. Here we go. I anticipated a tussle with an inebriated roué. Same old, same old. I read the man wrong. I read the man wrong. Little did I realise how his words would come back to haunt me when, two years later and approaching the birth of my firstborn, John would offer me a fortune to buy my child.

Pregnancy was the furthest thing from my mind that summer night in 1985, when one of the most revered actors of our time opened his heart to me in the pool house of a country estate. A gruff, boorish hellraiser by reputation, in the mould of fellow thespians and pals Peter O'Toole and Oliver Reed, the Hurt I encountered was gentle and unthreatening. At forty-five, he was almost twice my age. He was also, so I thought, contentedly married. When he reached for my towel, held out his wine glass and beckoned me to join him, something mournful between the cracks in his voice made me stay. I slipped on my clothes over my sopping swimsuit, and pulled up a chair.

We were at Quarwood: the fifty-five-room, forty-two-acre Stow-on-the-Wold, Gloucestershire home of Who bassist John Entwistle and his girlfriend Maxene. House parties were the Entwistles' forte. Stepping into their bar, hung with casts of marlin and shark that John had caught, I was confronted by a lively crew: actor Robert Powell, drummers Kenney Jones and Zak Starkey (Ringo's son), Midge Ure, Phil and Jill Collins, singer Jim Diamond, and John Hurt.

The house, eccentric pile meets musty museum crammed with skeletons, armour, Nazi memorabilia, Disney china and trainsets was, said Hurt, his kind of place.

'I've never had anywhere I could truly call home,' he said. 'All I've ever really wanted is some comfy bolthole, a sweet little wife and a clutch of kids. It's all any man wants,' he added, ruefully. 'I never once thought it would be too much to ask.'

I was confused. I'd met his wife Donna. They had married only a year earlier. The gutsy Texan waitress could match her husband slug for slug. But she was absent that night. They had met, he said, at the Rainbow Bar and Grill on Sunset Boulevard. Once known as the Villa Nova, it was where baseball star Joe DiMaggio had a blind date with Marilyn Monroe. It re-opened in 1972 with a bash for Elton John, and achieved infamy when 'Blues Brothers' star John Belushi ate his last supper there before expiring along the Strip at the Chateau Marmont. Phil Collins met second wife Jill Tavelman there in 1980. Max and John first got together there too. John Lennon, Ringo Starr and Keith Moon all favoured the joint. It was the kind of place you'd drop in at on a Friday for lunch, and finally make it home sometime on Sunday.

His romantic history, John confessed, had been a 'litany of heartache'. I sat quietly as he poured out memories of first wife Annette Robertson, whom he'd married at twenty-two in 1962 because she told him she was pregnant, and he was desperate for a baby.

'Why? Because I wanted the thing I felt I'd never been: the perfect child,' he said. 'I never felt my family really liked me. My mother (a draughtswoman) or Dad (an Anglican clergyman) would tell me that I must have some kind of depressive disorder, but I never thought it was that. I was an unhappy boy, certainly. The youngest of three boys. Suffocated by piety. I did feel ignored, and that my parents mostly put their own needs first. I didn't much matter to them. When I was sent far away (from Derbyshire) to a boarding school in Kent, I knew they could live without me. I diddled a bit with other boys. In the absence of girls, it was what one did. But I always wanted a wife, and to be a father. Of a little girl, especially. Girls fascinated me. My mother was remote. My elder brother became a Catholic monk, quit, had a family, then went back to being a monk again. Figure that out. My parents adopted Monica after the middle brother died. But she and I were not close. I didn't know much about females, but I wanted to. When my college girlfriend told me she was pregnant, I jumped for joy. I was desperate to be a father. I needed to put right all the wrongs of my own childhood. I rushed into marriage like an utter fool. In the end, there never had been any baby.'

The love of his life, French model Marie-Lise Volpeliere-Pierrot, died in a riding accident in 1983. After sixteen years together, they were planning a wedding.

'I married on the rebound after that,' John admitted. 'All I knew at the time was that I needed to.'

Poor Donna. Despite having applied themselves assiduously to the cause, conception had eluded them. Now, John's patience was running out.

'She drinks too much,' he blurted. 'That's rich coming from me, I know, but it's not doing her eggs any good. I've read enough pregnancy manuals (he quoted the late birth guru Sheila Kitzinger) to know that she needs to stop to get up the duff.'

In April 1987, songwriter, producer and 'Wombles' creator Mike Batt was filming a production of his musical 'The Hunting of the Snark' at the Royal Albert Hall. I'd been invited to interview the cast. John Hurt, the Narrator, was the last to go. He suggested that we repair to 'our drawing room' to talk. The Groucho Club had opened in Soho the year before. We were both founder members. When we arrived, he offered me champagne, which I declined, telling him that I was five months' pregnant. John fell silent. His lightly tanned face turned mauve. He dropped to his knees, threw his arms around my middle, and pressed the side of his head to my melon-shaped bulge.

'Does it kick?' he whispered. 'Can I feel it?' His eyes were brimming with tears when at last he stood up. He pulled me into a corner, helping himself to someone's rosé as he passed, accepting champagne from a PR lady who sent a bottle over. We dropped into a velvet sofa. John held my hand. All too soon, because a top-up was all it took, he was out of his skull.

He had never been shy about his love affair with the bottle. He'd given up more times, he'd say, than I'd had hot dinners. But he was drinking more than ever because he could not have the thing he craved the most.

'It's a damned unfair world, this,' he lamented, staring into his empty glass. 'It's not easy to have a child. You're very lucky indeed if you can do it. I say, I could buy your baby, couldn't I? I know you've finished with whatshisname. I'm sure you can't manage on your own, and I don't suppose you want to. The only thing I have to offer is money. If it would help ...' his words ran dry. Guess what, it was a no from me.

Mia Clementine was born at London's Whittington Hospital that August. Although John and Donna sent flowers, they never came to visit. The next time I saw John was in February the following year, on my first outing back to the Groucho Club. He leapt at me as I entered, dragged me off to his corner, and demanded know every gory detail. Did I have pictures? I showed him some snaps. It was then that he reached inside his jacket, and took out his cheque book.

'A hundred thousand,' he declared. 'All yours.'

'For what?'

'For Mia!'

'Oh, John,' I said, 'I told you before. My baby's not for sale. Besides, we'd get banged up for it.'

He nodded, and slumped. 'For sale: baby shoes, never worn,' he sighed.

'What?'

'Hemingway. The six-word novel. Maybe it wasn't really his idea, you know how people are, but I still like to think it was. The saddest short story ever told.'

After a while, he tucked the cheque book back into his inside pocket. He asked for a hug, and sobbed in my arms. He told me that he and Donna had spent £3,000 on IVF treatment at a private London clinic. During a ten-day stay, eggs were removed, fertilised in vitro, and implanted. They'd been warned that there was only a fifty per cent chance of success. They had tried everything, he said, even giving up booze.

'You see?' he said, 'I can stop any time I like. It's simply that I like to drink. I suppose Donna and I are fighting a lot these days. But she yells at me for all the right reasons. I've always gone on benders. I know a lot of actors never touch the stuff when they're working, but I tend to. It gives me a leg-up into the psyche of the character, I think. When I did 'Midnight Express', I had to play a man who was in a permanently messed-up state. I was drinking seven bottles of wine a day.

'During 'The Naked Civil Servant', I was evenly drunk throughout. But 'The Elephant Man' was a different approach. I didn't touch a drop.

'Now they say that I'm too old to be a dad. But I find myself reverting to the childlike state as I get older. I know I could be in tune with kids. I understand what they're about. I would make a good father. I'd be not half bad at all.

'I'm not happy,' he then blurted.

'My wife has thrown me out tonight. She wasn't impressed by my behaviour. It was on-your-bike time for me. It's all a mess. We have everything: a beautiful new house we've just built in Kenya. A West End flat for when I'm working over here. I've got a film out ('White Mischief', with Greta Scacchi and Charles Dance), and a new flick coming ('The Storyteller', directed by the Muppets' Jim Henson). I'm king of the world, aren't I. Get me. And yet, without a child, I really have nothing.'

What about adoption, I asked. John scoffed.

'Old lushes like us? They'd never let us through the door!'

Resorting to a string of expletives and obscenities which in sobriety would have horrified him, John dropped his chin and scowled at the hyped-up throng.

'I have always been pessimistic,' he murmured. 'Perhaps it's why every character I've played has been tormented. Joseph Merrick, Quentin Crisp, Bob Champion. More to come, I suspect. If I live long enough. What does it say about me?'

'That you have empathy,' I said. 'To identify with the afflicted is compassionate. To portray suffering with such honesty is your gift. Do you still believe in God?'

'I don't know. I don't need to know. I'll find out when I get there.'

I turned to face him, only to find that he had fallen asleep. A dishevelled drunk sat dribbling into my shoulder pad.

After that, I didn't see John again for nearly eight years. He divorced Donna, married American production assistant Joan Dalton, and had two longed-for sons: Alexander, known as Sacha, and Nick are now both in their twenties. The divorce was almost final when I ran into John at Scott's in Mayfair in 1996. He enveloped me like a long-lost child, and made a fuss of everyone at my table.

'And who's this pretty thing?'

I introduced Mia, who was now nine years old. John gasped, almost inaudibly. His crinkly eyes flashed.

'At last,' he whispered, 'at last.' Tears threatened. He bent down and picked her up, and smiled.

'My little girl,' he said.

John subsequently embarked on a seven-year relationship with Irish writer and presenter Sarah Owens. They separated in 2002. The following year, he met 'Welsh Brummie' advertising film producer Anwen Rees-Myers at the bar in, where else, the Groucho Club. They married in 2005, and were together until he died of pancreatic cancer on 25th January 2017.

John Hurt, LAJ & Kenney Jones, drummer, Small Faces/Faces/the
Who/the Law/Jones Gang, at Entwistle's home Quarwood,
Stow-on-the-Wold, 1986

PART THREE

27. STAYIN' ALIVE

What are the stand-outs?

Bowie at Madison Square Garden on the Serious Moonlight tour, 1983. I interviewed David in his dressing room, pre-show: he always preferred to do the chats early, to get them over with. We had dinner together afterwards.

The Who revisiting their rock opera 'Tommy' at the Universal Amphitheater LA, 1989: one of the last before I came off the road full-time. It was a charity fund-raiser. I'll never forget it. Elton, Steve Winwood, Phil Collins, Billy Idol and the rest performed with Pete, Roger and John, who had just called time on their partnership with Kenney Jones after a decade, sadly, so Simon Phillips was on drums. The after-show was a train wreck. We lost three days.

The Stones, 1982, for Tattoo You, an extension of their massive arena tour across America the previous year. The tour on which Keith whacked a fan, at Hampton Coliseum, Virginia, in December 1981. A guy leapt from the shadows and charged across the stage towards Mick during 'Satisfaction'. Where were security? Keith walloped him with his black Fender Telecaster and carried on playing as the guards woke up and dealt with the interloper. The guitar stayed in tune.

Live Aid. Queen stole it. Who remembers much else about that day? We remember Bowie, cool in powder-blue, or was it grey? The sound going down on The Who. Phil Collins boarding Concorde to perform at JFK Stadium in Philadelphia, right after his turn at Wembley. Paul McCartney playing live for the first time since John Lennon died. His piano mic going down at the start. Bob Geldof, Bowie, Pete Townshend and Alison Moyet singing back-up on 'Let It Be'. Madonna defying gravity. Simon le Bon's bum note of all time, on Bond theme 'A View To a Kill'. But it was Freddie and Queen who owned Live Aid.

I saw Prince play an impromptu gig at the Kensington Roof Gardens. I watched INXS perform for the first time at the Montreux Rock Festival in 1986. I couldn't take my eyes off Michael Hutchence. Ten sex symbols in a white denim jacket and dirty strides. There was so much of the Mick Jagger about Michael even then. Even his hands were hypnotic.

Women? Pat Benatar. Tina. Whitney. Dolly. Debs. My favourite Blondie show was at Hammersmith Odeon, in January 1980. All the girls fell for Debbie Harry that night. One way or another.

I sometimes wonder, which will be the last gig? Will I know it's the final one? I am reminded of this thought whenever I see Steve Harley perform, as I do whenever I can. He has promised to sing 'Make Me Smile (Come Up and See Me)' at my funeral. Every time we get together, he asks if I've got a date. My magician friend Nick Fitzherbert and I used to laugh about it. Now Nick's gone too. Life seems all a matter of death and death. It will get worse.

Only when confronted by a couple of thousand people paying homage on the streets of Soho did the reality of Bernie Katz's death begin to sink in. 'It's like a State funeral,' said someone. 'Not since the Krays has there been a turnout like this,' commented someone else. For all the Sienna Millers, Noel Fieldings, Dominic Coopers, Sadie Frosts, Jude Laws, Jaime Winstones and other famous faces, it was the tears of ordinary Groucho Club members for their beloved front-of-house manager, for whom the place had been our front room for decades, that said it all. The brass band did a turn with 'It's A Long Way to Tipperary' and 'We'll Meet Again' before the cortege wended north. Even none-the-wiser bystanding builders wept and sang. The trek to Golders Green Crematorium was hot and long. The chapel was jammed, as many outside as in. The eulogies seared. I could barely look at Bernie's little mum Rhoda. The stark words of his sisters broke us all. Jude Law jerked a laugh with his take on the Prince of Soho: 'He would put you in your place with a stamp of his Cuban heel, or find you a place at the best table in the house.' His description of Bernie's club looks – 'Greatcoat Bernie', 'Red Velvet Bernie', 'Leopard Print Bernie' – were spot-on. He spoke from the gut. His words, though loud and clear, were hard to hear.

But nobody mentioned how Bernie died. Nor why. I was shocked to the core to learn later that he'd hanged himself. So it appeared. Why would he do that? What darkness contorted his heart that he just couldn't share? I wept for the tragic, futile loss of a man who understood, more than any other man I've ever known seemed to understand, that the currency of life is not wealth, but love; that pure kindness, of the kind at which Bernie excelled, must be our underpinning; that we all have a point, however pointless we may feel. I longed to wrench him back from the grave and knock some sense into him. To say to him, as he had said to me – don't look back. Focus forwards. Keep going. Keep heading down the middle, chins up, chest out. Come the end of it, love, I promise you, there will be morning.

Media Business International: Garry Jenkins, Martyn Palmer, LAJ,
Roger Tavener, 1991

LAJ at David Bowie's Britannia Bay House, Mustique, 1991

LAJ, Bridie, Henry & Mia, Andalucia, Spain, 2000

Andy Hill, Jane Wroe-Wright, Nick Fitzherbert, Suki Yamamoto, LAJ, Henry Shine, the Other Palace Theatre, London, 2015

Ed Bicknell, Simon Napier-Bell, LAJ, Brian Bennett, the Ivy, London, 2016

Bernie Katz's funeral, Soho Square, London, September 2017

Bridie, Henry, LAJ, Mia with Jess Mackney (in the portrait),
Christmas 2018

ACKNOWLEDGEMENTS

In 2013, I had a drink in a New York bar with Malcolm Payne, whom I've known since we were teenagers. As usual, we sat regurgitating stories. 'You should write a book about your own life,' he said. 'Who'd be interested?' I asked him. 'Everyone.' Jane Wroe-Wright thought so too. She has been pestering me for years to write it. So Malc and Janey, this is for you. I owe you both. I also owe Francis Booth and Andy Hill for having refused to allow me to give up on it during the dark hours; Francis in particular, for seizing the ball and running with it, for sleeves-up editorial graft and technical expertise, and for daring me to be brave. I thank everyone who has ever employed me (with a couple of exceptions), and the following:

Charles Armitage, R.I.P.
John Blake
Clare Bramley
John Chenery
Natasha Coombs
Jim Diamond, R.I.P.
Simon Drake
Robert Elms
Nick Fitzherbert, R.I.P.
Jeremy Fox
Karen French
Rod Gilchrist
Robert Glassbrook
Nick Gordon, R.I.P.
Roy Greenslade
Gönül Güney
Phil Hall
David Hancock
Andy Hill
Bob Hill, R.I.P.
Dave Hogan
Richard Hughes

Julie Ives-Routleff
Allan James
Sian James
Russ Kane
Kabir Khan
Berni Kilmartin
Simon Kinnersley
John Koski
Herbert Kretzmer
Lynda Lee-Potter, R.I.P.
Harvey Mann
Leo McLoughlin
Piers Morgan
Jonathan Morrish
Simon Napier-Bell
Philip Norman
Sarah Oliver
Matthew Parris
Roger Scott
Rick Sky
Geoff Sutton
David Stark
Phil Swern
Roger Tavener
Martin Townsend
Lisa Tsang
Frank Warren
Stuart White
Michael Watts
Geoff Wilkinson
Sandy Williams
Annette Witheridge
Clair Woodward
Chris Wright

For my mother, Kathleen, and my father, Ken; and for Henry, Bridie and Mia.

Special thanks to my cousins Trevor and Debbie Jones for their invaluable memories and research.

This book is dedicated with fondest love and thanks to Suki Yamamoto.

LAJ, 2019

YOU GOT TO ROLL ME ...

'Tumbling Dice' is a track from the Rolling Stones' 1972 album 'Exile on Main Street': arguably the finest LP they ever made, and frequently voted one of the greatest albums of all time. The song tells of a gambler who is incapable of being faithful to any lover. It was recorded, along with most of the rest of the album, in the basement studio of the chateau Villa Nellcôte, Villefranche-sur-Mer, in the south of France. In the absence of Bill Wyman on the night that it was recorded, Mick Taylor played bass on the track.

Said Mick Jagger, who wrote the song to a riff created by Keith Richards,

'It's about gambling and love, an old blues trick.'

Released as a single on 14th April 1972, it made the Top Ten in both the UK and the US. It has been covered many times, notably in 1977 by Linda Ronstadt for her album 'Simple Dreams'.

I have always believed that the song's wider theme is risk. It's about the consequences of taking chances. But as life reminds us every single day, we have no choice.

NOTES

---

[i] Jack Tinker died of a heart attack in October 1996, aged fifty-eight. The West End's lights went down that night in tribute, an honour usually reserved for celebrated thespians.

[ii] Banksy's take on the philosophy was a sculpture of a TV set with this statement on its screen: 'In the future, everyone will be anonymous for 15 minutes.'

[iii] The self-regulatory body the Press Complaints Commission and its Code of Practice were established in 1990. The Leveson Enquiry, created to investigate the News of the World phone hacking affair, was set up in November 2012.

[iv] 'No Mercy', released in December 1986, was a violent swamp of a movie which performed poorly at the box office.

[v] No kidding. Tiffany was his mother Doris's maiden name.

[vi] To paraphrase the playwright Arnold Wesker.

[vii] To be fair, I was never bad at these. Gere was married to former supermodel Cyndi Crawford from 1991 to 1995. He was voted 'The Sexiest Man Alive' in 1999. In November 2002, he married model/actress Carey Lowell, and the couple had a son, James Jigme. They separated in 2013 after eleven years. He married publicist/charity executive Alejandra Silva in April 2018.

[viii] Following the Weapons of Mass Destruction/Tony Blair fiasco, Saddam was found guilty of crimes against humanity, and was executed on 30th December 2006.

[ix] 'Smoke on the Water', a track from Deep Purple's 1971 album 'Machine Head'.

[x] 'Return of the Piss Prophets' is an album by the Candy Stains, released June 2011.

[xi] 'Patch' Moore remained a would-be musician and actor. He wound up a drug addict, sleeping rough on the beach outside his father's Marina del Rey mansion. Dudley Moore died in 2002.

[xii] Marilyn Manson, 'Antichrist Superstar', 1996.

Camp founder Gilbert Klein retained his sense of humour, and retired to Baja, California. The rock'n'roll fantasy camp formula lives on. In recent times, it was David Fishof who was credited with the 'original' idea.

When the legend becomes fact, print the legend. ('The Man Who Shot Liberty Valance', 1962).

[xiii] 'Going Underground', the Jam, 1982.

[xiv] 'Frank, Liza and Sammy: The Ultimate Event' ran for five nights at the Royal Albert Hall, 18-22 April 1989, the singing stars performing their greatest hits accompanied by a 40-piece orchestra with Frank Sinatra Jnr conducting. All five concerts sold out before they were advertised. The tour visited a further 27 countries. Sammy Davis Jnr. died from cancer the following year. Dean Martin succumbed on Christmas Day 1995, aged 78. Frank Sinatra died in May 1998, at the age of 82. Liza Minnelli, 72 at the time of writing, is still going strong

[xv] Although the industry had now relocated, Fleet Street's name remains synonymous with the British newspaper industry and printing – just as Madison Avenue denotes New York's advertising industry, and Wall Street the financial markets.

[xvi] Stevie Nicks toured with the Pretenders during 2016 and 2017. She appears on Lana Del Rey's fifth studio album, 'Lust for Life' (July 2017), singing her song 'Beautiful People Beautiful Problems'. That month, she performed in London's Hyde Park, supporting Tom Petty and the Heartbreakers.

[xvii] Self-confessed philanderer Albert Roux divorced Monique in 2001, and married his second wife Cheryl Smith in 2007. A decade on, he left Cheryl for a forty-year-old Ukrainian cloakroom attendant.

[xviii] A default News of the World throwaway deployed by reporters caught in compromising positions while on a job, usually one with a sexual dimension. The phrase is said to have been coined by Australian journalist Murray Sayle (1926-2010), former foreign correspondent for the Sunday Times and revered investigative journalist, 'the most forceful of Fleet Street's finest'.

[xix] 'The Hollow Men', T.S. Eliot, 1925

[xx] Voluntary Service Overseas

[xxi] 'Wuthering Heights', Emily Brontë

[xxii] The 'white picket fence' was a favourite theme of John's. He wrote about it in the Bad English song 'Ghost in Your Heart'.

[xxiii] 'Touch', from John Waite's 2001 album 'Figure in a Landscape'.

[xxiv] Paul McCartney married third wife Nancy Shevell at Marylebone Register Office on 9th October 2011.

xxv Drew Barrymore entered rehab for the first time at the age of 13. She got her life back eventually, but would be the first to admit that she still bears the scars of her childhood.

xxvi Tatum O'Neal and John McEnroe had three children together, and separated in 1992. They were divorced two years later. She became addicted to heroin. He got custody.

xxvii 'Four Weddings' also claimed the BAFTAS for Best Picture, Best Direction, and Best Actress for Grant's co-star Kristin Scott Thomas.

xxviii In 2007, News of the World royal editor Clive Goodman and private investigator Glenn Mulcaire were convicted of illegal phone-hacking. The scandal escalated when it came to light that the practice was more widespread than at first thought. A large investigation was mounted. After the revelation that reporters working for the News of the World had hacked the voicemail of murdered schoolgirl Millie Dowler, there followed a public enquiry chaired by Lord Justice Leveson in 2011. Several more arrests were made, and prison sentences bestowed. After 168 years, the venerable News of the World ceased publication on 10th July 2011, bidding farewell to its '7.5 million loyal readers'. Hundreds of good journalists lost their jobs. It's always the beautiful who are damned. I hadn't worked at the paper for 16 years, but its demise broke my heart. In November 2011, Hugh Grant delivered a damning testimony on phone hacking to the Leveson Enquiry, thus reminding the world yet again of his misdemeanour.

Hugh Grant and Elizabeth Hurley called time on their long relationship. The mother of one married Indian textile heir Arun Nayar in 2007. The couple separated in 2010, and divorced a year later. Hurley became engaged to Australian international cricketer Shane Warne the same year. Rain stopped play in 2013. Grant is now a '4 by 2': a father of 4 children by different girlfriends. Stuart White made his excuses and left the newspaper industry in 2003. He is now a successful screenwriter.

xxix The Ritz Carlton at Double Bay, Sydney, reinvented itself as the Stamford Plaza. It was eventually demolished in 2009, and was replaced by a new apartment block.

xxx 'Suicide Blonde' is the title of one of INXS's best-loved hits. The first single from their album 'X', it reached Number Nine on the US Billboard Hot 100 in 1990, and Number Eleven in the UK. It became poignant after the deaths of Diana, Michael and Paula. May they rest in peace.

Printed in Great Britain
by Amazon